THE GEORGE GUND FOUNDATION
IMPRINT IN AFRICAN AMERICAN STUDIES

The George Gund Foundation has endowed
this imprint to advance understanding of
the history, culture, and current issues
of African Americans.

The publisher gratefully acknowledges the generous contribution to this book provided by the George Gund Foundation.

PEARL'S SECRET

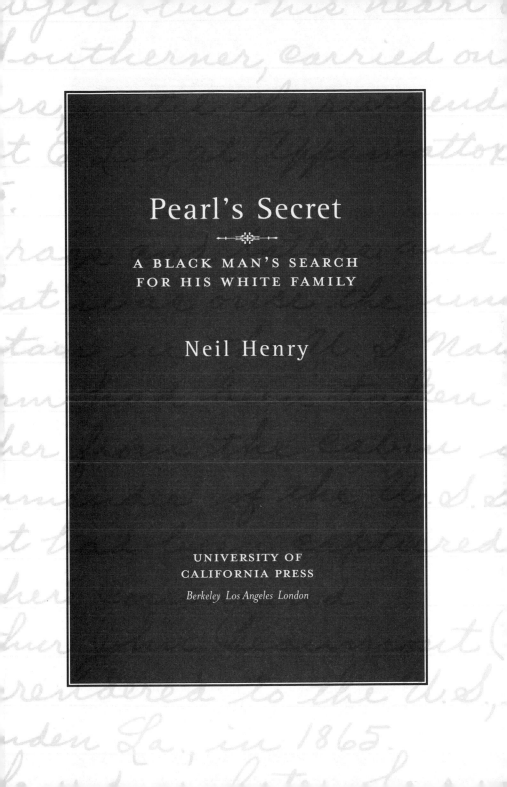

Pearl's Secret

A BLACK MAN'S SEARCH
FOR HIS WHITE FAMILY

Neil Henry

UNIVERSITY OF
CALIFORNIA PRESS

Berkeley Los Angeles London

University of California Press
Berkeley and Los Angeles, California

University of California Press, Ltd.
London, England

© 2001 by Neil Henry

Library of Congress Cataloging-in-Publication Data

Henry, Neil, 1954–
    Pearl's secret : a black man's search for his white family /
Neil Henry.
        p.   cm.—(The George Gund Foundation imprint in
African American studies)
    ISBN 0-520-22257-1 (cloth : alk. paper)
    1. Henry, Neil, 1954–   2. Afro-Americans—
Biography.   3. Afro-Americans—Race identity.
4. Beaumont family.   5. Henry family.   6. Miscegenation—
United States—History.   7. United States—Race
relations.   8. Racism—United States—Psychological
aspects.   9. Seattle (Wash.)—Biography.   10. Saint
Joseph (La.)—Biography.   I. Title.   II. Series.
E185.97.H46 H46 2001
973'.0496073'0092—dc21   00-053211

Printed in the United States of America
09 08 07 06 05 04 03 02 01
10 9 8 7 6 5 4 3 2

The paper used in this publication meets the minimum re-
quirements of American National Standard for Information
Sciences—Permanence of Paper for Printed Library
Materials, ANSI Z39.48–1992 (R 1997) (*Permanence of Paper*).

For Letitia and Zoë

Contents

PART TWO: DISCOVERY

Prelude

My great-great-grandfather was an Englishman named Arthur John Beaumont, who left his home in Kent when he was seventeen years old to sail for America, one of 200,436 immigrants who arrived in this country in 1856. A thin, pale-looking fellow with wispy dark hair and soft, penetrating eyes, he was called "A.J." for short by his friends and family. Like many young immigrants, he apparently came here with little in his pockets but with a heart overflowing with dreams of fortune and happiness.

To a large extent A.J. seemed to find what he was looking for, though it took a while, from what I initially gleaned about his life. Indeed, I knew relatively little about him when I started the research that culminated in this story of the dual racial legacy he left and my relationship as a black man to it. This much I did know: Soon after his arrival in America, the young man settled in a small town called St. Joseph on the Mississippi River in northeastern Louisiana, where he found work as an overseer on a cotton plantation.

A few years later, when the Civil War broke out, he proved his devotion to his new home by joining the Confederate Army and fighting as a lieutenant in an artillery brigade. Military service was something of a tradition in the Beaumont family, his father and grandfather having fought for king and queen against Napoleon at Waterloo, according to family lore. So Beaumont's own service in defense of Louisiana must have seemed a perfectly natural, worthy, and honorable fate. His unit was the 4th Battery of Louisiana Artillery, led by Captain Archibald J. Cameron, which saw action in numerous engagements ranging from Vicksburg to Red River over the course of the war, surrendering only when Robert E. Lee himself did, in April 1865.

After the war the English immigrant's dreams gradually came true. He returned to his beloved adopted town of St. Joseph, and over the last quarter of the nineteenth century, from Reconstruction into the Jim Crow era, he became a respected and admired figure in Tensas Parish as a plantation owner, merchant, town father, and civic leader. Indeed, his life story reads like the classic nineteenth-century American tale of the European immigrant who arrived young and destitute but died a natural death decades later in comparative prosperity as an old man.

I knew these details about my white great-great-grandfather's life largely by way of a yellowed newspaper clipping that had been passed down in my family for nearly a century, since its publication in the weekly *Tensas Gazette* on May 3, 1901. That was the year Beaumont died at sixty-two. The clipping, a very fragile thing about eight column inches in length, was his obituary and had been inherited and preserved by my mother in the top drawer of a bureau in her clothes closet with other family keepsakes.

But what had always fascinated me most about that brittle strip of newsprint was the story it didn't tell about A.J. Beaumont's life, a story I knew far more intimately through my family's oral history. This was his legacy as the inadvertent progenitor of an unusual black family—my family—that has endured proudly and exceptionally well over the century since his death. We were the ones, as my mother's brother, Uncle Sonny, sometimes said with telltale gruff irony when I was a child, who were "born on the wrong side of the blanket" long ago—descendants of Beaumont's post–Civil War sexual relationship with a freed slave in Louisiana, Laura Brumley, who became our ancestral matriarch.

I knew the details of our family's black history much better than those of its white history. Beaumont was always something of a mystery figure in our family's story—a white man remembered only vaguely and somewhat reluctantly through a faded old photograph and a newspaper clipping. By contrast, his longtime lover was a beloved and memorable figure, truly of flesh and blood. Laura's brilliant 1890 portrait and that of her beautiful mixed-race daughter, Pearl, my great-grandmother, hung proudly in the entryway of my house throughout my boyhood in Seattle in the 1960s.

These three people—A.J. Beaumont, Laura Brumley, and their daughter, Pearl—were perched near the top branches of my black American family tree as I knew it. And ultimately they were the inspiration for the story in the pages that follow, a personal history and narrative about my quest, 140 years after Beaumont's arrival in this country, to piece together the murky details about my family's racial past in the United States, a mixed ancestry with hidden branches not unlike that of millions upon millions of African Americans.

It is a story centered on a genealogy that was bifurcated from its start, rooted as it was in this nation's racist soil. While no obituary was ever published about Laura's life, it arguably was as fascinating and noteworthy as Beaumont's. In 1850, when Beaumont was about to enter adolescence in England, Laura was born on a cotton plantation just outside St. Joseph. The mulatto daughter of a slave born in Africa and a white physician who lived on a neighboring farm, she was the fruit of a taboo interracial relationship that was far more common in our history than we as a society have been willing to recognize.

The contemporary debate among historians over the significance of Thomas Jefferson's longtime romantic relationship with his slave Sally Hemings and recent DNA evidence proving that he fathered black descendants point to the ongoing volatility of this issue in American society. For many black Americans, however, what's perhaps most astonishing is how long it has taken for the interracial lineage of many African Americans to be considered a subject for serious public discussion and academic examination. Jefferson's family story, after all, is far from unique, as evidenced by a growing body of scholarly works devoted to black-white lineage, such as Edward Ball's *Slaves in the Family* and Henry Wiencek's *The Hairstons: An American Family in Black and White*. Certainly one reason the mixed-race history of many black Americans has not been seriously examined has been racism. Both blacks and whites have shown uneasiness about this history. For black Americans, miscegenation traditionally has connoted the stigma and shame of the slavery era. For whites, the discussion has been even more muted, and not only because race mixing was viewed as a cultural taboo. Were white society to publicly admit the obvious—that many blacks carry white blood—it would also have to accept their rights to fully equal citizenship—rights that the power structure could not allow. Nearly 225 years after the Republic's founding, we have yet to reach a point of equal acceptance of all Americans.

In the mid–nineteenth century, of course, there was little equality for a mulatto like Laura Brumley. Her mother worked as a cook in the kitchen of the plantation, and Laura grew up as a house slave, scrubbing floors, washing dishes, and changing bed-sheets. However, she was very much adored, according to family legend, by Sarah Tullis, the wife of the plantation's owner. A New Englander by birth, with firm moral principles rooted in the Bible, Sarah despised slavery, though she had married into a southern family that believed in it fervently. Her way of fighting the system was to educate Laura as best she could. And so the time-honored story of education providing a way out of oppression began to be written in our family. Using her family Bible as a textbook, the white woman defied southern laws by secretly teaching the mixed-raced child to read and write. She also trained Laura in a number of household skills, including sewing. By the time the Civil War ended, fifteen-year-old Laura, with her radiant brown face and dark curly hair, was a literate young woman who had experience as a seamstress—a trade that has often served as the first step on the ladder to improvement for generations of impoverished American immigrants. She seemed set to endure the challenges her people faced at the end of slavery, the only system they had ever known.

Sometime during this period immediately after the war, my great-great-grandmother Laura met and fell in love with the English immigrant and Confederate war veteran A.J. Beaumont.

It was the beginning of a long affair described as respectful and loving by those who remembered Laura, one that resulted in Pearl's birth in 1877.

This child—my great-grandmother—grew up looking very much like her namesake jewel, a pretty quadroon girl with brilliant alabaster skin, straight dark hair, and a fiery disposition. But she also was cursed to be born in an era and a place in which she was denied a meaningful connection to her father, a white man who was central to her life and her mother's, yet who existed, on the other side of the color bar, in a world where black people of all hues were forbidden.

This may have been part of the reason—no one in my family knows for sure—that in about 1890 Laura decided to move away from St. Joseph, her past, and everything she had ever known. She took Pearl and steamed north to St. Louis, where she eventually opened a boardinghouse for black travelers and laborers that she operated into the World War I era. It was there that Pearl grew into a woman, fell in love, and married a dashing black man named Frank Hall—a rake and reprobate who had an unfortunate fondness for ragtime honky-tonks and gambling. In 1896, at the age of nineteen, Pearl gave birth to their daughter, my grandmother Fredda.

My black family's last known connection to the white branch of the family tree occurred shortly after this period, when Pearl's tempestuous marriage fell apart in 1899. Pearl turned to her white father for support that year, sending him a letter to tell him about her life in St. Louis and about her baby—his granddaughter—and enclosing a photograph of herself holding the child. A month passed, as Pearl waited for a reply from Beaumont. Then a year. Nothing but silence.

Then one spring day nearly two years later, she received a letter from her white father, written by hand on stationery bearing
the letterhead of his flourishing mercantile business in St. Joseph.
This letter, like Beaumont's obituary, has been passed from one
generation to the next in my family. Now yellow and brittle with
age, preserved in its original envelope with its two-cent George
Washington stamp and St. Joseph postmark, it reads simply:

April 25, 1901

My Dear Pearl:
In looking over my papers in my safe I came across your picture,
also your daughter's, and your letter to me dated May 3, 1899. I
must acknowledge that you are my daughter and I feel that I have
done you a great injustice in not acknowledging the receipt of your
letter. If this reaches you, write to me.

Your affectionate father,
A.J. Beaumont

Along with the letter Beaumont sent a photograph of himself,
also still in my family. It shows the well-dressed figure of a content and prosperous southern gentleman with warm eyes, a soft
smile, and an impressive French imperial beard.

It's likely that Pearl felt elated by the letter and photograph, for
her white father finally seemed to be reaching out to her, after so
many years. But then, without warning, another letter arrived in
her mailbox. Inside, a friend in Louisiana had enclosed a clipping
from the *Tensas Gazette*—the obituary announcing Beaumont's
death.

The white man's letter essentially amounted to a deathbed
confession to his illegitimate black daughter, the kind of last-gasp

cleansing effort a guilty soul makes before entering eternity. Unfortunately, as often happens, the accompanying burden of regret was passed on to the living—to Pearl, according to my mother, who adored her. The stunned and saddened woman, then twenty-three, was left with the bitter realization that the love, reconciliation, and recognition she had always desired from her white father would now be impossible to obtain.

Beaumont's death was also painful for Laura, who, despite the passage of so many years, the distance in miles, and society's racial barrier, had never stopped loving him. When he died, people in my family recalled, a part of her died as well. Still, the former slave lived a proud, courageous, and independent life and became known throughout black St. Louis for many distinctive qualities. She was an expert equestrian who proudly rode her horse with an almost regal bearing; she was a devout Baptist fond of singing Negro spirituals around her boardinghouse; and she was a chaste, proper, and God-fearing soul who forbade her tenants to play the hot sound of ragtime or jazz, then in vogue, on the piano in her parlor, calling it the devil's music.

When Laura died in 1932 at the age of eighty-one, so many years and miles removed from the Louisiana plantation where she had learned to read and write under the guidance of the kind white woman whose family owned her, she was loved and respected in her adopted city. And those closest to her swore that after A.J. Beaumont she never took another lover, white or black.

Pearl's heartbreak lasted for the rest of her life.

My mother once told me of a rumor that the fiery Pearl had boarded a Mississippi River steamboat and traveled back to St. Joseph to try to claim an inheritance from her father's estate in

Louisiana, but that she was turned away by Beaumont's furious white widow. No one knew if that part of the family story was really true or even if A.J. Beaumont had ever married. But there is no doubt that Pearl held on to her father's letter, the obituary clipping, the yearly Christmas cards sent by the plantation mistress, Sarah Tullis, to Laura in St. Louis, and the old photographs, preserving them almost as if they were holy relics.

When Pearl died in 1944, these keepsakes were passed on to her daughter, Fredda, who had married in 1916. Fredda and her black husband, Edward Clifford Turner, lived a long and very happy life together in St. Louis, where they raised three children. She, too, cared deeply about holding on to these artifacts, for she always felt that one of the cruelest parts of being a descendant of slavery was feeling bereft of a sense of personal history and identity.

Before Fredda died in 1982, many of the old relics were passed on to her second daughter, Mary, my mother. Mary had settled in Seattle in 1956 with my father, John Robert Henry, a pioneering black surgeon who hailed from North Carolina. They raised me, my two older brothers, and my younger sister there.

Today A.J. Beaumont's photograph, his obituary, and his 1901 letter to Pearl still rest in my mother's desk drawer amid a host of other mementos passed down over the past 150 years—keepsakes that have both fascinated and perplexed me since I was a boy.

It was in Seattle, as a middle-class black kid growing up among white people during the era of racial integration in the 1960s, that I first came to wonder about the strange incongruity of my white ancestry. My mother and her family loved to talk about the characters in our family's past during regular get-togethers, so I grew up knowing quite a bit about our proud and colorful black history as it unfolded in places as far-flung as Mississippi, Louisiana, North Carolina, Missouri, and Washington State.

But for a long time I was also intrigued by the history no one seemed to know much about, especially the story of A.J. Beaumont. The white man's name was rarely mentioned in our house when I was growing up, and when he was referred to, my mother and her family would lower their voices, as if they were telling a secret too sensitive or perhaps even shameful for outsiders or youngsters to hear. I thus came to know him only vaguely as the "Englishman" in our black family album—the plantation owner, Confederate officer, and descendant of Waterloo veterans whose white blood was somehow mixed up with ours. (And mixed up with that of other whites who, unlike Beaumont, were nameless and largely unrecalled, their blood ties to us undocumented and untraceable across the color line.) How, I sometimes wondered as a youngster, could this prototypical white southern patrician in the photograph, this very personification in my mind of America's racist past, a past we despised so much as a people, be a part of us inside?

When I grew up, I became a journalist, and the unanswered questions I carried with me about A.J. Beaumont's life and legacy took deeper root somewhere in the recesses of my adult mind, fertilized to no small degree by my experiences with racism as a young black man coming of age in America. My profession had trained me to ask myself questions and to find ways of getting answers. So whenever I reflected about Beaumont, about the traces of white blood coursing through my veins, and especially about race in America—a subject nearly every black person in this country must think about quite often—my mind brimmed with questions, almost to the point of obsession.

Did Beaumont really marry and raise a white family in Louisiana not long after his relationship with Laura ended in the 1870s, as was rumored in my family?

Did he produce other children besides Pearl?

If so, what became of them?

Were there white descendants of A.J. Beaumont, cousins of mine, living in America today?

Where was this white family?

What stories did they have to tell about race in America from their "legitimate" branch of our shared ancestral tree?

How had their lives and experiences during the twentieth century differed from ours?

And, if these white relatives existed, could I find them, meet them?

As I imagined this white family, I naturally thought more and more about what it means to be black.

My family's experiences, like those of most black people in America, have mirrored the stresses and strains of our nation's racial history, from slavery through Jim Crow to the integration of the 1960s and on into the complex world of multiculturalism that seems to define the present. We have struggled through adversity, battled racial discrimination, loved, raised children, and pursued our dreams in many places around the country.

But, unlike many black families, mine has been comparatively privileged, favored by good fortune. From the 1850s, when Laura was a little girl on the Tullis plantation, to the present, we have been an upwardly mobile family, valuing education above all other gifts, seeing it as the only reliable avenue to security and freedom in a society often hostile to us because of our skin color. My grandfather—Fredda's husband—worked all his life as a postal clerk in St. Louis, and he felt the sting of witnessing less worthy men regularly promoted over him because they were white, yet he endured the pain of this discrimination stoically, never losing his deep religious faith. He did this not only because a government job was prestigious and rare work for a black man at the time, but also to ensure that his children received the loving home and education he knew they would need to survive in America.

My hardworking, strict, and ambitious father went to medical school to become a surgeon in the 1950s and eventually migrated to Seattle to raise his family because it was one of the few places in America then where hospitals would allow a black surgeon to practice. Growing up in the Pacific Northwest, my two brothers, my sister, and I were the first generation in our family to become friendly with white Americans, to live with them as equals in the same neighborhood, to understand and be allowed to compete with them in their own element. And to a large extent, as products of racial integration, we have succeeded in their world, at least according to their measures of success. My brother Wayne received an Ivy League education and became a lawyer. My other siblings, Bobby and Sharon, both carried on a family tradition and took up teaching in Seattle, Bobby in a private middle school and Sharon in the same public elementary school where she and I were among the first few black kids in the 1960s. I became a writer for the *Washington Post* after earning degrees at Princeton and Columbia in the 1970s, an educational and career progression unthinkable for most black people in America as recently as a generation ago. Our lives reflect the kind of unusual but significant progress made by advantaged black Americans over the generations since slavery, despite the hazards of racism and discrimination.

As I made my way in my career, traveling across America and to distant parts of the world to report for the *Post*, I sometimes thought about trying to find the white Beaumonts and comparing their family's story to my family's. I imagined one day writing a kind of flip side to Alex Haley's seminal adventure in *Roots*, where he traces his African forebears. But, within the frenetic pace of my newspaper career, I never seemed to find the time to pursue the search for my white kin.

Then in 1992 two things happened: I left daily journalism for a full-time teaching position at the Graduate School of Journalism at the University of California, Berkeley, and I became a father for the first time. Both events, occurring when I was thirty-eight, played a significant role in focusing my mind to research and write this book.

While the job change allowed me the freedom and time to investigate the project, fatherhood gave me a fresh sense of purpose in getting it done. Put simply, I wanted to be able to offer my daughter someday a better understanding of my family's racial history than I had had when I was coming of age and a clearer picture of the dynamic complexity of race and prejudice as they are woven into the fabric of America.

Little did I know when I started out on this journey that I would have to navigate some rough emotional and psychological terrain before gaining a far greater appreciation and understanding of my very blackness than I had ever realized was possible.

Nor did I know that by the end of the search I would find, like bits of gold at the rainbow's end, sparkling pieces of historical evidence—indeed, gifts bestowed on me from an unlikely source—that gave a deeper and richer context to our story as a family and a people in America.

But that is getting a bit ahead of things.

What follows, from its beginning, is a memoir of my search and the story I discovered on the other side of the tree.

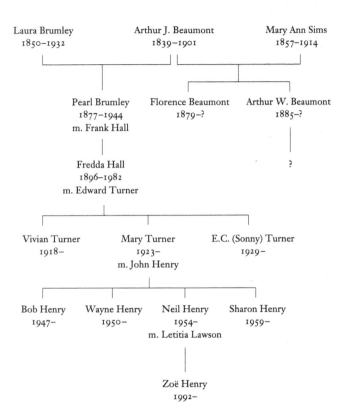

Laura Brumley · Arthur J. Beaumont · Mary Ann Sims
1850–1932 · 1839–1901 · 1857–1914

Pearl Brumley · Florence Beaumont · Arthur W. Beaumont
1877–1944 · 1879–? · 1885–?
m. Frank Hall

Fredda Hall · ?
1896–1982
m. Edward Turner

Vivian Turner · Mary Turner · E.C. (Sonny) Turner
1918– · 1923– · 1929–
m. John Henry

Bob Henry · Wayne Henry · Neil Henry · Sharon Henry
1947– · 1950– · 1954– · 1959–
m. Letitia Lawson

Zoë Henry
1992–

PART ONE

Search

CHAPTER ONE

Clues in Microfilm

How do you find the descendants of a white man who was born in England in 1839 and died quietly in a small town in Louisiana nearly a century ago? How can you discover if this man even left white descendants?

When I started my project years ago, I didn't know if the Beaumont family still existed, largely because it was my understanding that the fragile link my black family had to the white family before the turn of the last century was severed when A.J. Beaumont died. For all I knew, the Beaumont branch of my extended family tree ended sometime after the century's turn with Arthur's death and later that of his white widow, whose name I didn't even know.

My great-grandmother Pearl, the quadroon daughter Beaumont fathered with the freed slave Laura Brumley during the Reconstruction era, apparently tried to contact her white family in Louisiana sometime after her father's death in 1901 but was rebuffed. Anyway, that's what my mother vaguely remembered from stories she heard in her childhood in St. Louis. But even my mother didn't know for sure.

The whole Beaumont story was shrouded in mystery, a chapter in our distant past that no one in the family talked about very much when I was growing up, or wanted to talk about. I think this was largely because the real gist of that story—our blood link to racist white people who essentially had cast our ancestors aside as inferior and illegitimate long ago, during the plantation era— was certainly nothing to be proud of. And we were a family that, by contrast, had been blessed with many extraordinary black forebears to inspire us and accomplishments to celebrate.

I didn't have a lot of leads for my search, apart from Beaumont's old photograph, the brittle newspaper clipping that announced his death and noted his familial ties to Great Britain, and the fragile, yellowing letter the old man had written by hand on his personal stationery to Pearl shortly before his death, in which he guiltily acknowledged that he was her father. What I had were our family's oral stories and loving memories of Laura and Pearl, chiefly those of my mother and her younger brother, Uncle Sonny. They remembered Pearl from their childhood in St. Louis in the 1920s and 1930s and could recall the confusion and lonely torment she felt until the day she died, at sixty-seven in 1944, over her mixed racial background and the rejection she had suffered from her white father.

For about a decade, when time permitted, I dug into every resource I could find in search of the white Beaumonts—census records, court files, old microfilms of southern newspapers. At one point I even got some research help from both the British Imperial War Museum and the British National Army Museum, which I first contacted in June 1989 while on a two-day layover in London. I was en route to Kenya that summer, about to spend three years covering Africa for the *Washington Post* as a foreign correspondent based in Nairobi. I recalled that A.J. Beaumont's obituary stated that his father and grandfather had both served heroically as British Army officers during the Battle of Waterloo in 1815. So I contacted the military museum, seeking clues to the whereabouts of Beaumont's family in England. Perhaps they would know how to contact their American cousins—if they had any American cousins.

I pursued my unusual hobby in a number of crazy ways. I sought out genealogical societies on the Internet when I became computer literate in the 1990s, and I corresponded with numerous historical societies and libraries, from Kent in England to Natchez in Mississippi. I researched Social Security, immigration, and U.S. military records on CD-ROM and microfiche at various temples of the Church of Jesus Christ of Latter-Day Saints, which is headquartered in Salt Lake City and home to one of the finest libraries for genealogical research in America. At one point I even mailed letters to every Beaumont I could find in every telephone directory in Louisiana and Mississippi—thirty-five households in all. I got fascinating responses from people in many of those white homes, though none were able to provide a verifiable link to the genealogical history I sought.

But that wasn't the hardest part of my work. I now realize that one of the biggest obstacles in my restless searching was not a lack of resources or tools at my disposal or even places to hunt. It was the strange fear and unsettling ambivalence I often felt about what I was struggling to do. Essentially, I was trying to fashion a bridge over a chasm between white and black people that our nation's racial history and separatist customs had created. The difficulty of this struggle often played itself out in an internal emotional war over my feelings about race, about white and black people, and about the story I was attempting to uncover—feelings that went back to my growing up as a black kid in white middle-class Seattle in the 1960s.

I had little luck in my periodic search for a number of years. No luck in London. No luck in the historical archives in Louisiana. No luck with those letters I sent to all those households in the South.

But then one hot Thursday afternoon, on August 7, 1997, I finally happened upon an important clue.

During my summer break from teaching journalism classes at Berkeley in 1997, I decided to spend nearly all my time in a last concerted effort to find answers to the Beaumont puzzle. Nearly every day that summer I went to work at a microfilm reader in the public library near my home in Davis, California. The Yolo County Public Library in California's Sacramento Valley might seem an unlikely place to hunt for elusive clues to a family story buried long ago in the Deep South, but it turned out to be perfect for what I needed to do. Located just ten minutes from my house, the one-story building on the edge of the city's Community Park possessed two newspaper microfilm readers in good working order in its reference area, and it was these readers that were key to my search.

Day after day I flew back in time, my eyes peering closely at the reader as I scrolled from week to week in the years 1901 to 1916. I was hunting for clues to the whereabouts of A.J. Beaumont's white survivors in a newspaper called the *Tensas Gazette*, one of a number of old southern small-town newspapers copied on reels of microfilm that I had procured through my university library at Berkeley. The *Gazette* was Laura's and Beaumont's hometown weekly. It was started in the early 1800s and remains today one of the oldest continuously published newspapers in Louisiana. Printed in the old levee town of St. Joseph, the county seat of Tensas Parish, hard on the banks of the Mississippi River in northeastern Louisiana, it contained news from throughout the region.

In truth, as the summer was drawing to a close, I was starting to feel depressed by my lack of progress. For weeks I had been working on a set of six *Gazette* microfilms, on interlibrary loan from Louisiana State University, and I had a sinking sense that I might never find what I was looking for. When I began this latest tack in my research, I thought for certain I'd find a clue somewhere in time, some old footprint in the snow of history to tell me what happened to Beaumont's white survivors after he died in 1901.

Did they take over his business and cotton-growing interests in Louisiana? I wondered. Were they as prominent and successful after the turn of the century as he appears to have been in the 1880s and 1890s? Did they move on and settle somewhere else in America after his death?

St. Joseph numbered no more than 720 residents (and Tensas Parish, 19,070) at the turn of the last century, most of them engaged in cotton growing and related river work, and the local pages of the *Gazette* between 1890 and 1914 often read like notes from a church social. Almost everybody in St. Joseph's white society and that of the surrounding parish seemed to know everybody else, from Mayor Bondurant and Sheriff Hughes to society belles like Mrs. B.F. Bonney and Miss Inez Losey to Dreyfus, the druggist; Kershaw, the tool dealer; and Collins, the kindly old "colored" man who worked as a bailiff at the parish jail. Members of the Tullis family were frequently mentioned, including the *Gazette*'s publisher and editor Hugh Tullis, a lawyer who would go on to a distinguished career as a state judge. This was the same Tullis family that had once enslaved my great-great-grandmother Laura Brumley and many others on their plantation in St. Joseph and who remained prominent social and political leaders in the parish for many years after the Emancipation Proclamation. It was the same Tullis family whose matriarch, Sarah Tullis, had educated Laura, in defiance of the law. The old newspaper was filled with events and scenes from the lives of white people in the Delta region before and after 1900. The people who toiled to support their way of life, my black ancestors, provided little more than an anonymous and faceless backdrop to the stories.

Entire columns in the *Gazette* were given over to breathless descriptions of the most arcane happenings, and I ineluctably found myself swallowed up in the rhythms of the small town's life as I journeyed through the years.

A Negro man living on Buckhorn plantation was kicked by a mule on Tuesday of last week and after extreme suffering died on Friday.

We desire to return thanks to the officers of the steamboat Goldman for highly appreciated courtesies on her trip down last Monday and up Thursday.

A large buck was run into town last Tuesday by some hunters, and after a hot chase was finally killed in the duck pond field.

There were weekly write-ups about family visitors from neighboring villages and towns, like Rodney, Natchez, Hard Times, and Waterproof, about Mississippi River fishing derbies and moonlight hayrides, about baseball games between rival city clubs, and about mint julep soirees on Tensas Parish's finest plantations. Even the smallest changes in weather in St. Joseph were noted in fascinating detail in the *Gazette:*

> The weather for the past week could not have been improved for the purposes of the cotton planter, and under the rays of a summer sun cotton is growing rapidly.

But it was the weddings, illnesses, and death remembrances in the small town's comfortable white society that received the most consistent and devoted attention, and I studied each of these news items for clues about the Beaumonts:

> Mr. Guy N. Hunter paid a beautiful tribute to Mrs. Guice's memory when he said she was a sweet, unselfish Christian gentlewoman, who never thought of self, whose greatest happiness was in giving pleasure to others. She was ever ready to comfort the sick and distressed, and the world was made better by her influence and gentle ministrations to others.

It seemed a reasonable hunch that I would find the name Beaumont in those pages somewhere, some year, some month or day, after the turn of the century. After all, A.J. Beaumont had lived in St. Joseph for more than forty years after his arrival in Louisiana in the late 1850s and had become a well-known figure there before he died nearly a half century later. From my research a year earlier, using the same microfilm readers in the

Davis public library, I already knew that Beaumont was something of a town leader, frequently mentioned in the *Gazette* between 1870 and 1900. His obituary in 1901 took up eight column inches on the local page.

This English immigrant, I had learned, served on the city council for a short period in the 1880s; he was also a school board official, a private investor in civic improvement projects (including a lucrative wooden plank toll road on the city's levee), a saloon and billiard hall owner who specialized in fine cigars and German brews, a cotton grower, and a prosperous dealer in plantation supplies, whose store occupied a central place on the town's main thoroughfare, Plank Road, not far from the Tensas Parish Court House. Indeed, Beaumont frequently advertised for business in the *Gazette*, especially in the weeks when the Tensas Parish Circuit Court was in session and St. Joseph filled with lawyers, jurors, and others on business from throughout the state. His name appeared in listings of liquor license applications; it could also be found among the faithful attendees of Tensas Parish Democratic Party meetings during Reconstruction and the rise of Jim Crow.

Each detail I had mined about Beaumont's life in St. Joseph during my earlier research fascinated me. On the paper's society pages, for example, I had discovered:

> Mr. A J Beaumont will open his billiard and pool room early
> next week, the entire room has been refitted, the pool and
> billiard tables recovered, and everything put in first class condi-
> tion. This room is the prettiest and most comfortable of any in
> the State, outside of New Orleans, and well supplied with every-
> thing that can contribute to the comfort and pleasure of his
> guests. (November 21, 1885)

A J Beaumont invites lawyers, clients, witnesses and jurors to call at his palatial saloon and billiard rooms during court. . . . Everything imaginable for the comfort of the inner man can be found at Beaumont's. (April 30, 1886)

We return thanks to Mr. A J Beaumont for a pitcher of mint juleps kindly sent to this office. (May 7, 1886)

At other times I had found Beaumont's name hidden amid the dark lines of type in local news stories about events large and small:

Fire was discovered in the house in the rear of the saloon of Mr. A J Beaumont on Monday night about 11 o'clock. The alarm was given and the blaze was soon extinguished, doing little harm to the buildings. The fire was evidently the work of an incendiary, as the building caught from the outside. The house was occupied by the barber, Wm. Thomas. (July 6, 1894)

There is a herd of unbroken ponies that grazes around St. Joseph and every evening about sundown goes to the lake in front of town to water, and then dashes across the levee and down the road through town like onto a charge of cavalry. This is a great source of danger to people who are driving their wagons and to children whose nurses take them walking about that hour. Quite recently this cavalcade of horses going at full speed startled a team of mules hitched to a wagon in front of Mr. A J Beaumont's store and caused a run-away. Had it been a carriage with ladies in it the danger to life and limb would have been great. We do not know of any way to correct this evil and would be glad for someone to suggest one, short of killing the ponies. (August 21, 1896)

Some items in the newspapers before the century's turn had offered intriguing glimpses into Beaumont's prosperity in business:

Mr. A J Beaumont is having his store beautifully painted and decorated. Mr. Sam W. Hazlip is doing the work and this in itself is a guarantee that the job will be well done. . . . Mr. Beaumont also has fitted up a room in his store next to his office for the accommodation of customers. Comfortable chairs and tables are there, and the strictest privacy can be obtained by those desiring it. (September 18, 1896)

Other lines had provided a passing glance at the mundane details of his life:

FOR SALE A good large iron safe. Very cheap. Apply to: A J Beaumont, St. Joseph. (June 4, 1897)

Indeed, I had spent the previous summer, in 1996, combing through the years before Beaumont's death, meticulously collecting each of these items, finding in their accumulation a slightly more detailed portrait of my great-great-grandfather and his white family, one that added color and context to my search. From all the information I had gathered, it seemed clear to me that Beaumont had been a beloved and respected member of the white landed gentry and merchant class in St. Joseph, a quintessential nineteenth-century immigrant who saw his dream of prosperity and freedom in America come true.

With each morsel of information I obtained, I grew convinced that Beaumont's name must have lived on in St. Joseph after his death, through his white survivors. But, so far, no matter how closely I searched the microfilms, I couldn't find the clues I needed. The surname Beaumont seemed to largely disappear from the life of St. Joseph after 1901.

By the time I got to the year 1914 in early August, I didn't know if I could carry on much longer. My research had already turned from a hobby into something of an obsession and had pervaded slices of my personal and professional life in one form or another for nearly a decade. Yet deep down I felt torn about this project, tantalized by my discoveries but frustrated by the obstacles. Often, during that sweltering summer, I returned home to my wife and daughter feeling distracted and moody. I agonized, knowing there had to be an answer somewhere—but where? At the same time I loved the hunt and felt immense excitement over even the tiniest historical discovery. Like the electrifying moment more than a decade earlier when, sitting at a long wooden desk at the National Archives building in Washington, D.C., I discovered that A.J. Beaumont did indeed marry a white woman and have children with her after his long affair with my great-great-grandmother Laura.

I had been investigating 1880 and 1900 census records on black sheets of microfiche over a stretch of hours that summer afternoon. The Archives building on Pennsylvania Avenue, with the famous words "The Past Is Prologue" etched into a granite cornerstone near its ornate front door, was filled with hundreds of people that day, all searching for clues to their origins and ancestors among the library's many historical files and databases. Most of these people were not professional researchers, just ordinary Americans looking for personal meaning and identity in the details of our shared national history. Some were excitedly hunting through the manifests of the hundreds of passenger ships that arrived at New York's Ellis Island before and after the turn of the last century, hoping to uncover parents' or grandparents' names and the exact name of the ship they arrived on and its date of arrival. Others were scanning the state-by-state records of

Union and Confederate muster ranks, hoping to find their ancestors' names and priceless evidence of their small marks on our national history. Still others, like me, were searching copies of the original handwritten notes in our nation's census records for bits of information about their people, their blood kin.

Throughout the 1980s, spurred in no small measure by Alex Haley's exploration of his family's black heritage in the 1976 bestseller *Roots*, the nation's libraries and archives of genealogical materials experienced heightened use by Americans searching for clues to their past. Before then, genealogical research in this country was not nearly so popular. It was usually the hobby of people seeking validation of Old World nobility or royalty in their bloodlines. But after the enormous success of *Roots*, both in print and as a television miniseries, many Americans, white and black, began searching enthusiastically for even mundane details of their ancestors' lives, as a way of connecting personally to history and their racial and ethnic identity.

I was just one among many curious people in the Archives that day in 1986, my hunt for the footprints of my white forebears just another among many searches through time. My search, though, represented perhaps a new twist in the usual process. Whereas once the interracial heritage many Americans share was largely off-limits to public discussion or even research, the explosion of interest in genealogy in the 1980s helped shatter the taboo. Haley himself, in an interview in the *Washington Post* shortly before his death in 1990, pointed to the mixed-race heritage of many black Americans as the next frontier he hoped to explore in his sociological research.

As I was looking through census records on microfilm and microfiche that afternoon in Washington, I suddenly came upon Beaumont's name and household. It was startling. There in fine cursive writing penned by the 1880 census taker were Beaumont's full name and that of his wife, Mary Ann, whom he had married in St. Joseph in 1878. The marriage came one year after Laura gave birth to Beaumont's mixed-raced daughter, Pearl. I also found in the Archives' census microfiches the names of the white children Beaumont subsequently produced with his wife— Florence, born in 1879, and Arthur W., born in 1885, both in St. Joseph.

I scribbled this information down on a piece of scratch paper and later filed it away in my desk drawer at home, elated by the discovery but not knowing what, if anything, to do with it. Still, this tiny proof that Beaumont had indeed had children with his white wife intrigued me and formed the germ of my search. Perhaps Beaumont's children had had children of their own who were living somewhere in America today, distant cousins of mine.

When I found more time to pursue the chase in the 1990s, I discovered wonderful material in the newspaper microfilms, including details about the historical context of Beaumont's life in the late nineteenth century in St. Joseph. This information riveted me. For example, while relationships between white men and black women in the Old South were certainly not uncommon during and after slavery, one story I found in the *Gazette* pointed up unusual demographic imbalances in St. Joseph that may have contributed to an even greater number of such relationships. In February 1873, during the period Beaumont and Laura were meeting in St. Joseph, the newspaper published the following note about city life, which, while written in humor, nonetheless illustrated a reality about life for young white men laboring in a small, rural, out-of-the-way river town 150 miles north of New Orleans:

> The most serious topic in St. Joseph seems to be the scarcity of young ladies.
>
> Our little town has 15 promising young men, including lawyers, merchants, preachers, steamboatmen and planters, all anxious to get married and there is not a single young lady, not promised, in town. We understand that these young men have had several meetings recently, to consider what steps could be taken for their relief. The last proposition we have heard suggested is to start General Stephen Routh out with full power of attorney to act for the unfortunate young men who are unable to leave their business—each one binding himself to accept the selection made by General Steve. Two have volunteered to accept widows not older than forty.
>
> Poor boys!

Uncovering such slices of a bygone life fascinated me intellectually, but I was troubled by my growing obsession. I often felt a vague uneasiness and inexplicable hurt deep inside the more I worked on this project and sometimes wondered if, in the end, my search was pointless or, worse, harmful in some way—if, indeed, I was doing something vaguely disloyal to my own people by devoting so much time and mental energy to trying to find a different sort of "roots" in the white family of a man whose good life seemed dependent on the very system of injustice and inequality under which black people had suffered for so long.

A.J. Beaumont and I were distantly linked by blood and DNA, but the differences between us could not have been starker. I was a forty-three-year-old black man, a husband and father living at the dawn of the twenty-first century in a postindustrial America that was contending with new challenges of ethnic and racial "diversity" and sharpening disparities between the rich and the poor, the informed and the ignorant.

The contradictions of my America were staggering. It was a time of seemingly boundless opportunity and sickening hopelessness and alienation, an age of unsurpassed economic riches when children gunned down children in schoolyards. The wealthiest society the world had ever known, we nevertheless seemed unable to guarantee that young people graduated from high school knowing how to read and write. Still, we were witnesses to stupendous wonders nearly every day. Scientists sent robots to Mars to test for life and made genetic copies of sheep and other living creatures, while ordinary people could find information about practically anything within the blink of an eye by the mere touch of a finger on a computer keyboard.

On the one hand, African American men like me had an 81 percent chance of being either dead, jobless, or in jail by the time they were twenty-one. On the other hand, it was an age in which black Americans had rocketed to outer space in proud, patriotic service to their country, pronounced landmark judgments on the U.S. Supreme Court, headed the nation's Joint Chiefs of Staff in wartime, and led public opinion polls for president of the United States.

A.J. Beaumont was a white man from a far different age, a poor immigrant who, like millions of others, came to this country in the nineteenth century in search of a dream. He benefited tremendously from his adopted nation's racist way of life in Louisiana, becoming a proud and successful member of the landed white southern gentry. And by all family accounts he, like so many other white men of his age, did not feel any meaningful moral responsibility for his mixed-race offspring, my great-grandmother Pearl.

I looked at Beaumont's old photograph countless times during my quest, the one he had sent to Pearl in 1901 as an expression of his regret over his failures as a father to her, the one that had been handed down from Pearl to Fredda to my mother. Cradling it in my hands, I often wondered what his life and times must have been like.

He lived between 1839 and 1901, a period that saw the full flowering of the Industrial Revolution in England and the rise and greatest glory of the Victorian Empire. He lived during the time of the potato famine in Ireland and the Opium Wars in China. The invention of the telegraph and Morse code and the heyday of the railroad age occurred during his lifetime, which ended at the dawn of the internal combustion engine and the age of flight. His contemporaries were giants like Darwin, Hugo, Marx, and Lincoln; Tchaikovsky, Monet, Whitman, and Edison. And he lived during the times that had always fascinated me most, not the least because of their lasting effects on my racial and family identities—the eras of slavery, Civil War, Reconstruction, and the rise of Jim Crow in the American South. It was an extraordinary period in human history, and I found it infinitely interesting to study.

But at times I found myself seething with an almost atavistic resentment at Beaumont's photograph as I worked at my computer and in the library, frustrated by my failure to locate his white heirs and growing embittered by the Gilded Age prosperity and smugness I saw reflected in his unchangingly pale and silent face. I couldn't help seeing in his portrait the face of every white man I had ever come to despise in my life and every white man whose racism, arrogance, and privilege had translated into oppression, injustice, and untold pain for so many. I saw in it all the obscenities of slavery and all the evils of the plantation era, when white men like him whipped and tortured my ancestors and took black women like Laura for their pleasure whenever they liked. I saw the degradation my mother had suffered in the 1940s whenever she had to travel on squalid Jim Crow railcars to attend her segregated library school. I saw all the cowardly white administrators who, terrified by the idea of a black physician ministering to white patients, said no and shut hospital doors in my father's face when he sought to establish his career as a talented young surgeon in the 1950s. And I saw in Beaumont's face the faces of white strangers in Seattle whose ignorant prejudice marked my coming of age during the era of racial integration in the 1960s.

Indeed, it was in that decade of my childhood that my family first got to know what white people were like, on their own turf. In many ways, I realize in hindsight, the genesis of my search for the Beaumonts lay in that era.

Up until the 1960s all generations of my family lived in a racially segregated America—in St. Louis, Winston-Salem, and Nashville. Even in Seattle, where my parents migrated in 1956, after my father finished his surgical training in the Deep South, the neighborhoods and schools were segregated by local custom if not by Jim Crow law. The city's black residents were largely confined to a several-mile-square patch of real estate in the inner city called the Central Area, where the public schools were predominantly black and abysmally staffed and supported, compared with schools in white areas.

Infused by the ideals of equal rights and opportunity that galvanized their generation of black professionals, and buttressed by legal advances of the civil rights movement elsewhere in America, my mother and father decided in 1960 to test Seattle's de facto system of racial segregation. Unable to buy a house outside the Central Area because of their race—and thereby unable to gain access to premium public schools for their children—my parents secretly commissioned a white middleman named Franz Brodine to purchase a piece of property for them in the city's south end, in a middle-class subdivision called the Uplands, where the public schools were good. For many years, under a 1920s-era racial covenant governing the subdivision, blacks and Asians—unless they were working as domestics—had been barred from residence in this pleasant neighborhood on the shore of Lake Washington.

Although such racial covenants governing neighborhoods and housing were ruled unconstitutional by the U.S. Supreme Court in 1948, the restrictions were still observed in practice in many American cities. My parents' clandestine method of purchasing property in a white neighborhood was typical of the sleight-of-hand upwardly mobile black people in northern cities had to resort to in order to better themselves, to secure equal educational opportunities for their children, and to force the nation to honor its constitutional guarantees. It was one thing for the courts to decide that racial segregation was illegal, as they did throughout the 1950s and 1960s, but it was up to individual black people like my parents to test those decrees, to force the change, and to deal with the personal consequences.

It was on a beautiful street lined with lush, vase-shaped elm trees and tall, elegant pines, amid rows of stately homes overlooking the lake, that my mother and father decided to build a house. After Brodine signed the property deed over to my parents, they commissioned the city's only black architect, Benjamin McAdoo, to design and build the house. A relatively new arrival in Seattle, with a growing reputation for his work, McAdoo took special care with our house, in part because he wanted to make sure our historic move went smoothly. He had already designed and built several other houses for white families in the neighborhood and was well aware that he couldn't live in any of them because he was black. Our victory would be his as well.

For months, as our house was being constructed, the white neighbors were unaware of who owned it. Then, shortly before we moved in that December, they found out the new arrivals were a black family. Terrified of us and distressed over an assumed deflation of their property values, our prospective white neighbors convened emergency block meetings to cobble together strategies to thwart us. When the city's mayor, Gordon Clinton, got wind of the controversy, he urged civic mediators to quell it somehow. But the white neighbors persisted. They sent petitions from house to house throughout Seattle's south end to gain wider support for their efforts and pooled their money to offer my father a buyout at 200 percent of his purchase price. Anything to stop us.

But my parents were determined. We moved into our new house at 6261 Lake Shore Drive South a few weeks before Christmas 1960, the first black family in Seattle's uplands subdivision. From that day, my life changed forever. I was six years old, the product of a proud and loving black world, embarking on a new childhood in a world where my family and I were clearly alien and unwanted.

My closest friends, my teachers, my neighbors, the first kid I ever fought with my fists, the first girl I ever kissed on the lips—practically everyone who populated the universe of my school-age childhood—was white. I was the quintessential poster child of the era of racial integration, a drop of color on a field of snow. I was the first and only black kid in my class from first to seventh grades. I was the only black kid on my Little League teams, in my Cub Scout troop, and at swimming school. I learned to read, write, and enunciate English with perfect diction and grammar, to use a protractor and slide rule expertly, and to sing first tenor in classical ensembles in the school choir.

Indeed, I outdid most of my white classmates in practically every school subject and was popular enough to be elected president of the student body in junior high school by a landslide. At the height of the Vietnam War in 1968, when I was fourteen, I was awarded a prestigious American Legion medal by local war veterans for civic leadership and academic achievement. I was, in their eyes, the ideal young citizen, a model American.

But I was also hopelessly mixed up.

For the incongruities that defined my childhood were profound and difficult to comprehend. From early on, I felt a weight attached to my childhood on Lake Shore Drive. I knew that, as a black kid, I was in some way carrying a flag for my race and must never let it touch the ground in disgrace. My mother especially taught me to be proud of being black, repeatedly explaining that living amid the white middle class in Seattle was a pioneering and noble venture. Not many black people got the chances my siblings and I had, and we should make the most of them, both for ourselves and for other black people who might come behind us. My parents made it clear that failure—in school, in our behavior, in life—was not acceptable, a lesson my father used his leather belt to reinforce.

So I definitely knew I was black. It was precisely because I was black that I had to make excellent marks in school, that I had to prove I was as good as any of the privileged white kids. No matter that my skin was a light brown color, I knew that, in the eyes of most white people, I was as black as any African American boy in this country. Throughout the civil rights struggle in the 1960s, as my family, from our distant vantage point in the Northwest, followed events in the South through the newspapers or on television, I certainly knew what was at stake and whose side I was on. I knew that when Martin Luther King, Jr., and Medgar Evers led boycotts, sit-ins, and marches, they were fighting for me, not just the striking sanitation workers in faraway Memphis or the brave voting rights workers in Mississippi. The fire hoses, police dogs, and bloody nightsticks I saw to my horror on the *Huntley-Brinkley Evening News* could just as easily have been trained on me or anyone else in my family, had we been living in Selma instead of Seattle.

At the same time I became aware of the subtle paradox that black people are not all alike, that as a race we have recognized and fostered divisions and pecking orders among ourselves based on the very sorts of physical differences in skin tone and hair texture that have fed white racism. My hair was what my mother, her family, and her friends in Seattle's small but close-knit black bourgeois society called "good hair" because it wasn't rough and nappy, like that of most dark-skinned black people, but curly, comparatively straight, and soft, like the hair of whites. My skin, in their eyes, was a pretty "tan" or "yellow" or "red" color, not dark "as the ace of spades." I was said to be fortunate because I didn't have "liver" lips or kinky, unkempt hair that looked like "dust on a jug." While my mother instilled in me a deep sense of pride in our race and our history of struggle as a people in America, she also made it plain that black families like ours were somehow different and more blessed within our own society precisely because we had fairer skin and were closer to being perceived as "white."

When my mother was growing up in her bourgeois family in St. Louis, her dark-skinned father often used to say half-jokingly that America's race problems never would have festered so long had Abraham Lincoln not freed the slaves. With all the interracial children produced under slavery, America would have become fully racially mixed in time and the system of slavery and human inequality would simply have "withered away." "You must try to improve the race," Grandpa from time to time instructed my mother during her adolescent years in the 1930s, encouraging his daughter to choose a light-skinned man as her mate. Light was simply better than dark, and the more white in us, the better.

Even as a child in Seattle, in my deep unconscious I was never able to reconcile such an appalling contradiction. How could we feel truly proud of being black inside if the less black—the whiter—we appeared seemingly made us "better," more favored in society and among our own people? If being black was indeed something to be proud of, why did we have to leave black people behind in so many ways in our endeavor to live with and model ourselves after whites? How could such outward racial pride and traces of inner self-loathing coexist?

I remember feeling shame the first time I read *Nigger*, Dick Gregory's searing 1964 memoir about his impoverished childhood in the 1940s in St. Louis. He wrote bitterly about the racism that he, with his dark skin, encountered from the black bourgeoisie, who generally had lighter skin. Although this bigotry stemmed in part from the animosity of many established black St. Louisians toward poor, backward black sharecroppers who, like Gregory's family, had migrated north during and after the war, it was also based on skin color. Gregory was constantly made to feel as if he were little more than an ignorant, dirty, shiftless "nigger"—not by whites, but by the snobbish blacks who occupied a higher social station based not just on livelihood and income but also on lighter skin color, straighter hair, and other physical features. Their bigotry was just as malicious and crippling as any he ever felt from white people, Gregory wrote. That he grew up in St. Louis in the same era as my mother, in the same neighborhood, yet came away deeply wounded by the very classist and racist pathology she had been conditioned to believe in, confused me as a teenager and left me despairing whenever I tried to figure racism out. How was the racism of my loving family any different from the white racism we all loathed?

"Good" hair. "Light" skin. "Thin" lips. "Proper" articulation. Such were the subtle messages and code words about race that filtered into my unconscious mind as the child of a black professional family. "You come from good stock," my mother used to say to me with pride, an expression that was somewhat meaningless to me as a little kid but became infinitely fascinating and richly ambiguous by the time I entered adolescence. *Good stock.* What did that mean? "You've got good blood," she would reply, usually after an impatient sigh over my obtuseness. "You come from good ingredients, like a good soup." Still, the phrase would flit around my brain like a firefly in the dark, intriguing and yet not quite reachable or knowable. I knew the expression must have something to do with race, with black and white, as did so many things in my life. In time I came to an understanding of my mother's pet phrase that somehow satisfied me both emotionally and intellectually. "Good stock" suggested I had the best qualities of both races in me. But more important to me, the expression seemed to connote such human qualities as strength, rootedness, intelligence, devotion, and identity, admirable qualities that many in our black family line epitomized. That had to be it. "Good stock" must encompass both character and color. Such was the truce I eventually made with my mother's expression.

For the longest time when I was a kid, I had no idea where my family's lighter features and relatively straight hair came from. I rarely thought about it, actually. My parents always made it clear that the overriding reality we needed to understand, for the sake of identity and survival—despite all the contradictions and nuances of race as they manifested themselves in our family—was that we were black in a racist society dominated by white people.

Still, as a small child I used to gaze at our family's photographs in albums and on the living room walls in Seattle and admire not only how handsome and beautiful many of our black relatives and ancestors were but also how breathtakingly varied they were in skin color and physical appearance. Our family album was a living, breathing testament that "black" people in America come in all shapes, sizes, and colors, ranging in skin tone from my grandfather Clifford's rich chocolate brown to my sister Sharon's creamy ivory. Yet we were all one family, each of us definitively "colored," "Negro," "black."

It wasn't until I was about twelve that I began to put a few things together about our family's mixed racial past, almost by accident. My grandmother Fredda—Pearl's daughter and the granddaughter of A.J. Beaumont—was visiting us in Seattle from St. Louis with her husband, my grandfather Clifford. How I loved it whenever they visited, bringing with them their soft Missouri drawl, which filled our house in the distant Northwest with loving echoes of our southern heritage. One warm summer evening I was standing at Grandma's side while she played Scrabble with my mother and grandfather on our living room table. She asked me to help her craft a word with the tiles in her wooden holder, but as I snuggled next to her, my eyes kept falling on her gentle hands as they held the tile holder, hands mottled slightly by age spots but clearly white in color. They were as white as the hands of my white teacher, Miss St. Martin. My eyes traced a path from her hands to her bare white arms to her face, a kind, expressive face with warm hazel eyes and skin as white as that of any white woman in my neighborhood. It was as if I had never really *seen* my grandmother before that moment. I was stunned and slightly amused by the strange revelation that my beautiful black grandma was not "black" in appearance at all. I next noticed my dark-skinned grandpa at the table and then gazed at my mother, one of their three children, a perfect blend of the two, a woman with tan-colored skin and wavy dark hair. I realized there was something mixed up about us. We were probably not unlike the milk shakes my sister and I loved to make in the summertime, using chocolate and vanilla ice cream and mixing them with milk in a bowl to make a creamy brown. But where this mixture in us, as people, came from I hadn't a clue as a child. While the revelation stayed with me, inside my mind somewhere,

I rarely thought about it consciously in my childhood and never asked any questions, so busy was I with the fun of growing up.

In many critical ways my childhood *was* happy, so "integrated" with the lives of white people in the Uplands that it lent validation to the ideals of the age. We proved—in an isolated, microscopic fashion, at least—that a black family could live in a sea of white people of the same advantaged class, with shared values, if everybody could get over the initial fear and ignorance of each other. My childhood was not unlike *Leave It to Beaver*, with my siblings each cast as Wally, my parents as Ward and June, and me as the Beaver. Were it not for the color of our skin, we could have passed as just another family in our pleasant town, which resembled the Mayfield of the Cleavers. Decades later my memories of those days in Seattle remained filled with happy family summer vacations to Washington's pristine Olympic Peninsula, salmon-fishing charter trips with my father in the Pacific Ocean off Neah Bay, rafting escapes on Lake Washington, and endless pick-up baseball, basketball, and football games on lazy summer afternoons with my white neighborhood pals.

But amid the happy times were a number of cockeyed, wretched experiences that colored my awareness of the white world as a black child. Sometimes happiness seemed to come in tandem with hurt, precisely because of race. Once, when I was seven, I skipped up the block to visit a white school pal at his home for the first time, only to see his front door slammed in my face with a loud bang by his mother, who hadn't known Tommy's friend was black. In another incident, at nine, I visited another house up the street where two little white girls had invited me to play, only to have their grandfather chase me from the yard with a long wooden stick in hand, snarling, "You

black . . . !" And then there was the time, at ten, several schoolyard jerks encircled me as I headed to my classroom, taunting me
with shouts of "Chocolate! Chocolate!" Too scrawny to fight
back, I looked up at the bullies through my thick horn-rimmed
eyeglasses and repeatedly muttered the only thing that came to
mind: "Vanilla! Vanilla!" The crowd of white kids watching this
scene fortunately began to laugh uproariously at my rejoinder,
and I managed to slip into class without a bruise or a scrape. A
sharp wit, I learned, could be as useful in a schoolyard pinch as
the solid right cross my older brother Wayne preferred.

My mother and father explained that these racial episodes,
these occasional scrapes with white fears and ignorance, were not
my problem. I didn't cause these incidents and they were not my
fault, my parents told me. They were simply part of the complicated and challenging experience of being black in America. All
black people in all strata of society had similar encounters. My
parents said racism was *their* problem, those ignorant and hateful
white people's problem, and that the best thing we could do was
show our resilience in the face of the storm and continue pursuing our life goals. Get over it and deal with what matters most,
they insisted, things like school and family and friendships. Don't
let the occasional bigots defeat you or force you to lower yourself
to their level. Thus my method of coping with prejudice, like my
mother's and father's and that of so many other black Americans,
became to swallow the hurts, to stow them away in a little box inside my soul somewhere, and try to get on with my life without
allowing them to cripple me.

But, of course, the hurts accumulated. They festered over
time. And somehow, many years later, they seemed to be coming
to a head inside me during my search for my white kin. The old

photograph of A.J. Beaumont became a kind of key to a locked portal to my psyche, releasing all sorts of long-pent-up personal memories about race as I pursued the white branch of my family tree.

Taken and developed sometime in the 1880s in a studio called Washburn's on Canal Street in New Orleans (according to the label on its border), Beaumont's portrait, which for posterity had been mounted onto a sturdy slice of cardboard, seemed fairly typical of studio portraits of that era. Pictured against a grayish backdrop, he posed very formally for the camera, apparently seated, wearing what appeared to be a dark tweed jacket and a satiny floral tie. His head was facing slightly to the left, his hair neatly combed with a crisp part, his French imperial beard classically trimmed. It seemed the unmistakable image of a proud, middle-aged Confederate veteran, a man obviously very comfortable with his civilian life some twenty years after the conflict.

Now, more than a century later, the photograph had become a kind of symbol of so many racial incidents in my own life. It was Beaumont's image that came to mind whenever I recalled the white administrator who headed the Princeton-in-Asia office on campus, which sponsored students spending semesters abroad for academic credit. One day during my junior year in 1975, I visited the office to inquire about spending a year in Taiwan or Japan, since I was majoring in political science with Asia as a focus. I took a seat and, after an exchange of small talk, the administrator looked me up and down nervously for a moment and cleared his throat. Then he confessed that the program had never sent a black student to Asia before and that he felt many alumni and host families would object to my participation. "It's not that I object," the white man said as he squirmed in his chair. "It's just . . . I'm sure you understand."

I also saw Beaumont's image clearly in my mind whenever I recalled a newsroom confrontation I had as a young journalist in 1982 with Larry Kramer, an editor at the *Washington Post.* I had just written a feature article about cockfighting in the Maryland countryside, a story so colorful and newsworthy it was scheduled by the paper's top editors to be published on the front page the following day. Now, though, Kramer was worried. One year after the scandal of Janet Cooke, a talented young black writer who had fabricated a sensational story about an eight-year-old heroin addict, the pudgy white editor was questioning whether I, too, a young black writer, had fabricated my story. After all, weren't we all alike?

I wanted to strangle the editor, just as surely as I wanted to murder the Princeton administrator. I wanted to pound the white bastards with two-by-fours and grind them into the floorboards under my feet. But instead I swallowed my emotions, told myself to work harder, and stowed away the hurt and resentment for the sake of moving on.

"Thanks for your time," I told the white Princeton official before shoving my books under my arms and trudging back to my dormitory room, seething with anger and sadness.

"No, Larry, it's true," I told my white editor, struggling to contain my emotions. "I didn't make it up. It's a great story."

Maddeningly, as I reflected on my past, I saw the face of A.J. Beaumont as an all-purpose emblem of white racism. Yet it was this very white man, this seemingly archetypal plantation-era figure whose life during Reconstruction seemed to represent all that my people despised and feared, whose blood was a part of mine. I began to hate the thought of him as much as I hated the warped, ugly pathology of racism at the heart of American culture, the system that ranked people according to their place in the wide spectrum of human skin tone and hair texture, lending grudging favor to black people like me whose looks were marginally closer to the white ideal while unfairly classifying darker people as ugly, undesirable, or unintelligent. I hated this insidious injustice, which ran directly counter to the ideal of human equality that gave direction and powerful meaning to my black ancestors' lives and, by extension, my own. And I hated the thought that it was only by a quirk of ancestral fate that I had been born "lucky" in this regard, that I was somehow more blessed in my culture because Beaumont's blood and the blood of other white people in our ancestral tree coursed with the black in my veins.

But most of all I hated this: the thought that I, too, had ineluctably internalized this racist pathology as the product of a privileged class. After all, didn't I prefer lighter-skinned women when I became a man, just as my society and family background conditioned me to? Didn't I often think they were prettier than darker women and that straight hair was finer than kinky? When I was feeling especially insecure about my abilities, in school and later in my careers in journalism and teaching, didn't I feel vaguely inferior to white peers because of my blackness? Indeed, didn't the sickness of my culture manage to seep its way through the gate to my soul, teaching me to distrust myself because of the black in me?

There was an old street saying about racism that my brothers and I sometimes cynically recited as we made our way to school in the rain and wind in Seattle—"If you're white, you're all right;

if you're yellow, you're mellow; if you're brown, you stick around; if you're black, you go back." It seemed as true when I was an adult as it did when I was a child. Was it, then, at least partially true that my family and I had endured comparatively well in America precisely because we had drops of white blood mixing with the black? Was that was our most telling advantage in the end?

Since leaving Seattle, I had been a journalist for twenty years—exciting, deeply challenging years that had seen me pursue news stories around the world for the *Washington Post*, from the cotton fields of Mississippi and the tough streets of Washington, D.C., to the embattled countrysides of Nicaragua, Liberia, and Ethiopia. But in very few of those hundreds upon hundreds of reporting projects had I felt the level of unsettling rage and anxiety that my search for my white cousins brought out. I often felt in my research as if I were peeling back the pulpy layers of some forbidden fruit—inexorably, almost involuntarily—and I was deeply troubled about the truths I might find at the core.

It had all seemed so simple that night in 1981 when my search essentially began. I had been a professional journalist living in Washington, D.C., for five years and was visiting Seattle on vacation. My mother and I, as we often did, were chatting about our family history over beer, and I was laughing with her as she recalled stories from her childhood about her grandmother Pearl, who she said was whiter in complexion than even my grandma Fredda. Mom regaled me with stories about Pearl's mother, Laura, the freed slave who was the offspring of a slave born in Africa and a white physician living on a neighboring plantation in Louisiana. There was also white blood on my father's side, Mom told me, in the form of a nineteenth-century

German-Jewish plantation owner in North Carolina named Lowenstein. Mostly, though, she talked glowingly about Laura's loving affair with the Englishman, which produced Pearl.

I had heard all these stories before, and I never got bored hearing her tell them. My mother was a wonderfully gifted storyteller who loved to punctuate her words with gales of laughter.

"We've got America in us," she told me that night. "We've got the story of America."

"But how do we really know all this is true?" I asked.

It was then that my mother rose from her chair, padded to her desk, opened a drawer, and almost nonchalantly pulled out the artifacts at the heart of my search: the photograph of A.J. Beaumont, his obituary, and the letter he had written by hand to his mixed-raced daughter, Pearl, shortly before he died. I gently held the fragile paper up to an overhead light and was startled by the clarity and beauty of the old man's penciled handwriting.

I had vaguely known such keepsakes existed somewhere in our family archive since I was a child. But now, as a working journalist, I suddenly began to recognize their remarkable value. It was as if in these artifacts I had stumbled upon an original work by Picasso or a long-lost manuscript by Langston Hughes.

One of my story editors at the *Washington Post* used to teach young reporters that stories had little value in journalism unless you collected a paper trail of evidence to back them up. "Make sure . . . you get . . . the documents," Bob Woodward would say in his telltale monotone voice, which made for mimicking behind his back in the newsroom.

Well, here, before me, on my mother's desk were documents of a sort, small threads of evidence that this old story from our family's past was true. And it was a story that must, I was sure, be filled with important lessons about race in America if I could fill it out.

Where did the white family go?

The key thing I needed to do was pinpoint where Beaumont's descendants went after his death so I could pick up a trail that might lead to the present day. I believed that if I found where his wife and children settled after leaving St. Joseph, assuming they had left, I could go to the county courthouse closest to their new home and research all kinds of property, probate, and tax records, which might provide clues to other places these descendants—if there were descendants—had resided over the subsequent decades.

I didn't know if the Beaumont surname had lived on. I didn't know if his children had children. All I knew from my research was that Beaumont's immediate survivors must have departed St. Joseph sometime after his death, because their names didn't appear in census or property records there after the turn of the century. There were no Beaumonts listed in any directory in Tensas Parish.

All I had to go on, really, were the newspaper microfilms, which offered fascinating clues to the family's comfortable way of life in St. Joseph society before A.J. died, like this snippet about the ninth birthday of his son, the white half brother of Pearl:

> MASTER ARTHUR BEAUMONT entertained his young friends on Monday night at a charming birthday party, which was largely attended and highly enjoyed by the young folks. (November 2, 1894)

I happened upon just two mentions of his survivors' names

after Beaumont's death in 1901. One was this advertisement, published among dozens of others on the front page of the *Gazette:*

FOR SALE CHEAP—One dump cart, practically new, and one dog-cart and jumper nearly as good as new. Either or both can be had at a bargain. Mrs. AJ Beaumont, St. Joseph. (April 21, 1905)

The other item was a review on the society page of a musical concert in which Beaumont's widow performed:

The St. Joseph Dramatic Troupe entertained their friends Tuesday evening at the Masonic Hall. A large and enthusiastic audience attended [showing] their appreciation with frequent applause. . . . Miss Eva Caldwell and Mrs. Arthur Beaumont delighted the audience with several rare musical selections including "Schubert's Serenade." (April 1906)

After that—nothing, literally nothing, for years and years on microfilm. Beaumont's survivors essentially disappeared without a trace after 1906, in an age when few records existed that would provide a paper trail for U.S. citizens as they moved from place to place.

And so on that hot August afternoon in 1997, I focused on the year 1914, studying the *Gazette* as I had for so many other, earlier years, searching it page by page, column inch by column inch, my eyes scanning the glass screen for any clue in the advertisements or news and society pages. I turned the knob of the microfilm reader, watching closely as the events of June 1914 glided slowly by. As I wandered from aay to day, history came alive. I saw several stories and news items in those weeks about "coons" and "the Nigger problem" that attested to the racial crudities of the day in Louisiana:

A few days ago a darkey named Beverley went into Dreyfus'
store and reaching over the counter gently drew from it a pocket
book containing $100. Immediately, Dreyfus missed it and
accused Beverley of taking it. . . . Beverley, finding himself
cornered, quietly drew the pocketbook from the back of his
neck. The darkey was last seen in the company of the sheriff
and will be invited to spend the next few years with Major
James at his "training band" at Baton Rouge.

I passed on.

On June 26, 1914, the big news was about the arrival of U.S.
troops in Veracruz, Mexico, where they had been dispatched by
President Woodrow Wilson in response to a crisis between the
two countries. "Pathetic Scenes in Vera Cruz," cried a headline
over photographs showing Mexican refugee children receiving
food from American soldiers. On page 3 of the same day's
Gazette a compelling photograph showed two men and two
women, dressed all in black, picketing on a sidewalk in New York
City. The headline read, "Mourners in Front of Rockefeller's
Office." The story detailed a labor strike in a Colorado mine
owned by the widely hated industrialist John D. Rockefeller and
the nationwide protests over his use of violence to quash it.

Amid all the stories were fabulous old advertisements for
"wonder" cures like Lydia E. Pinkham's alcohol-laced elixir for
"feminine troubles," for a new refreshment called Coca-Cola,
which promised "vim" and "vigor" to all who drank it, and for
the Edison Phonograph, described as a revolutionary new "sound
producing machine." I loved looking at the ads, which seemed
like vintage Madison Avenue antiques coming to life before my
eyes. But as fascinating as they were, the displays were a diversion
from my true task, and I tried my best to ignore them. I wan-

dered on, page after page, scanning each line of type in the old newspaper—not sure of what I was looking for exactly and not even sure it existed.

Then suddenly it happened.

Scrolling through the issue of June 26, 1914, I saw something strikingly familiar out of the corner of my eye. I turned the knob gently to reverse the film. I thought I had seen the letters "BEAU . . ." in a small headline on page 12 with the local news.

The words and letters were maddeningly tiny in the *Gazette*, and the paper was so old and brittle that the film image couldn't reproduce the entire page. I had to keep fiddling with the enlargement and focus knobs to find what I thought I saw amid the splotches and blemishes left in the newspaper by time.

There it was again. "BEAU . . ."

I enlarged the item so that it filled the entire screen and adjusted the focus. I wasn't mistaken.

DEATH OF MRS. A.J. BEAUMONT

Last week we inadvertently omitted mentioning the death of Mrs. Mary Ann Beaumont, relic of the late A.J. Beaumont, who was for so many years a resident of St. Joseph.

Mrs. Beaumont at the time of her death was living with her son, Mr. Arthur W. Beaumont, at Vicksburg.

Mrs. Beaumont was a good Christian lady who bore ill will to no one and was always a faithful, loving wife and affectionate mother. Together with her husband she lived in St. Joseph many years, including in her list of friends her every acquaintance in our town, and after the death of Mr. Beaumont in 1900 [*sic*] she made her home in Vicksburg, where her son had employment and has since continuously resided.

Mrs. Beaumont was a faithful and consistent member of the

Catholic Church and died in full communion with that Ancient Faith. Her remains were taken to Natchez for interment. The many friends in this parish extend her son deepest sympathy in his bereavement.

I read the article several times closely, then pressed the "copy" button to try to capture a printed image of the story. A moment later I pulled the warm sheet of paper out of the machine, the story somehow feeling more real and believable as I held it in my hands. I noted the mistake in the date of A.J.'s death and smiled inwardly at the article's stuffy Old World language, particularly the reference to Mrs. Beaumont as a "relic."

As I read the word "Natchez," so many memories about my search came to mind. I remembered receiving from the St. Joseph public library a few years earlier a listing of headstones in the historic Natchez City Cemetery and finding A.J.'s and Mary Ann's names in the lists. I remembered reading about the tradition in those days for white people to be buried in Natchez, about sixty miles south of St. Joseph, since the city was located high on a bluff and not prone to flooding from the Mississippi River like so many other Delta towns.

But it was another word in the small newspaper story that stood out as brightly as a beacon from all the rest. I heard myself read the word aloud, the sound soaring into my mind like a trumpet note, echoing over and over.

Vicksburg.

The family had moved to Vicksburg, the storied old city located just north and across the river from St. Joseph in Mississippi.

I felt a new surge of energy and returned to work. I looked at the screen some more to scan other stories and ads near Mary

Ann Beaumont's obituary, which was near the bottom of the page. One ad touted a surefire rheumatism cure called "rub-my-tism." It was next to an official Louisiana state notice of a forthcoming exam for teachers' certificates.

I enlarged the image on the glass screen to look at each page in quadrants. The story of Mrs. Beaumont's death was in the lower left quadrant of the local news page amid a host of other short social items.

> Mr. and Mrs. Carneal reached home Monday after spending several days visiting friends in New Orleans. . . .

> Mr. and Mrs. Salvador Baragoan are receiving congratulations on the coming of another baby-girl. This now gives Salvador five queens and one king. . . .

I scanned up and down the page before heading to a new page of local news and on to another. Then, almost instantly, my eyes were grabbed by an item on page 6. I saw the letters "Beau . . ." again and felt the same sudden jolt of excitement that had filled me just moments before. The item rested amid a series of local announcements, sandwiched between an ad for an anthrax vaccine and another announcing an upcoming St. Joseph school board meeting. It stated simply:

> Mr. and Mrs. Arthur Beaumont and little daughter are visitors to St. Joseph this week.

I read the sentence several times more, admiring each word as if it were a pearl in a long necklace. I finally had the piece of evidence, the illusive footprint in time that I had been searching for. In 1914 A.J. Beaumont's surviving son, also named Arthur, had a child. I had advanced the white family's story by a generation.

It was then that I realized that my odds of bringing Beaumont's white family story forward from his arrival in America in 1856 to today had increased from the nearly impossible to the feasible in the short span of several minutes. Perhaps I really could accomplish what I had wanted all along in my research, to compare my black family's history over the past 150 years with that of our white cousins.

I couldn't believe my luck. After a long spell of frustration I had picked up their trail.

A couple of hours later I packed up my notes, the photocopies, and the reels of microfilm and headed out to my car, my brain filling with questions, my heart still throbbing with excitement. I switched off the Giants baseball game on the radio as I merged with traffic on Covell Boulevard to travel home on the outskirts of Davis. I headed west in the direction of California's coastal range, which glowed purple and blue on the horizon in the radiant late afternoon sky.

Think, I told myself as I drove, feeling a nervousness in my fingertips as I held the steering wheel.

Think.

A.J. Beaumont's son was still a young man in 1914—just twenty-nine. What if he had had other children later, maybe even a son or two? They could certainly be alive somewhere in America today, I conjectured, and perhaps even the name Beaumont had lived on. Somewhere. Maybe.

If so, that would certainly make the search easier.

I made a left turn at the Circle K store onto Lake Boulevard, heading south toward my house, and soon a series of familiar imaginary scenes started playing in my head, the same fantasies that had both fueled and haunted my search from the start, the ones in which I envisioned myself meeting the living white descendants of A.J. Beaumont in the flesh.

The scenes invariably transported me from the here and now to some other reality, a different sort of consciousness. My body certainly was driving my old blue sports car that afternoon, but my mind was being swept far away, under a crazy momentum all its own.

These mental images were always the same. I saw myself calling a phone number I had gotten from a phone book or information operator in some town or city in America. I saw myself dialing it and feeling my stomach tighten as it rang.

"Hi," I would say, after a voice finally answered. "Is this the Beaumont residence?" I would introduce myself, then say, "You're not going to believe this, but . . ." And then I would tell the voice the long story about my work and the relationship between my family and his.

I would tell the voice I was a writer and now a teacher of journalism at the University of California, Berkeley. I would say that I was calling because I hoped to tell a story about America in the parallel lives of our families, to write a book about race relations, about how some things have changed and how other things have stayed the same through the long years our families have lived in our country.

The voice in these scenes would sound stunned, startled, nearly speechless. On my bad days I would imagine the Beaumont descendant not believing a word of what I had to say to him. But on my good days my imagination would be more forgiving and I would sense understanding, or at least intrigue, on the other end of the line. The voice would tell me "Sure" in my imagination, "of course" I could come visit his house to ask questions about his family, his ancestors, and their lives over the past century.

The next thing I knew I would find myself flying to some town or city in America. I would rent a car and find the house I was looking for by studying a city street map or asking strangers on street corners for directions, as I had done so often when hunting down news stories around the world.

I would park in front of the white family's house, walk up the path, and knock on the door. In my imagination the wooden door with its leaded glass window was eerily like so many front doors I remembered from all the houses in the white neighborhood I grew up in.

When the door opened, I would see the white Beaumont descendant in person, finally, after all the years of searching. I would smile, extend my hand, and shake his. Then I would be invited into the white stranger's house, as I had been invited into strangers' houses in many other places for my work. I would enter bearing copies of Arthur Beaumont's photo and Laura's and Pearl's, along with copies of his obituary, the letter he wrote to Pearl in 1901 before he died, and copies of other material I had acquired over the years. I would take a seat on a comfortable sofa and glance around the living room as the white Beaumont family members examined in amazement what I had brought.

The living room would be like any other in America on a weekend afternoon: a football game playing on a television set near a fireplace where several logs were burning. Above the mantle would hang family photographs of smiling husband and wife and three or four cheerful children. On another wall, near a picture window, I would spot other photographs, much older ones, brown with age, of Beaumont ancestors dating back more than a century.

At this part of my imaginary scene, I would rise from the sofa to get a closer look at a photo near the center of the collection. I would feel my heart race as I recognized it, the very same photograph of the English immigrant and Confederate war veteran that had lasted an entire century in my family, the one he mailed in 1901 to my great-grandmother in St. Louis. It would be the final bit of proof I needed.

The scene played on as I drove home that afternoon, my mind still racing at breakneck speed.

I would return to the sofa and take out my notebook and pen from my jacket pocket and get to work. I would start interviewing my subjects just as I had interviewed countless sources for my newspaper stories. I would try to make them feel at ease with me and wouldn't interrupt them as they spoke. But I would be persistent in my questioning as I gently guided the conversation.

"Did you know anything about this? Did anyone in the family ever talk about it? What did your ancestors remember about A.J. Beaumont?

"What do you do for a living? Where were you born? Who were your parents and what did they do? What did they dream? What kinds of lives did they want you to have? Which dreams did your ancestors realize in America and which were dashed?

"Yes, I would love to have some coffee, thanks."

I would get an array of answers:

"No, we never knew anything about this. Had no idea! It's amazing, simply fantastic! So this makes us related, I guess. . . ."

"Well, very distantly," I would say, feeling a vague uneasiness.

"Oh, we've been many things in our family over the twentieth cen-
tury, Mr. Henry. Yes, we have. Steel fitter, prison inmate, Ku Klux
Klan member, Communist, and priest; circuit court judge, baseball
player, beauty queen, and vagrant; social worker, army veteran, school-
teacher, con artist. Methodist, Democrat, PTA member, Mason.

"We've wanted our kids to live better than we did. Don't all
Americans believe in that? Our dreams are the same dreams the coun-
try over. . . ."

Eventually I would get around to the questions I cared about
most, the ones about race and bigotry in America that had driven
me all along in my research. And I would feel an old welter of
emotions—rage, hurt, sorrow—begin to rise inside me.

Did you ever feel anything deep inside, as our family surely did,
about the great events and seminal figures in our nation's racial and so-
cial history over all these years?

What did you white people think about the Scottsboro Boys and Paul
Robeson, W.E.B. Du Bois, and Martin Luther King, Jr.? What did
you feel about George Wallace and Malcolm X, about the integration
of baseball and the army? Where did you stand on affirmative action?
How did your ancestors feel about Plessy v Ferguson *and* Brown v
the Board of Education?

While my family was struggling to make its way in America over
these many decades in the face of racial prejudice and discrimination,
from Nashville and St. Louis to Seattle in the far Northwest, where did
you, our white cousins, stand?

Are you people any different today? Are you any different from the
way I imagine your bigoted white ancestors were so long ago when
Laura and Pearl left Louisiana to make a new life for themselves in
St. Louis?

CHAPTER TWO

Road Maps

I pulled into my garage in Davis that afternoon and entered our house through the kitchen door, carrying my notebooks, artifacts, and microfilms in my black canvas shoulder bag, feeling enveloped by the harsh, penetrating heat of the desert evening. It was late when I stepped into the kitchen, nearly 6 P.M., so I immediately began to cook dinner for my wife, Letitia, and our five-year-old daughter, Zoë, filling a big iron pot with water to cook pasta, then chopping onions and garlic to go along with a few links of Italian sausage. I still felt exhilarated by my discovery in the *Tensas Gazette* a few hours earlier, but my excitement was now tempered with some uncertainty and anxiety as I pondered the possibilities. What if I did find this white family? Could I ever gather the nerve to meet them and talk to them?

I went outside to pick some tomatoes for salad from our small garden in the backyard, where we had also planted zucchini, watermelon, basil, parsley, and a variety of peppers. Amid them all was a stand of gorgeous yellow sunflowers, sturdy, straight, and tall, where my daughter loved to play hide-and-seek with her friends. The garden was a splendid sight, rich with life and glowing with color and greenery in the desert heat. I heard blue jays squawking and sparrows chirping near our rooftop, gazed at the white butterflies dancing amid the tomato plants pregnant with fruit, and I took a deep breath, longing to capture forever the magical moment in my mind's eye. Such beauty, such peace, I thought, right in my own backyard.

I loved Davis and the Sacramento Valley, especially at that time of year, and felt thankful that Letitia and I had decided to make the town of 54,905 our home. I even had grown to love the dry heat, which often soared above 100 degrees for days at a time in the summer. I had first moved to Davis late in 1991, after finishing my tour of duty in Nairobi, Kenya, as my newspaper's Africa Bureau chief. Letitia was then earning her Ph.D. in political science at the University of California's campus in Davis, and I joined her there after getting an appointment as a visiting lecturer for a semester at Berkeley's Graduate School of Journalism. I took a leave of absence from the newspaper, and when my Berkeley appointment turned into a full-time faculty position later that year, I quit the *Post* for good. It was time. I had put in fifteen years in daily journalism and needed to make a change for the sake of my personal life. I wanted to start a family and have the time to see it grow, a luxury I couldn't easily enjoy while chasing news stories around the world.

Letitia and I thought about moving closer to Berkeley, an hour's commute west on Interstate 80, but by then Davis had curiously grown on me. It had the comfortable size and feel of a small town, with an easy, gentle pace of life (fittingly, the official logo was a bicycle, a favored mode of transportation). It was the kind of town where smiling strangers said hello to each other on the sidewalks and jogging trails and where residents and grocery salesclerks knew each other by their first names. Davis was the first place I lived as an adult that remotely resembled the Seattle of my childhood in that way.

The city possessed a comparatively affluent, highly educated, and tolerant population whose professional lives centered around nearby Sacramento, the state capital, and the well-regarded local university. Their political attitudes were generally progressive. For many years the local representative from the Davis and Yolo County area was Democrat Vic Fazio, one of the most liberal members of Congress. It was indeed an eccentric little city, whose officials once proved their environmental sensitivity by authorizing $13,000 to build a special tunnel under a local high-way to protect endangered toads and once enforced a local noise ordinance by citing a woman for snoring too loudly in her apart-ment. The city council at one point voted to change the name of a local street called Sutter Place, after being aroused to indigna-tion by allegations that its namesake, California pioneer John A. Sutter, was an immoral "sexual predator" and enslaver of Indians. But the council eventually backed off, partly because it realized there were many other streets in town, such as Conquistador Drive, with similarly questionable origins, and that the expense and endless political arguments sure to follow such changes might not be worth the bother.

If there was any form of political feeling in town that might be considered extreme, it had to do with abuses committed against animals and vegetables rather than people. Animal rights groups, for example, regularly protested outside the UC Davis science research facilities, with the more radical groups sometimes expressing their outrage over the treatment of monkeys and rodents used in research by pouring blood and other debris on the driveways leading into the premises. The temporary mayhem and the police arrests that followed such acts were sort of an annual rite that citizens in Davis had grown used to. In the late 1990s, when stunning advances in biotechnology and agricultural engineering were made at research institutions like UC Davis, protestors found new reason for outrage, sensing conspiracies by scientists and multinational corporations to redo the planet's genetic makeup to the detriment of humanity and all flora and fauna. A group calling itself "Reclaim the Seeds" claimed responsibility for destroying a UC Davis research field full of genetically altered vegetables one night, pulling up each and every plant by its roots.

Such idealistic naïveté occasionally brought national attention to the town. Arch-conservative commentator Rush Limbaugh—who got his start in talk radio in nearby Sacramento in the late 1980s—sneeringly dubbed it "The People's Republic of Davis." Davis's population was about 4 percent black, 8 percent Latino, and 13 percent Asian, but the city's largely white heart was often in the right place when it came to issues like diversity and human rights. Admittedly, Davis suffered very little in the way of homelessness, violent crime, joblessness, and other ills plaguing bigger cities. People in Davis could afford to be proudly liberal by nature and tolerant of human differences largely because they didn't have very many significant differences to tolerate.

Still, I enjoyed Davis despite its provinciality and often precisely because of it. I enjoyed playing softball and golf and fishing with pals I had made in town. I enjoyed pedaling with Letitia and Zoë on the bike paths leading along Putah Creek toward Lake Berryessa to the west. And I loved jogging through the groves of olive trees and ancient valley oaks and the abundant tomato and corn fields that surrounded the city in the lazy summers. Davis was a tranquil place, where I didn't worry if I forgot to lock my door or left my windows open at night. It might seem plain, but it was conducive to reflection and raising my family. I found time and space there to think and to live.

After many years as a nomad, living in places from New York City to Nairobi, I was tired of packing up and moving every couple of years. The Sacramento Valley was where I landed at thirty-eight and finally decided to make a home, a place to call my own despite its flaws and quirks. The long commute to work was difficult but worthwhile for two chief reasons: housing in Davis was eminently more affordable than the depressingly overpriced Bay Area and—most important—the city's public school system was recognized as among the finest in the state. I realized that in putting our daughter's public school education first Letitia and I were making lifestyle trade-offs not unlike the difficult ones my parents made for similar reasons a generation earlier in Seattle.

Sometimes life's realities struck home in Davis, shattering my sense of calm and triggering a deep-seated rage over prejudice and racial ignorance that often scared me. One day a black father who lived in my neighborhood decided to teach his two teenaged children how to drive a stick-shift car in a large abandoned parking lot just outside town. The lot was located on the grounds of a hospital that had recently closed and relocated elsewhere, but inside the building several employees were still at work. One of them noticed the car and its black occupants driving awkwardly in the lot and telephoned the county police in fright, thinking the father and his children were going to rob the premises. Within minutes three squad cars sped to the scene. The white officers surrounded the car and at gunpoint ordered the occupants out. The father and children were badly shaken by the incident, which aroused great regret and breast-beating about injustice in the community. To me it confirmed what I and other blacks and Latinos in Davis had known all along: the reality behind that old acronym DWBOB—Driving While Black or Brown—was something the liberal, self-satisfied white community knew nothing about.

Many whites in Davis did not even realize the depth of their own ignorance or prejudice. To my never-ending anger and stupefaction, the local newspaper, the *Davis Enterprise*, occasionally confirmed this. One evening, for example, the newspaper prominently featured a news story about an attempted kidnapping downtown. The paper's crime reporter soberly wrote that the suspect in the case, who had fled the scene, was not "the typical suspicious-looking sort by usual police standards. He was a white male adult . . . [and] had no noticeable accent."

Here my small hometown newspaper was doing its naive and racially ignorant best to caution my comfortable white neighbors about the dangers presented by people who didn't "look" or "speak" like them, in an article that was deeply insulting to me and my family. The worst part was that the newspaper didn't realize the offense it was blithely committing, the racial prejudice it was condoning and perpetuating, until I and several other Davis readers angrily demanded an apology in writing.

At the same time deep down my anger was exacerbated, I knew, by the tormenting statistics that black people were involved in crime—and suffered as victims of crime—at a higher rate than any other group in America. My unspoken frustration and outrage over black crime were almost as profound as my spoken anger over white stereotypes about us. It was easy for white people to perpetuate a godawful stereotype, after all, when examples of black crime abounded. And I knew, to my inner guilt, that one reason I had chosen to raise my family in Davis was that the city was so tranquil and safe, unlike other urban areas I had lived in previously, including the inner cities of Washington and Baltimore. There life had never been completely secure, and I often lived as if under siege, behind barred windows and triple-locked doors and beneath the piercing nighttime glare of police helicopter searchlights. On the one hand, I wanted my daughter to grow up with an open mind about life and people and their many wondrous varieties. On the other hand, I wanted her safe from the world's many dangers, dangers that so many other black children in America's inner cities had to face every day.

My love-hate relationship with my adopted hometown often manifested itself so suddenly, without warning, that it was hard to prepare myself for the occasional shock to my equilibrium. I remember October 3, 1995, the day the Los Angeles County Superior Court jury rendered its verdict in the O.J. Simpson murder case. I watched the verdict that morning on television at my house and was stunned by the predominantly black jury's not guilty decision. Hadn't they seen the same mountain of evidence that millions of others had seen in the televised trial—the bloody footprints, the history of spousal abuse, and other incriminating records against Simpson? Contrary to the view that the news media frequently presented, that blacks in America were a monolith of agreement that Simpson was innocent, some of us felt that he was guilty and shared in the outrage that broke out across the land over a perceived miscarriage of justice. A few minutes after the verdict, however, I went with Zoë to a shopping center in Davis, to purchase a bag of doughnuts. It was there that I began to sense something else, something strange and unnerving in the wake of the verdict. I noticed it most clearly in the faces of the white strangers I ran across that morning, inside the doughnut shop and in the walkway outside. A small group of UC Davis students, an elderly couple, a trio of young women—all almost uniformly cast sharp, sudden glances my way before quickly averting their eyes, dismay and outrage at the verdict still etched on their faces. I felt as if I had stumbled into a gathering where I was obviously not welcome. Conversations seemed to cease or at least become much more muted in my presence. It was as if in me, the only black man in the vicinity, my white fellow citizens suddenly saw the living incarnation of the injustice they had witnessed only moments before on national television. It was as if a black jury member or O.J. Simpson himself were in the doughnut shop, not me. Because I was black, I must somehow have been a party to all that was horribly wrong in the Simpson saga.

Whether this was in fact how these white people felt, I cannot be sure. No words were spoken. But certainly there was a telltale tension in the air. And I knew that racism and bigotry often manifested themselves in public in the stony, awkward wordlessness of silence. It was a cold and eerie feeling, one that stayed with me during the emotional weeks that followed and soon tempered my outrage over the verdict itself. Indeed, after that experience in the doughnut shop with Zoë, a part of me naturally began to ponder the many godawful miscarriages of justice against black victims of white violence in our history, reflections that helped me conclude bitterly at times, "An eye for an eye . . ."

It was racism in Davis, and the city's continued reluctance to recognize its hallmarks, that prompted me to chat with a woman named Tansey Thomas, a black longtime Davisite who served on the city's human relations commission. We were discussing an incident that Letitia had witnessed in the city's community park one day, in which a group of seven-year-olds in a summer city program were playing a chase game. Two black boys were playing with about a half-dozen white girls in the game, in which the black boys were dubbed "monkey" and "gorilla" while chasing the squealing girls. The boys called themselves these names, and so did the girls. All of this happened under the supervision of white city recreation workers. Letitia was so outraged by the blatant racial overtones of the game that she wrote a letter to the newspaper to complain about it. Her letter soon triggered another angry letter to the paper, from one of the white girls' parents, who said Letitia didn't know what she was talking about, that the game wasn't racist at all, largely because the black boys "had created the game" themselves. This troubling aftermath reflected a breathtaking ignorance about race and racism on the part of the white parent as well as the city—which seemed perfectly willing to assume that two seven-year-old black boys had a better understanding of the rudiments of racism than adults of any color did. I was so disturbed that I brought the matter to the attention of the city council. It was then that Thomas contacted me.

"It's especially hard in a town like Davis for black boys," she said. "I raised a boy here. It's always like they're the ones who are the scary outsiders and 'bogeymen' in these children's games. It seems perfectly innocent at first, especially to white kids and white parents, but the repercussions can be pretty severe in the long run." Thomas told me about the problems her child had encountered in a Davis elementary school, where he was one of only a few black boys and often came home complaining about being called names, including "nigger."

Thomas said she had complained to teachers and administrators but was told that her son was too "sensitive" in his play with other children. Someone suggested that he should just ignore the name calling and the kids would eventually stop. "Besides, they're only words," this person added. Thomas told her son he could not hit others for calling him names, but he could use words to fight back. So her son did just that, using the one slur he hated most to hurt his tormentors back: nigger.

"Pretty soon he was calling everybody who bothered him nigger, unbeknownst to me," Thomas said, chuckling softly at the memory, "no matter what they looked like, no matter how white." A few weeks later Thomas heard a knock on her door. Opening it, she found a distraught white mother with her little boy, who pleaded with Thomas to tell her son to stop calling the white boy names.

"It was the most amazing thing that ever happened in my life," Thomas recalled. "Here on my doorstep was the mother of a blond, blue-eyed boy begging me to have my boy stop calling him nigger." She said her son had learned that white people were not that much different than he was, for they, too, hated to be called names. But, as Thomas pointed out, the incident also showed the extraordinary, sometimes ridiculous lengths to which you sometimes had to go in order to force a largely white, affluent, "progressive" community to wake up to its intolerance and prejudice.

Not surprisingly, my deepest fury erupted whenever such cases of mind-boggling racial ignorance involved my daughter, even remotely. She was born on a warm September night in 1992 in a small county hospital in the nearby town of Woodland. (Letitia and I named her Zoë because the name's classical meaning in Greek, "life," seemed so simple and joyous to us.) From that moment my existence became a whirlwind of bottle feedings, diaper changes, soccer games, ballet lessons, singing recitals—all the scenes and sideshows that make up the crazed theater of child-rearing. It was a joyous transformation of my life that I happily embraced.

But into this new life came episodes that confirmed with startling clarity the endurance of racial ignorance in America. I sometimes was driven to despair over the realization that my little girl would have to struggle with it as all of us had, in one way or another, from the beginning of slavery on this continent. Far from ending after one generation's long fight, such ignorance continued, festering like some kind of bacteria, from one generation to the next.

When my daughter was three, I remember, I called a local preschool, the Davis Parent Nursery School, to see about enrolling her because a few friends of ours had recommended it. One of the questions I asked the school official who answered the telephone had to do with the ethnic and racial diversity of the kids. She answered that the school was largely white, "unfortunately."

"We sure would like to have more black and Hispanic kids," she told me, "but it's hard. Our kids generally come from two-parent households, you know." For hours I darkly ruminated over her comment. What was she really saying? Obviously, she assumed that black and Hispanic families weren't normally blessed with both a mother and a father, like the white families in Davis. And this belief gave her a "reason" for saying it was difficult to mesh "different" cultures in one school. Whatever her nutty and uninformed point, I stewed over it in frustration and sadness.

Some months later, while Zoë was attending a different preschool, the white teacher asked the kids in her class, who were mostly white, to cut out magazine pictures that looked like their parents to make a collage of their families. It was an innocent enough project. But in the magazines the teacher chose to pass out there was not one black or Asian or Latino face. The minority children had to construct their families using all-white faces. The next morning, after hearing about the incident from Letitia, I stormed into the school to confront the teacher. I was probably more stunned than she was by the hot anger I heard in my voice.

There were, of course, mundane incidents with vaguely racial overtones that cropped up in our everyday life in Davis—just as they crop up in the lives of black people all over America. Like the morning Zoë and I went to a Blockbuster video store downtown. As soon as we entered the door, the white saleswoman made sure to ask for my book bag for security reasons. I glanced around the store and spotted a middle-aged white man in clear view of us, browsing freely with a big paper shopping bag in his hand. I pointed my finger at him, then heard myself curse at the store clerk and call her a bigot as I felt blood rush to my face in sudden rage. I was stunned at how unnerved I had become, instantly ashamed that I had sworn at the baffled white clerk.

Zoë, who was five then, had absolutely no idea why I was so livid. She had no idea why I grabbed her hand abruptly or why we left the store so briskly without getting the Bugs Bunny tape I had promised her. And I found I couldn't really explain it to her when I returned to the car. Or at least I didn't know how to begin, what words to use.

Even the most seemingly trivial incidents could drive me to distraction in those days. Once Letitia told me that a blond-haired girl in Zoë's class had informed Zoë, innocently enough, that she was black and would stay black "even when you're grown up." The girl's words didn't bother Zoë in the least, nor did they bother Letitia. But I dwelled on the incident for days, turning it over in my mind to look at it from every conceivable angle, wondering if there was some ulterior meaning and, if so, what the girl's parents had done to educate their child about the significance and meaning of skin color. I felt weak, powerless, no longer able to just accept some things and let them slide, as I had done so often in the past. It was as if in approaching middle age, as I continued with my search for the white family on the other side of my genealogical tree, a Pandora's box periodically opened up inside me, spilling out demons left and right.

I saw these race demons increasingly in my daily scanning of popular culture too, and wondered at times if I was losing my mind. Were the demons dancing only for me? In my obsession I began to keep a running tally of the number of times famous and accomplished black people were referred to by their first names in newspaper and magazine headlines and on television. Within weeks my list filled a small notebook.

Why were Steven Spielberg and George Lucas always "Spielberg" and "Lucas" in the press, I wondered, while Spike Lee was often simply "Spike"?

Was it mere happenstance that actors like Richard Gere, Tom Cruise, and Bruce Willis were always "Cruise," "Gere," and "Willis" and Denzel Washington nearly always "Denzel"?

Why did headline writers and television commentators often refer to white political figures such as Bob Dole, Jerry Falwell, and George Bush by their last names, yet feel perfectly free to refer to Jesse Jackson as "Jesse" and San Francisco's Mayor Willie Brown simply as "Willie"?

It was the sports world that presented the most glaring and frequent examples of such incongruity. The surnames of white superstars appeared in sports page headlines and on magazine covers, and television and radio announcers uttered their names reverently on the air—Marino, Gretzky, Clemens, Bird, and Elway, for example. Black star athletes were more likely to be mentioned informally by their given names or nicknames in print and on the air—Deion, Michael, Keyshawn, Reggie, Shaq, Magic, Rickey, Latrell, Ozzie, Charles, and Bo among them—as if little more identification were necessary or even pertinent or merited.

A sane mind, I figured, would be capable of accepting such evidently innocuous cultural conventions and move on, especially since such conventions seemed to bother so few others, including the black personalities themselves. Besides, these black celebrities, among them the women known to the multitudes simply as Oprah and Whoopi, were earning far more fame and money every year than most white people could dream of. What was the big deal?

But the more I thought about it and the longer my cultural

tallies grew each day (based chiefly on local papers like the abysmally provincial *San Francisco Chronicle* and local television news stations), the more despairing and obsessed I became. The not-so-subliminal message seemed to be that white Americans owned surnames worth respecting and honoring—sure evidence, in short, of roots, of identity, of a birthright and valued past. Black people, by contrast, no matter our level of achievement, could expect to be treated in a far more condescending and informal fashion in popular culture, as if our status were on a par with children, say, or household help—because by definition the last names of black Americans didn't really count, at least to white America.

Indeed, it wasn't much of a mental stretch to recognize in such modern cultural conventions a peculiarly enduring legacy of nineteenth-century antebellum America, when white slaveowners commonly forbade blacks their rights to surnames in order to discourage them from feeling connected as families and to facilitate their sale and separation. In this sense, demeaning first-name-only references in popular white American culture were not too far removed in spirit from the age of the plantation, of Aunt Jemima and Uncle Ben. At least that's how my tormented mind increasingly began to see it.

Sometimes late at night, when I couldn't sleep, I found myself wondering if my mother and father had felt the same things I did now when they were entering their own middle age in Seattle in the 1960s and reassessing their lives. Did they feel the same simultaneous sense of African Americans' progress and deep disappointment over lingering racism as I did? Did they ever wonder how many generations had to pass before such latent and blatant prejudice was finally wiped away? Why would my daughter likely have to contend with the same old hurt and struggle, the same maddening inexplicability of race?

I picked a handful of basil leaves from my backyard garden, taking a moment to inhale the herb's sweet odor as it mixed with the perfume of Letitia's climbing white roses. I then plucked a half-dozen plum tomatoes from a vine, cradling the produce gently in my hands, and returned to the kitchen screen door, which I opened with my foot. I re-entered the kitchen, placed the tomatoes on the countertop, and began to wash the basil. Letitia was getting a drink of cranberry juice from the fridge for Zoë, who was down the hall in the living room, lying on the floor on her stomach and cradling her head in her hands as she watched her *Pocahontas* video.

"Pasta okay?" I asked.

"Sure," Letitia said softly, swiping a lock of her dark brown hair from her forehead as she poured the juice in a cup. She looked tired and emotionally frazzled after a long, sweltering day of watching Zoë and obviously wasn't in the mood for talking. It was so unbearably hot and everyone was so tired.

But I just had to tell her what I had discovered in the library. I had to share my excitement over finally making progress in my work, which had been proceeding at such a glacial pace.

I rinsed the tomatoes in the kitchen sink, then took a sharp knife and began to cut the red fruit lengthwise on my cutting board, placing the sweet, juicy slices atop thin wafers of fresh mozzarella. On top of the salad I would sprinkle chopped basil, salt, and pepper, then olive oil. It was Letitia's favorite summer repast, and I loved making it for her.

"I think I had a little breakthrough," I said as I watched Letitia sip a drink of water.

My wife looked at me without speaking, an invitation to go on. A cool and exacting academic with expertise in political theory and African economic development, she was often befuddled by the emotional fits and starts that accompanied nearly everything I touched in my work. But to my never-ending amazement Letitia was never-failing in her emotional support. She listened to me with supreme patience and for some reason had as much innate faith in what I was trying to do as I did.

Until I met Letitia at thirty-five, my experiences with the opposite sex had been nothing short of a tangled mess, a tempestuous jumble of false starts and ill-fated choices, all in a lush variety of shapes and hues. I was certainly an "integrated" black man in that sense, for as the product of racial integration and the new cultural liberties of the 1960s, I had felt free to enjoy the company of women from many different races and backgrounds. In my coming of age I did not feel in the least restricted, partly because of my naive belief that race didn't really matter when it came to the ways of the heart and partly because most of the girls I was around when my adolescent hormones began belatedly to stir were white. I simply didn't know many girls who were my color.

Still, at seventeen my first choice in love turned out to be the beautiful black daughter of a surgeon who had trained with my father at Meharry Medical College, a historic black school in Nashville, and, like my father, migrated to Seattle in 1956. Southerners by heritage, she and I had both grown up in the virgin world of the Pacific Northwest, though in different neighborhoods, and I was certain our lives were destined to be linked forever. When she broke off our two-year relationship during my first year at Princeton, I was crushed. Soon afterward she became betrothed to a white student she met at the University of Washington.

A few years later I fell madly in love with a woman I met in graduate school in New York City. Like me, she dreamed of becoming a famous journalist, inspired by the heroic stands of the press during Watergate and over the Pentagon Papers. Both of us were also filled with youthful wanderlust, dreaming of international travel. Also like me, she was short and rather slender, with very curly dark hair, dark brown eyes, and light brown skin. But unlike me, she was an orthodox Jew from a first-generation Syrian immigrant family in Brooklyn. Her family detested me for being both black and a gentile, in their eyes a pagan. Still, she and I were idealistic enough to try to make the relationship work. Love could conquer all, my hopelessly romantic heart figured. Despite my receiving numerous late-night phone calls from her brother in Brooklyn, in which he vowed to drive down Interstate 95 to Washington and gun me down if I persisted in seeing her, she and I decided to elope a couple of years after we met. We were married in a civil ceremony at the old state courthouse in Annapolis, Maryland. In the three years that followed, she would sometimes awake late at night and weep over missing her family, who didn't want much to do with her after the terrible sin she had committed. Whether her family actually pronounced her dead and sat *shiva*, the Jewish ceremony of mourning, I wasn't sure, but the effect was pretty much the same. After a few years my first marriage collapsed from its own emotional weight, the victim of many pressures and deceptions, not the least of which derived from the wide divergence in our family, racial, and religious backgrounds. That breakup, too, was devastating.

I was certain I was fated to fail miserably in love, partly because I was such a cultural oddity, evidently born to straddle the very complicated worlds of black and white people. Indeed, the inner turmoil spurred by the breakup of my marriage in 1986 led me to examine many other aspects of my life and emotional history. In the months after the rupture I was propelled into psychotherapy, finding in the Connecticut Avenue office of a kind, Harvard-trained black psychiatrist named Dr. Henry Edwards a badly needed sanctuary where I could vent my deepest pains and sorrows twice a week—a wailing wall for all my anger and frustration, much of which derived from race. Unlike so many other black men in America, especially those who were impoverished and arguably had far greater and more urgent cause to feel alienated and adrift, I was fortunate, as an employee of a rich American corporation, to enjoy generous medical insurance that paid for my treatment. The many months of turbulent sessions with my insightful and intelligent black doctor certainly helped smooth the rough edges of my emotional upheaval.

I remember that year of the breakup, 1986, as one of intense inner despair personally. But paradoxically, it was also a year of growth and success professionally. I was the only black reporter on the *Post*'s prestigious National Staff and traveled to the far corners of America in pursuit of fascinating stories, from astronomers' discoveries at Kitt Peak National Observatory in Arizona to the heroic efforts of public health nurses in rural Mississippi to reverse trends in infant mortality. And it was a year of many women in my private life, women from differing backgrounds and walks of life. How I feasted at the table of delights of the opposite sex that year, finding myself gravitating toward women who, like me, were somewhat outside the social and cultural norms. In the ashes of my first marriage I aimlessly (and often comedically) drifted from one relationship to another in Washington and elsewhere, like a sailor with a defective rudder.

Few of these relationships worked, but all the women were certainly fascinating for their sheer range of personality and ethnic diversity. One was a blue-eyed Swedish news broadcaster with long blond hair who once modeled blue jeans in Stockholm and cooked terrific meatballs and pasta. I met her on the subway coming home from work one rainy night and offered her the use of my umbrella when we disembarked at the Eastern Market station. In truth, I was simply dazzled by her beauty. But I broke up with her some months later when I realized we didn't have a great deal to talk about, her understanding of race and racism in America in particular being very limited. Another brief affair was with a fiery half-Chinese, half-Filipino woman from Manila, a legislative assistant I met at a party on Capitol Hill one night. Just one week later, on a whim, I found myself traveling to France with her for a vacation. That relationship ended almost as quickly as it began, like a Roman candle fizzling in air. I went out briefly with a pretty and very talented black jazz singer who specialized in crooning the blues in smoky clubs and at Smithsonian museum recitals. Later I dated an accomplished young black newswoman with whom I enjoyed talking late into the night about writing and reporting. But that relationship, too, quickly failed because her assertiveness, which had served her well in the daunting climb up the ranks of her magazine's newsroom, had a brashness I wasn't used to.

I found myself going in and out of quite a few such relationships, most fairly brief and fraught with weird disconnects, cultural divides, and communication gaps. A number were slapstick comedies like something out of a Marx Brothers movie. I was a very active and adventuresome (though somewhat reluctant) bachelor during those chaotic years after my first marriage and, in retrospect, a pretty hapless and lost one too, a bit out of my element and depth.

Then, one night in January 1989, I met Letitia. I was at a conference in Lusaka, Zambia, where I had traveled to prepare for my posting in Africa. There she was, standing in a long black dress with her arms folded in the middle of a cocktail party crowd. She was a tall woman with short dark hair and a pretty face. I was certain I had seen her somewhere before, but I wasn't sure where.

"We've met," I blurted out innocently enough as I strolled up to her, a pensive look on my face and a drink in my hand.

"Oh yeah?" she said somewhat skeptically. "Where?"

I was serious, but she thought my line was a come-on.

We both started laughing sheepishly over the cliché and later went for drinks, where I learned she was an Africa scholar working for a nonprofit agency in Washington, D.C., that informed Congress about African issues. Educated at Smith College and Columbia University, Letitia was extremely bright and knowledgeable about Africa. She cared about the continent with a passion that was infectious, and over the next few weeks, back in Washington, helped educate me about my upcoming assignment overseas. In a sense, I violated a cardinal rule of journalism: "Never ever get involved romantically with a source," I warn my students at Berkeley. But I fell in love with Letitia.

A child of poverty raised by a single mother, Letitia grew up understanding nearly as much, if not more, about the black experience in America as I did, an improbable circumstance, given that she was white, of Hungarian, Swedish, and other European ancestry. She spent part of her childhood in the 1960s as one of only a few white kids in the black, low-income Anacostia section of southeastern Washington, D.C. Indeed, her background was almost the mirror opposite of mine. Her teachers, neighbors, school pals—all were black. She was even baptized, at eight, in a pool of righteous water one Sunday morning at a black evangelical church.

Letitia knew about the sting of racism too, on a gut level that jibed closely with mine and helped cement our devotion to each other early on. While I understood prejudice from a black middle-class perspective, Letitia had experienced its more blatant, white working-class form when she was child.

Once, while traveling to visit relatives in West Virginia, her mother and a black male companion were stranded on a desolate rural road when their car broke down. Car after car sped by on the lonely highway without assisting them, as Letitia, then a little girl, stood nearby. One car driven by a white fellow did slow to help, but when he noticed the black man with Letitia and her mother he scowled and sped off. Hours later a kind, elderly black man in a dilapidated pickup truck finally stopped and rescued them.

"You remember this," Letitia's mother had told her, tears of shame and rage filling her eyes. "You remember who it was who didn't bother to help us and who it was who did."

Letitia despised racism and never forgot all the other episodes of petty cruelty and ugliness she experienced growing up with poor whites in West Virginia, blacks in Washington, D.C., and Latinos in south-central Los Angeles. Her intelligence awed me as much as her sensitivity to and simple understanding of prejudice and the complexity of human existence. Still, she and I often laughed over her first impression of me. Assessing my brown skin, my mustache, and my curly hair that starry night in Zambia when we met, she thought at first that I was Cuban, then Puerto Rican. It was almost by a process of elimination that a day or two later she deduced I was African American.

Her reaction was one I often got from strangers in my travels in America and around the world, who at first glance would appear perplexed about my racial origins. In college a friend once described me as a "universal ethnic," suggesting I could pass for practically anything if I wanted to. It turned out to be oddly true, often to my amusement. In Athens, Greeks asked me for directions on the street, thinking I was one of them. Same thing in Mérida and Mexico City with Mexicans, and in Managua with Nicaraguans. From Asmara to Kingston, I received similar friendly responses from East Indians, Eritreans, Ethiopians, and other darker-skinned people who thought I was one of them. But in Uganda, in East Africa, the initial reaction of some strangers was strikingly different. Because interracial relationships between Africans and immigrants from India and Pakistan were traditionally reviled by Ugandans, who had killed and evicted thousands of Asian immigrants under the reign of Idi Amin in the 1970s, I was viewed quite contemptuously by strangers in Kampala who thought I was a "half-half" before realizing I was an American. In their eyes, a brown-skinned, curly-haired "half-half" like me was little more than a mongrel, a half-breed sullying Ugandan national pride and ethnic identity.

In America when I met a white stranger for the first time, either socially or during interviews in my work, my appearance would often spark a quizzical expression that would linger as the person struggled to identify me racially. A typical conversation would go something like this, with the stranger aiming mightily to identify me without actually broaching the touchy, discomfiting subject of race:

"Nice to meet you, Neil. Where are you from?"

"Seattle," I would say. "I grew up on the West Coast."

Hearing this, the stranger would nod, hoping I would go on to answer the question more fully so it would be possible to figure out what my blood origins were. But I usually remained quiet.

"So, your folks were from there?" the stranger would ask after the pause, taking a crack at the puzzle from another angle.

"No," I would answer. "They were from Missouri and North Carolina."

Another nod would be followed by another awkward pause, a more deeply furrowed brow, and then: "And they, uh, were also born in this country?"

I often had fun with that question too, explaining succinctly that yes, indeed, my people's roots went quite a ways back in America—"waaaaaaay back!"—long before the birth of the Republic, since slavery was certainly older than the United States itself. In time, though, I would relieve the white stranger's agony with a smile and say, "I'm black. I'm an African American with many other things mixed in."

The bond between Letitia and me was sealed during my time overseas between 1989 and late 1991, when I traveled across Africa to report on wars, famines, and the dynamic political change that broke out as the Cold War ended. I had been picked for the Africa beat by my white bosses at the *Post* not because I wanted the position and had applied for it. I hadn't, in fact, and

Arthur J. Beaumont (1839–1901), ca. 1880. The author's great-great-grandfather arrived in America from England when he was seventeen and found prosperity as a plantation owner and merchant in Louisiana, after fighting for the Confederacy during the Civil War. Photo courtesy Vivian DeShields Raspberry.

Laura Brumley (1850–1932) (left) and her daughter, Pearl (1877–1944), ca. 1890. Born into slavery in Louisiana, Laura was educated by the plantation mistress. She gave birth to Pearl after a long affair with A.J. Beaumont. Photo courtesy Mary Turner Henry.

Pearl Brumley Hall, ca. 1900. The quadroon daughter of A.J. Beaumont and Laura Brumley, Pearl was briefly married to Frank Hall, a black gambler, and gave birth to Fredda Hall, the author's grandmother, in 1896. Photo courtesy Mary Turner Henry.

Pearl Brumley Hall, ca. 1920. A fiery, passionate woman, Pearl longed for a relationship with her white father and his family but was rebuffed because of her race. Adored by her black family, she died in St. Louis at the age of sixty-seven. Photo courtesy Yvonne DeShields Days.

Fredda Hall Turner (1896–1982), ca. 1916. The daughter of Pearl, Fredda easily could have passed for white, but she felt that love was far more important. She married Edward Clifford Turner, a black postal clerk, and lived happily in St. Louis, raising three children there, including the author's mother. Photo courtesy Mary Turner Henry.

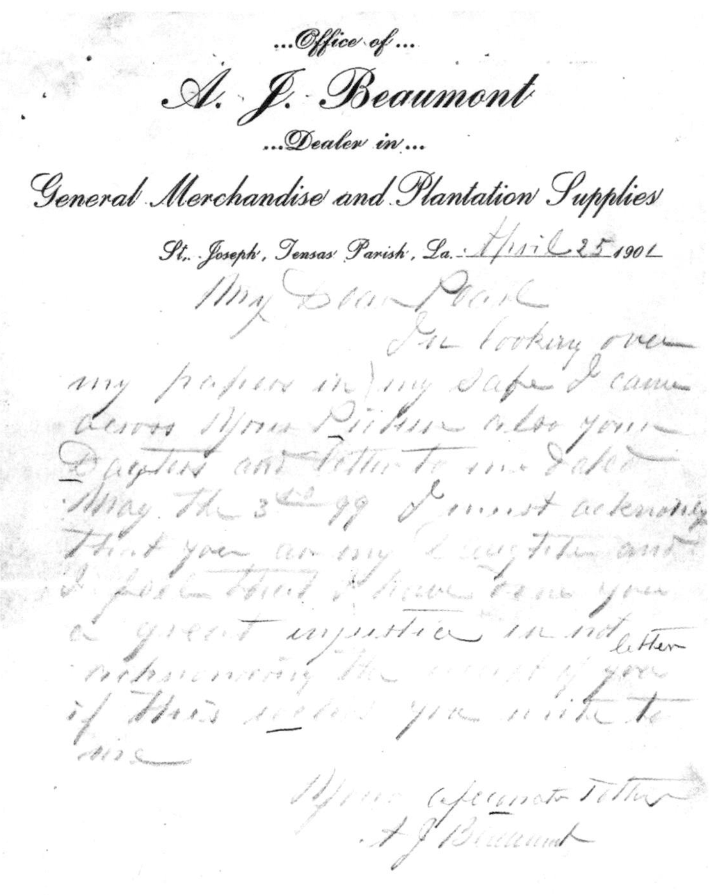
...Office of...

A. J. Beaumont

...Dealer in...

General Merchandise and Plantation Supplies

St. Joseph, Tensas Parish, La. April 25 1901

My Dear Pearl

In looking over my papers in my safe I came across your Picture also your Daughters and letter to me dated May the 3rd 99 I must acknowledge that you are my Daughter and I feel that I have done you a great injustice in not acknowledging the receipt of your letter if this reaches you write to me

Your affectionate Father
A J Beaumont

A.J. Beaumont wrote this letter to Pearl shortly before his death in 1901, finally acknowledging her as his daughter. The letter and its envelope remained keepsakes of Pearl and her black descendants. Courtesy Mary Turner Henry.

A family reunion in 1958. Foreground: Neil at four (center, arms raised); brother Wayne (left); brother Bobby (right). Back row: John Robert Henry, Jr., the author's father (second from left); grandparents Fredda and Edward Clifford Turner (third and fourth from left); Mary Turner Henry, the author's mother (fourth from right); Edward Clifford Turner, Jr., Uncle Sonny (third from right). Photo courtesy Vivian DeShields Raspberry.

The author in 1968, at fourteen, receiving an American Legion award for exemplary scholarship and citizenship. Though popular, he felt "mixed up" racially during the era of integration in largely white Seattle. Photo courtesy the author.

At twenty-one the author found fulfillment in writing; here he is typing an article about African students he met during a trip to China in 1975. The piece was later published in *The Crisis*. Photo courtesy Mary Turner Henry.

The children of Dr. John and Mary Henry in 1977 in the backyard of the family home in Seattle, built in 1960 against the protests of their white neighbors. Left to right: Neil, Sharon, Wayne, Bobby. Photo courtesy Mary Turner Henry.

Dr. John Robert Henry, Jr., in 1945, as a young physician after graduating from Meharry Medical College in Nashville, a legendary institution that trained many generations of the nation's top black doctors. Photo courtesy the author.

The author's mother, Mary Louise Turner, at twenty-two, as head librarian at Bennett College in Greensboro, North Carolina, in 1945. She would marry Dr. John Robert Henry, Jr., the following year. Photo courtesy Mary Turner Henry.

Mary Turner Henry at thirty-one, as a young mother in 1954 on the porch of the family house in Nashville. Neil, as an infant, on her lap; Bobby, center; and Wayne, right. Photo courtesy the author.

The author's grand-parents Fredda and Edward Clifford Turner, ca. 1930, in St. Louis. Fredda, like her mother, Pearl, and her daughter Mary, felt that the cruelest part of being a descendant of slavery was feeling bereft of a sense of family history and identity. Photo courtesy E.C. Turner, Jr.

knew little about the continent when I was first approached by Mike Getler, the foreign editor. If there was any part of the world outside America I was keenly interested in covering, it was China, a country that had fascinated me since my college studies of Mao and Chou En-lai. But, from my previous reporting, my editors saw an unusual spirit of adventure in me, a spirit that certainly was needed to cover a difficult assignment like Africa. They knew me as a clear and concise writer, and my blackness was a critical plus in their eyes for covering a region that often was treated as an afterthought, if that, in the paper's coverage of the world. So I became the fifth black foreign correspondent in the paper's history, an assignment I accepted not so much because I had eagerly sought it, but because I was living in an era in which pioneering opportunities for black men in American professions were still too rare to be refused. It was important, in other words, to take on all challenges, to grasp all new opportunities, whether you sought them or not, if for no other reason than to set a benchmark, to plant the race's flag, for those coming behind you.

Letitia visited me in Nairobi numerous times, bringing welcome relief to the otherwise frenetic pace of my existence in Africa, which marched to the pounding rhythms of news in the thirty-five countries on my beat. Unlike some black Americans who travel to Africa in search of identity or elusive "roots," I entertained no such fantasies when I ventured there. I knew who I was and what I was in Africa to do. My job was to write about a continent in tragic turmoil, and that I did, counting rotting corpses of victims in the ethnic strife of Liberia and Somalia, traveling with heroic aid workers through rebel-held Ethiopia, witnessing unruly police gun down demonstrators protesting for democracy in Kenya. My work was both challenging and heart-breaking, and I grew to love and admire many of the people who struggled for liberty in the nations I visited. I felt enormous respect for their courage and their aspiration for political change. But as an African American I never felt I was "one" culturally with any of Africa's wondrously diverse millions, who despite breathtaking poverty, enjoyed a strong sense of place and ethnic identity, which I secretly envied and admired. Sometimes, in fact, I sensed that Africans looked at me somewhat sorrowfully, despite my wealthy American-ness, as a cultural orphan of sorts, a comparatively "rootless" being who, unlike them, didn't know where his ancestral village was. To many Africans there was no sadder fate than that.

The challenges in my work were all-consuming, and in many ways they brought me face to face for the first time with my own sense of mortality. With each month that passed and each danger I confronted on the continent, I grew more and more cognizant that I was living on borrowed time. Such is the feeling many Western correspondents in Africa face at some point, because the beat so often requires covering war. In the course of performing my job there, I survived the wreck of an ancient Kenya Airways 707 in Ethiopia, counted corpses shortly after their slaughter in Liberia, and had a submachine gun trained on me first by a crazed soldier in Sierra Leone and then by a cop in Kenya. With each incident I found my journalistic nerve, my inner youthfulness and sense of invulnerability in pursuing stories, become harder and harder to summon. I became somewhat wary in my assignments, a quality that I knew could only sap my practice of the craft. I had always prided myself on my intrepidness in searching for the complete story, whether it was about the destitute in the flophouses of Washington, D.C., the convicted killers in the prisons of Maryland, or the migrant workers earning slave wages in the tomato fields of North Carolina. But the raw truths and terrors of the Africa beat began, over time, to wear me down inside, to weaken my soul. My experiences left me feeling, for the first time, powerless as a journalist to convey adequately the sheer magnitude of the human stories I encountered—and to get my distant readers in America to care.

Part of my professional crisis, too, stemmed from my inner re-realization that Africa's many, and maddeningly inexplicable, fights were ultimately not my own. I didn't want to die covering a story I didn't have an intense personal stake in, and the longer I worked as a journalist in Africa, the more I felt there was a real chance I might have to die, and probably senselessly. That stark realization came to me perhaps most clearly one night in Somalia several days after the fall of the dictator Mohamed Siad Barre in 1991, as I watched hundreds of tracer bullets soar into the sky from celebrants' pistols and submachine guns, knowing that the same bullets would fall seconds later somewhere in the city, possibly wounding or killing people at utter and senseless random— as indeed happened to several people, I discovered the next day. I also grew increasingly convinced that the most meaningful story for me—the story I *was* willing to wage war over, the one simmering in the cauldrons of race—was located somewhere in America. And that it was that fight I needed somehow to rejoin, to examine again, to find answers about. America was the place I needed to return to before my time was finished, the locale of the story I needed to face, the source of the roots I needed to redis-cover and somehow come to understand better.

Letitia was my link to sanity in those years in Africa in many ways, a wellspring of patience, devotion, and understanding. Despite the pressures of my job, she and I managed to find time to enjoy the splendors of the continent on our own terms. We hiked together in the beautiful rocky landscapes of Zimbabwe; enjoyed safaris in the wildlife preserves teeming with wildebeests, lions, and elephants in Kenya; drank libations with a village chief in Ghana, where Letitia's mother was serving in the Peace Corps; swam in the warm turquoise waters off the Seychelles in the Indian Ocean. By the time my work in Africa was coming to an end, Letitia and I realized we wanted to make a life together.

Now, six years later, she was my wife and a mother, somehow keeping our home and family together in Davis while continuing to research and write about Africa and teaching courses in African politics to top U.S. and African military officers at the Naval Postgraduate School in Monterey. She remained no less a marvel to me now as when I had first met her.

I stood over the stove, folded my arms, and looked into my wife's eyes as I waited for the pot of water to heat up. Letitia was the only person who truly understood what I was trying to do in my peculiar search, understood how even the most arcane discovery could nonetheless carry significant emotional repercussions for me. I told her about the *Tensas Gazette* microfilm I was working with and the year 1914. I told her I had found the obituary for A.J. Beaumont's wife. Not only that, but I had discovered that the white family moved to Vicksburg after Beaumont died.

The water began to boil. I snapped the spaghetti in half and tossed it in the pot.

"And the son had a daughter, Tish," I said. "That was in the microfilm too. He had a little girl in 1914, probably about Zoë's age."

"So maybe she's alive?"

"I don't know. Maybe. Or maybe the little girl had kids who could be alive somewhere today. Or maybe there was later a son or two who could be alive. The thing is I've brought the story forward by thirteen years."

A little light came to Letitia's dark green eyes then and she smiled. The child-care fatigue in her face seemed to lessen.

I went on: "I don't know what the hell to make of it, but I think I found them, at least where they were in 1914. I can't believe I found them."

She stood with her arms at her sides, hands folded before her, and her back against the kitchen counter. Then, lifting her arms and walking toward me, she asked, "Squeeze my back, will ya?" I folded my arms around her waist and held her tight, lifting her firmly to stretch her vertebrae into place. I heard the bones in her back crack into alignment. It was her regular therapy for fatigue, our regular kitchen hug.

"Vicksburg, is that in Tennessee?" she inquired.

"No, Mississippi," I said. It was the site of a famous Civil War battle, in the very heart of the South. "Remember the siege of Vicksburg? It was Grant's first big win, the battle that made his reputation," I explained, recalling all the Civil War books I had read voraciously years earlier as I tried to put Laura's and Beaumont's lives into context in my mind. "Vicksburg fell the same day the Union won at Gettysburg. On July 4, 1863. It helped turn the tide of history."

I felt myself growing excited talking about it.

"So you're going there, right?"

"I guess so," I said hesitantly after a pause, suddenly brought back to reality, feeling vaguely ambivalent once more about what

I was attempting to do. "But shit, Tish, you know—it's like finding a needle in a haystack. . . ."

She ignored my negativeness and asked me to show her Vicksburg on a map. We went to our bedroom on the other side of the kitchen, where all my files and Civil War and civil rights history books were cluttered in messy heaps next to our computer. I reached into a pile of papers atop a cardboard box near the desk and pulled out a dog-eared road map of Arkansas, Louisiana, and Mississippi, where I had marked the towns of St. Joseph and Natchez with little red dots. I sneezed from the dust.

"How do you find anything in this mess?"

I opened the map and spread it on our bed. I pointed out Vicksburg and circled it in blue with a pen.

"About forty miles from St. Joseph, see?"

"How far is all this from Atlanta? You're going to Atlanta again this semester, aren't you?"

I grunted in reply. Georgia was not on the map, so I reached into my pile of papers and pulled out a fold-up map of the United States. I opened it and placed it atop the other map on our bed. Here I had marked Seattle, St. Louis, and Winston-Salem, North Carolina, in red.

Letitia found Atlanta, then glanced at the distance legend at the bottom of the map. She used her left forefinger to measure the miles between Atlanta and Vicksburg. "Look, there's a major highway that goes right there," she said, pointing to the meandering blue and white line marked I-20. "Probably about four hundred miles."

She knew I was due to travel to Atlanta for two days in October to attend a professional and graduate school fair put on by the city's historically black colleges, Spelman, Morehouse, and

Clark Atlanta University. Every year scores of educators and administrators representing the nation's top professional and graduate school programs convened there to set up placards and booths on the floor of Atlanta's Omni Convention Center and try to recruit the city's top black undergraduates.

With affirmative action eliminated in California through the passage of Proposition 209, Berkeley and other schools in the state were under tremendous pressure to maintain minority enrollments. My journalism school decided to put money into a new recruiting initiative to attract black students. For many years the school had sat back on its reputation as a top institution of journalism education and presumed the best students of all backgrounds would find Berkeley without much work on its part. Now the school's administration realized that we needed to do much more—to go out and find *them*. It was not just a matter of believing in the educational benefits of "diversity" in the student body. It was also a question of economic imperative, for we had to keep the school competitive with other top programs, like those at Columbia and Northwestern.

At Berkeley we were in the difficult position of being legally forbidden from factoring in race or gender in our evaluation of applicants. We supposedly couldn't even discuss race or gender or ethnic background at our admissions committee deliberations. Yet at the same time we were under great pressure from representatives of American news media corporations who would baldly ask us every year at graduation who our top black and minority prospects were, having increasingly come to realize that a diverse news staff could result in a finer and more credible product. They wanted to hire them.

It was a kind of warped, Alice-in-Wonderland, Through-the-

Looking-Glass predicament in which we were attempting to hew to the letter of California's new anti–affirmative action law while at the same time doing our damnedest to get around it for the sake of education, the quality of the craft, and the future of journalism.

"Why don't we just go to the black schools in Atlanta to get some top people from there?" I had urged our school's administrators the year before, when faculty members were asked frantically for ideas. The next thing I knew, I was given money to fly to Atlanta to trumpet the benefits of a Berkeley journalism education to the city's gifted black college students. I believed in this cause with all the zeal of an insurrectionist and loved meeting the young adults. What's more, I felt a special, rare kind of inspiration and pride in Atlanta, a oneness with a generational, racial zeitgeist—believing that I was performing a small role in advancing an old cause of my people and, especially, my family.

For at its heart my family's story, and that of many other black families in America, has always been about education. Nothing else has been more important to black Americans' survival and fulfillment than that. *Education*. And getting *access* to education. Such critical opportunities were being limited, I felt, by the rollbacks in affirmative action, with possibly devastating results for the new generation I was charged with training. In my own time affirmative action had played a significant role not just in opening doors for people like me, doors that had long been barred to dark-skinned people, but also, and perhaps more important, in changing the culture of America's schools and workplaces. Changing the culture held the promise of improving American society, establishing a certain tolerance and acceptance of differences and a commitment to the principle that all people, regard-

less of race, background, or gender, should be allowed the chance
to prove themselves. I didn't know where the post–affirmative
action age would lead us, but I did know one thing: that without
access to opportunity, especially access to education, we were lost
as a people. Education was certainly the critical link in my family history, dating back to Laura's learning to read and write as a
child on the Tullis plantation in Louisiana. And education surely
was as profoundly important to my generation more than a century later. Without education we were at the mercy of whatever
hell white America wanted to foist on us. Education was our only
protection as a race, the greatest birthright and legacy we could
leave to those we loved.

When I was in Atlanta the previous year, trying to recruit
black students for our program at Berkeley, I thought often
about my mother, who attended a segregated, all-black Atlanta
University in the 1940s while earning a graduate degree in library science. I reflected on how her values about education had
been passed down to me during my childhood in white Seattle.
To my mother, education didn't mean just schoolwork, academic
achievement, or training for a livelihood. It meant education
about the world too, about the different kinds of people who in-
habit it, and it meant moral enlightenment, particularly when it
came to racial issues. In many ways she was the fire and spiritual
force behind our family's transition from the black world to the
white middle class in Seattle in 1960. Despite her own experiences with racism, she somehow maintained an abiding faith that
most white people, under their skin, would prove to be as decent
and caring as other people if they could get over their fears and
ignorance about us. My mother had always felt our biggest challenge as a family was to sustain this faith and not become so em-

bittered by our experiences with racism that we became blinded to the basic goodness of most white people. The worst thing I could do was hate white people back, she often told me. To hate in reaction to prejudice only served the ends of the racists, she felt. I somehow had to be better than that.

This spiritual framework of my mother's life, and by extension of my own, was erected early on in St. Louis, where she was born Mary Louise Turner in 1923. She was the second of three children of Edward Clifford Turner, a genial postal worker who was the son of a freed slave, and Fredda Turner, the shy daughter of Pearl and granddaughter of the English immigrant A.J. Beaumont. My mother grew up in a very stable and loving family centered in the Ville—short for Elleardsville—an admired St. Louis neighborhood known throughout the Midwest as a mecca of black culture and achievement in the first half of the twentieth century.

My mother always spoke lovingly about her childhood in the Ville, for it was a place where a black child, especially an advantaged black child, could grow up feeling proud of her color. The Ville in the 1920s and 1930s was to the black Midwest almost what Harlem was to the East during the Harlem Renaissance years, a source of rich culture and identity. The inner-city neighborhood was home to a thriving black middle class made up of steady government workers like my grandfather, as well as doctors, dentists, artists, undertakers, chauffeurs, and craftspeople. The Ville featured numerous movie and musical theaters and boasted elite black schools, including Charles Sumner High School, the first black public school built west of the Mississippi River, where my mother finished first in her class in 1940. As a child in Seattle, listening to her describe life during the heyday of the Ville, I felt the same sense of longing and loss that a white child born in America must feel listening to immigrant parents tell stories about the wonders and joys of Budapest or old Warsaw. The only world I knew was the world of white people. As a black child growing up so far removed from the lives of most of my own kind, I tried to imagine such a wondrous place made up entirely of black people, all my people, many of them very successful and accomplished, living, as she described it, like one big extended family that ate together, worked together, played together. It was magical to my child's mind.

An old adage about the Ville from my mother's youth held that a black child could be born, raised, and receive a fabulous education—from grade school at John Marshall Elementary, to Sumner High, to Harriet Beecher Stowe College, all the way to medical education at Homer G. Phillips Hospital—without ever having to leave the five square miles and forty-three blocks of her or his neighborhood. It was in the Ville that my mother was bred to be proud of her color and her advantaged class, despite the degradations of racial segregation, and to value learning.

As my mother told me, her own life choices as a black woman were made plain to her from the time she was little, when she accompanied her mother, Fredda, on trips downtown to pay the family bills. Fredda, the granddaughter Beaumont never met, informed her that of all the people in America, "colored" women had the hardest lives, and that if she wanted to have a happy life, she had to prepare early. One day in 1935, when my mother was twelve, Fredda made a point of taking her to Stix, Baer and Fuller, a bustling St. Louis department store, where Fredda wanted my mother to see the efficient and very attractive uniformed black girls, many of them light-skinned like my mother, working as stockers, elevator operators, and in other menial positions.

"Aren't they pretty?" Fredda asked her. My mother was indeed enchanted, she remembered, by the black girls' beauty and zest as they called out "First floor! Lingerie, perfume, hats!" and opened the elevator doors with a flourish.

"So pretty!" my mother replied.

"Now look down, Mary," my grandmother told her. "Don't just look at their faces and pretty hair. Make sure you see their feet."

My mother said she lowered her head and what she saw was clearly imprinted in her mind more than a half century later. Each of the beautiful young women wore shopworn, threadbare loafers beneath horrifically swollen ankles, testimony to their hard lives and the poor pay they received for their labor.

My mother and grandmother turned away.

"They didn't study, Mary. They didn't take their schooling seriously, do you hear?" Fredda said as they left the store. "And they're the lucky ones, because at least they have jobs. Such pretty, sad girls. They spend their lives on their feet and can't even afford shoes.

"Your father and I can't afford to send you to college," Fredda added. "You'll have to earn it on your own. But you remember these girls. . . ."

My mother finished at the top of her class at all-black Harriet Beecher Stowe College in the Ville and set her eyes on becoming a trained librarian, a profession that, in her day, was among the most prestigious a black woman could enter. In 1944, while studying for her degree in library science at Atlanta University, she met my father in Greensboro, North Carolina, during a semester working at a small black college library. After a few dates she fell in love with the handsome young medical student from North Carolina and soon realized she had two divergent paths before her: one leading to a doctoral degree in her field and perhaps the directorship of a university library someday if she worked hard enough; the other to a life with John Henry as wife and mother.

When their courtship stalled after a year and my father confessed to her that he probably wasn't ready to marry, my mother quit the South. She was accepted into a graduate program in library science at the University of Michigan in Ann Arbor, one of just a few black students in the program.

But one night my father phoned her from North Carolina to tell her how much he missed her. Then he wrote a love letter to her. Then he phoned her again and asked her to marry him. She said yes, quit school immediately, and happily hopped over to the other path. And on a beautiful snowy afternoon, Christmas Day 1946, she and my father were married at All Saints' Episcopal Church back home in St. Louis before scores of family and friends. She always said it was the happiest day of her life.

My parents dreamed a big dream that many other postwar, upwardly mobile black people shared in those days: that they could be the first generation of black people in America's long racist history to enjoy the same freedoms and access to good neighborhoods and public schools for their children as white people did. It was the guiding principle of their age. The time, they believed, was long past for America to honor its constitutional ideals by applying them to all its citizens. This was particularly imperative after a long, bloody world war in which millions, including many black American soldiers and sailors, had died to bring such freedoms to people in Europe and Asia. Some generations are lucky to be marked forever by an overriding passion or human ideal. For my parents' black generation it was equal opportunity and racial understanding.

Unlike my father, my mother possessed a strong religious faith to buttress her political convictions, and it, too, was a legacy of her upbringing in the Ville. She was raised in the Episcopal church, the denomination of choice of the city's black bourgeoisie. She believed that faith was as critical to a meaningful life as a good education and that in many ways the two went hand in hand. In Seattle years later, my mother was the driving force behind our attendance at a predominantly black but racially integrated Episcopal church, St. Clement's, each Sunday, where our Sunday school education complemented our grade school lessons. (This weekly ritual was not observed by my comparatively taciturn father, who was a pragmatist at heart and an atheist by nature. He pointed out to me on more than one occasion when I was a child that more wars had been fought in the name of God than any other power.)

Faith was perhaps most important to my mother when it came to grappling with racism. She felt that our family's inner strength, forbearance, and understanding of the racial obstacles we encountered in Seattle—our character—would somehow be rewarded in the end, much as Christians believed that God always redeemed the good and the just.

One of my mother's favorite prayers was the "Serenity Prayer," which was etched into a ceramic plaque that her mother had hung on the wall of her kitchen in St. Louis during the 1950s and that remained there long after her death in 1982. I often gazed at it as a child during our occasional summer visits to our ancestral home from Seattle in the 1960s, contemplating its meaning:

God grant me the serenity to accept the things I cannot change, the courage to change the things I can, and the wisdom to know the difference.

The prayer was most often associated with Alcoholics Anonymous, whose members used it to assist them spiritually toward recovery from addiction. For my mother and her mother the prayer offered support and comfort in the struggle not against booze but prejudice and racism. At the same time, while upholding the prayer's sentiments, my mother's beliefs were mixed with a sizable degree of gritty moral outrage and worldly skepticism, especially toward white prejudice.

Often when I was a kid in Seattle, my mother wrote letters home to her family in St. Louis, spilling out her deepest fears and dreams for us as we made our pioneering entrance into the world of white people during integration. This one, which I found in my mother's old house in St. Louis during a visit in the 1990s, was typical, filled with the passions of her age. Written by my mother several months before we moved, it was addressed to Fredda, who had feared our migration from Seattle's black neighborhood to a white one would be a terrible mistake. Fredda had preserved the typewritten letter in a plastic casing in a bureau drawer, knowing it would one day become a keepsake as precious as any.

Saturday afternoon
September 10, 1960

Dear Mama:
    The boys started [at the all-white] school Wednesday, and they are not at [the all-black school in the Central Area]—thank goodness! We made a trip down to the school board and got a special

transfer. Bobby's going to the junior high school in the district where we will move and Neilly and Wayne are going to elementary school in the new district. I drive them every morning and pick them up, 20 miles a day. I looked at my poor little children when I let them out that first morning and thought what a burden they had to bear because they were colored. If somebody had dumped me out like that I would have stood on the curb and jumped up and down and cried to go home. I took them to their school rooms and met their teachers and left them to swing it alone. The rest of the day I paced the living room and prayed. . . .

Now, with only 3 days in school Neil has learned how to read 4 sentences and is carried away. Wayne is delighted. I have never seen him so completely relaxed and sure of himself and so dedicated to learning. Every afternoon when I pick him up he stands by the flagpole, smiling that little secret smile he has with a twinkle in his eye and leaps in the car to tell me what happened that day. He and Neil are the only Negroes in the school and he knows the score and is quite mature about it—much more mature than a lot of adults would be, including his Ma. . . .

Yesterday I was sitting here meditating, trying to understand your bleak attitude about our move [into the white neighborhood] and getting the kids out of these all colored schools. Suddenly, it dawned on me that you don't understand the problems we face in Seattle. (It took me a long time, too, living here with the problem every day.) In the olden days when I was a little girl, growing up and going to school in the Ville, there were no problems for you, as such, because the St. Louis school system was one of the best in the country. And though the schools were segregated they were for all practical purposes equal to the whites' inasmuch as the teacher supply came from the two separated but supposedly equal city colleges.

At that time the teaching profession attracted the best Negro women who for the most part were dedicated and took pride in a

job well done. . . . Here in Seattle the situation is entirely different
and mirrors the situation in all larger cities in the north and west.
The school the boys have been attending in the Central Area for the
past 4 years is now 99 percent Negro, which is quite alright if the
faculty were strong and sympathetic and dedicated.

   But they are not. Over half of the kids come from illiterate,
underprivileged homes and discipline is nil. These schools have
a very high percentage of teacher turnover every year. I have
watched Wayne become increasingly handicapped year by year
by one weak, undedicated teacher after another.

   After much haggling I finally managed to get him into a
colored teacher's room and he pulled himself up. Unfortunately,
the school board's policy is to disperse Negro teachers throughout
the system. I have worked with the PTA and the Urban League
and other organizations dedicated to raising the educational
standards and teacher qualifications of these Negro schools until
the city's segregated housing situation is relieved.

   But until then, what are we to do?

   Gradually it dawned on me that my boys were suffering and
being given an inferior education. Since a good education is the
best legacy John and I can endow them with we decided on the
move. Ponder that statement Rachel Robinson [Jackie Robinson's
wife] made not long ago—"What's wrong with our kids going
to an all-colored school? Nothing, if they're going to live in an all-
colored world."

   So yes, we have sacrificed a 35-year-old home with an $11,000
mortgage in a cozy black neighborhood for a brand new home with
no view and a higher mortgage on a street of hostile whites for a
principle—and for what we believe will enhance our children's
future.

   Who can say whether we are right or wrong? We take pride,
however, in having the courage of our convictions. And though we

are harassed by these white people by day, we sleep the sleep of the
just at night and take comfort in the fact that we are not alone—
in Seattle, or throughout the country—because other Negroes,
though small in numbers, are taking the giant step.

Here's hoping that this next generation will be armed for battle
with good and equal educations, ready and willing and able to take
their rightful places in the integrated society their parents and
grandparents fought and raved and shouted for. . . .

A longtime librarian for the Seattle public schools, my mother
was full of zest when it came to practically everything in life—
reading, politics, the social whirl among other black wives in
Seattle's small but growing black bourgeoisie—and often her
perspective on my experiences growing up with white people
could be sharp and biting. Despite her religious convictions, she
wasn't above calling a white person a "racist bastard" or "poor
white trash" when the occasion suited and her ire was sufficiently
raised. But she didn't like saying such things out loud in front of
me. At some point in the mid-1960s she shortened the expletive
"poor white trash" to "PWT" and later to simply "Pee Dub" in
her vernacular, to use whenever she felt compelled to explain
why certain white people acted as crassly or maliciously or stu-
pidly toward us as they did.

As a kid, I considered my mother one of the prettiest women I
knew. I don't know exactly why. Maybe because I paid more attention to her than to any other woman I knew. She had high,
round cheeks; soft, curly black hair, which she often wore close
cropped and which turned an elegant gray as she grew older; and
expressive dark eyes that reflected rage and joy with equal fervor.
I often could tell exactly how she felt just by looking into her eyes.
I thought she was pretty not only because her face was so radi-

ant and her eyes so full of life or because she had her hair clipped nicely by a hairdresser practically every week and often dressed in very fashionable clothes. Her prettiness, to me, went beyond her physical appearance. She carried herself with elegance and style, possessing a sureness and pride in her walk and bearing. Long after I became an adult, my friends and acquaintances would tell me that that was the first thing that came to mind on meeting my mother—that *this* was a woman with class. It was doubtless her background in the Ville that produced this quality.

Vivacious and highly opinionated, she was never sparing in pointing out the difference between right and wrong as she saw it in our everyday lives, often doing so with a sharpness that could deeply sting. Once when she was purchasing a lamp in an electric appliance store in Rainier Valley, an impertinent white shop-keeper made the mistake of calling my mother by her first name after seeing her full name, Mrs. Mary T. Henry, on her bank check. My mother—reminded of the demeaning manner in which white merchants and other strangers often addressed black women in the South, considering them little more than sub-servient "girlies" and "mammies" and "queenies" without last names—exploded.

"My name is Mrs. Henry, do you understand? You do not address me by my first name, *do you understand?*"

I was awed by her temper.

"Don't you ever let those people treat you like that," she said bitterly to me and my sister, Sharon, after we had returned to the car, her eyes filled with tears.

That was in 1968, the year Martin Luther King, Jr., was assassinated. I was fourteen, and the racial rage and violence that quickly broke out across America in the murder's aftermath made our home near Lake Washington seem the only shelter from trouble and fear. The Sunday after King's killing, my mother attended her racially integrated Episcopal church to hear words of spiritual consolation, guidance, and hope from the white clergy. She expected to hear something to help her deal with the pain she felt, something to commemorate all that King had struggled to do. But she returned home that afternoon enraged.

"The minister didn't mention Martin Luther King once, can you believe it?" she cried. "How can they go on and on about angels and archangels when the world is coming apart like this?"

She didn't attend church again for several years.

"You've been given advantages that a lot of people don't have," she told my older brother Wayne and me as we sat in our family room one windswept night that terrible spring, watching the news bulletins on television about the rioting in Washington. "You've gone to good schools, you've had clothes on your back and food in your stomach, and you've never had to want for anything. You've been lucky. But you can never afford to forget you're black in this country. Never, do you hear? And you should do what you can, you know, to help other folks come along, even if it's just a little."

Three decades later I was about to return to Atlanta to renew my own small initiative to help counter the effects of the end of affirmative action at my school in California. It was my modern-day battle in the old war for access to the American dream that my people had always fought, my way of doing "a little" to help the cause and to continue to honor the "giant step" my mother had written about so passionately in her letter to Fredda all those years before.

But could I also find a way during the same brief trip to find answers to our old family mystery? Could I follow up on the clues I had discovered in microfilm and piece together the white family story concealed somewhere on the other side of our ancestral tree?

It was going to be such a quick trip to Atlanta, and deep down I felt I would need weeks instead of hours or days to accomplish my task. I wondered if I would have time to squeeze in a visit to Vicksburg at all. I knew I would have only a few days in the South before I had to return to teach my classes at Berkeley.

"Of course you can," Letitia insisted, turning to me, her eyes peering into mine, her finger resting again on the map of Mississippi. "You're going to be in the South anyway. You've got to."

I knew she was right. So I thought quickly about everything I would need to do. There was so much. I would first rent a car and then make a rapid, hard charge in one day through Georgia, Alabama, all the way across Mississippi to Vicksburg. If I timed it right, I might be able to have a full day or perhaps even two full days there to research court records and historical documents, to see if the Beaumont family paper trail really existed and to determine how far I could follow it.

Vicksburg was the seat of Warren County in Mississippi. That meant that any civil, property, criminal, or probate judgments the Beaumont family might have been involved in would certainly be in the files there somewhere. With luck I would be able to find a copy of A.J. Beaumont's widow's will and perhaps the children's marriage certificates, if the family had resided in Vicksburg long enough.

I had a lot of preparing to do, I knew. A lot of phone calls and appointments to make.

Letitia called Zoë to the dinner table a few minutes later, and after I placed the pasta and salad before us, I said grace, as I usually did each night, using the same prayer my mother recited before meals in Seattle. It was funny, but I had spent my adult life in a profession, journalism, that valued earthly skepticism much more than spiritual faith. Yet somehow such faith remained rooted in me.

> Lord be our holy guest,
> Our morning joy, our evening rest;
> And with this daily bread impart,
> Thy loving peace to every heart.

We then ate the pasta, salad, and sausage as the sun set in the sultry evening air outside our open kitchen door, and afterward Zoë and I played tic-tac-toe as Letitia cleared the dishes from the table. I became so lost in thought that my daughter had to keep telling me, "Your turn, Daddy," and "Play, Daddy, play!" Still, my mind drifted again and again to Vicksburg, to Natchez and St. Joseph, and to the task ahead of me, to Laura, Pearl, and Arthur Beaumont.

All that time, all that searching.

Amazing, I thought.

I always knew I would travel somewhere, perhaps many places, in America when I started on the strange and vexing odyssey years earlier to find the white family whose blood my family shared. But deep down I guess I knew the truth all along, that the trail I sought, the clues I needed, and the answers I so badly wanted were ultimately buried somewhere in the South.

It had always been that way in my family.

Always, the South.

CHAPTER THREE

Natchez

I flew from Sacramento to Atlanta on Saturday, October 11, arriving in the Georgia capital late on a humid and drizzly night.
The next morning I rented a compact car at a downtown agency
near my hotel to begin the long drive west to Vicksburg. With
my wrinkled old road maps on the seat beside me, I was on the
move by 9:30 A.M., passing quietly through Atlanta's deserted
Sunday-morning streets. I soon found an on-ramp to U.S.
Interstate 20 and followed the freeway out of the city as it wound
its way on a southwesterly 450-mile course through the pine
forests of Georgia and Alabama and the kudzu of Mississippi toward the Mississippi River.

Fall semester at Berkeley was in full gear, and once again I was
overwhelmed with course work and lectures back home. The
focus of my attention was the eleven graduate students in
Journalism 200, an intensive course in news reporting and writing that students were required to pass if they wanted to go on to
specialized training in television and print journalism and even-

tual careers in the field. The course was a baptism of fire in the intricacies of the craft—much as anatomy is for medical students, perhaps, or torts for law students—and something close to hell for both me and them. I was teaching them how to gather information and interview sources and ordering them to write and rewrite staggering numbers of news and feature stories on deadline, all of which I had to edit. The assignments I issued each morning ranged from the mundane to the zany:

> The Berkeley City Council meets tonight. Cover the session. Write 500 words about the most newsworthy action, direct news lede. Deadline: midnight.

> Nudists are demonstrating at Sproul Plaza tomorrow as an expression of their First Amendment rights. Write 700 words. Interview at least one of the nudists in depth, and get reaction on the record from First Amendment experts on campus and onlookers. Deadline: 7 P.M.

> Find a vacant lot in Berkeley. Go to the county assessor's office with the lot's address and research its history as far back in time as you can go. Find out who owns it now. Contact the owner. Find out what he or she plans for the property, if anything. Write a memo about your research. 1,000 words. Deadline: Monday, 8 A.M.

The students were also invading the criminal courts in nearby Oakland to write about murder, armed robbery, and rape trials, and learning how to research civil and criminal court files and other public records critical to the work of journalism. One of my students, a twenty-seven-year-old black woman from Oakland, had taken my assignment to write a short profile about a figure in the judicial system and turned in a remarkable story about an old high school boyfriend who was doing time in Santa Rita State Prison for dealing drugs. I edited her piece closely, then fired off a quick note to her:

> Excellent work, Nandi. Here's what I'd like you to do now.
> Please make this a commentary. Tell the reader what you
> remember about going to school in Oakland and how you
> feel personally about the destruction of so many lives of people
> you knew, through drugs, crime, and alienation. Also provide
> more information about what life is like behind bars for your
> old boyfriend and what he foresees for his life when he gets out.
> Let's aim to get this piece published on a local op-ed page.

Another student, a thirty-one-year-old former schoolteacher from Oakland who had decided to change careers to become a journalist, was writing his master's thesis on the daily struggles of Eric Brooks, the lone black student in that year's entering class at the Boalt Hall School of Law on campus. The law school had seen a sharp drop in minority applicants in the wake of the anti–affirmative action Proposition 209. Many activist groups saw Brooks's lonely plight as a cautionary tale about the future of higher education in the state. My student's first draft of his thesis about Brooks was very rough but filled with potential. I ordered him to pursue the piece further:

> Rob: Wonderful job to get the access you have. You are the
> only member of the Bay Area or national press who has been
> able to get this story in the kind of depth it requires. But the
> key to making it work will be how well you are able to under-
> tand Brooks. Get to know him. Go to classes with him. Unwind

with him. He is an unusual man in a very unusual circumstance, and the better you are able to present him in flesh and blood as a human being, the better the reader will connect to the story and the important larger issues involved here.

But now I was in the South, taking a short breather from the fires of my daily life as an educator, putting my lectures and schoolwork aside for a few days to try to solve the old puzzle at the heart of my family's racial story while also trying to recruit a few more black students for our program from the black colleges in Atlanta.

It was a gray, still, and misty Sunday morning as I headed into the Georgia countryside, conditions that made the rolling farm-land and stands of tall pines passing silently by outside my car windows appear remarkably lush and timeless. As I flowed with the light traffic through the three states, alternately hearing preachers shout their sermons, church choirs sing soulful hymns, and broadcasters chatter play-by-play about a pro football game on my car's AM radio, I felt within me the sharp emotions I had harbored for the South since my childhood in Seattle.

Nearly every road sign I passed on the six-hour trip evoked a jarring memory of some racial or historic event that touched things deep in my soul. As I drove through Birmingham, I peered downtown, wondering where in this old brick- and rust-colored steel town was the small black church where four girls were killed by a white terrorist's bomb in 1963 as they prayed during a serv-ice. I could hear the words of George Wallace ringing in my mind's ear—"Segregation now, segregation tomorrow, segrega-tion forever!"—words the belligerent white governor had defi-antly shouted during his inaugural address in 1963. Six months later he mounted his "schoolhouse stand" to block two black students from enrolling at the University of Alabama in Montgomery.

I drove past a highway exit leading toward Philadelphia, Mississippi, the small town where three civil rights workers were gruesomely murdered in 1964 by white vigilantes out to stop black people from asserting their right to vote.

These places were key landmarks in the history of the struggle that I remembered vividly from my boyhood in Seattle. From our faraway vantage my brothers and sister and I had watched the civil rights movement in the South unfold in the 1960s on television and in the newspapers. The South was where bigotry had always been overt and brutal, in contrast to the sullen face of prejudice I had known when I came of age in Seattle, Princeton, and Washington, D.C.

But the South in my mind didn't just connote oppression and brutality. Like many of my attitudes about race and our family history, my feelings about the region were a complex mix, for the South was also deeply inspiring. It was the same region that saw black people in many of their finest moments in history, bravely joining the boycotts and marches for equal rights led by Martin Luther King, Jr., and Medgar Evers and showing supreme courage in individual acts of defiance, like that of Rosa Parks, the black woman in Montgomery, Alabama, who turned the world upside down by refusing to give up her seat on a bus to a white passenger.

As I drove on, my mind filled with King's words of April 3, 1968, the stormy night before he was killed, from a speech he delivered to a packed black church in Memphis. I remembered seeing King that night, in news clips on our television set in Seattle,

as he passionately affirmed his belief in the civil rights struggle
and racial integration while eerily expressing acceptance of his
own mortality. In my mind I heard the fire in his voice, the
crowd's ecstatic shouts and cries, and recalled feeling one with
our history, even as a fourteen-year-old black boy so far away:

> We've got some difficult days ahead, but it really doesn't matter
> with me now. Because I have been to the mountain top. Like
> anybody I would like to live a long life. Longevity has its place.
> But I'm not concerned about that now. I just want to do God's
> will. And he's allowed me to go up the mountain top. And I've
> looked over. And I've seen the Promised Land. I may not get
> there with you. But I want you to know tonight that we as a
> people will get to the Promised Land. So I am happy tonight.
> I'm not worried about anything. I'm not fearing any man. My
> eyes have seen the glory of the coming of the Lord.

On toward the Mississippi River I traveled, toward the muddy,
seemingly endless body of slow-moving brown water that in-
spired so many American writers, from Mark Twain and Edna
Ferber to Langston Hughes. It was the same river Laura and
Pearl had steamed northward along in the 1890s to begin their
new life in St. Louis, leaving A.J. Beaumont and their native
Louisiana behind. And I remembered one of my earlier visits to
Mississippi more than a decade earlier, in 1986.

I was working then as a national correspondent for the
Washington Post and came up with the idea of writing a long feature story about race relations at the University of Mississippi
nearly a quarter of a century after its first black student, James
Meredith, had been admitted under protection by federal troops
amid a hail of gunfire from white racist protesters. I wanted to

know how relations between blacks and whites had changed there over the years. Had ties improved? Or degenerated? Were there any real ties between the races at all?

Journalism had been a godsend to my life in that way, allowing me the chance to make a terrific living doing what I loved to do more than anything in life: satisfy my curiosity. Best of all, newspapering had offered a startling contrast to my college experience at Princeton, four years that were essentially a black hole in my life, which even now I recalled with anxiety and pain. But I couldn't help thinking about Princeton whenever I considered my fifteen-year career at the *Washington Post*, because the two experiences had such opposite but profoundly lasting effects on my life.

I went to Princeton in 1972 essentially because—encouraged by my older brother Wayne, who by then was enrolled at Brown—I had applied and been accepted. It was one of the best schools in America, and as a young black man whose ancestors had struggled hard to gain access to education, I felt honor-bound to take advantage of the opportunity, to push the walls of the racial envelope, to once again see how I measured up.

But from the moment I arrived on campus carrying my two suitcases, which had been marked "NH" in big letters by my diligent father with strips of masking tape, I was badly intimidated—by the prep school culture, by the aura of old wealth and alien traditions, by the strange political and scientific discourses of the era. One of the biggest controversies on campus during my years at Princeton was over a speaking invitation that a group of my white fellow students had extended in 1973 to solid-state physicist and Nobel Prize winner William Shockley. Shockley was a

Stanford professor who was far more noted nationally for his belief that black people were genetically inferior to whites than for
his work in physics. A predecessor of the contemporary conservative race and intelligence theorist Charles Murray, he also fervently believed that people of lower intelligence should be paid
money to be sterilized. That way, Shockley felt, the brighter
lights of the species, white people, could be protected from the
wasteful effects of miscegenation.

As I went through my daily routine of classes and studies,
often eating alone in the mammoth dining halls or retreating to
my dorm room, I couldn't help believing that Shockley was only
expressing aloud what most white people in America and on my
campus privately felt about black people already. And as much as
I hated his theory, I secretly wondered if Shockley—a supposedly brilliant scientist, after all—was correct in his beliefs, could
somehow prove black genetic inferiority, and I wondered in the
end what it said about me.

The controversy symbolized the tenor of my dismal years at
Princeton, along with my odd ways of coping with them. I was a
virtual recluse at college, someone whose picture you will not
find in any school yearbook and who participated in no campus
activities worth memorializing. I hung out with neither the rich
white preppies who favored weekend beer busts and Beach Boys
music nor the small band of black students who dined together,
lived together, sat together in lectures, smoked herb and danced
to the Ojays and Tower of Power together, and otherwise tried
to find security as a group in the midst of the white majority on
campus, much as conscripts might move en masse from bunker
to bunker in hostile territory.

I was something of a loner by nature and didn't trust companionship based solely on my skin color, mainly because it was so alien to my background, and Princeton's ivy and gray-stoned foreignness only made me even more aloof. Actually, by the time I went to college, I had become somewhat wary of other black people, thanks to some painful experiences with blacks of my own age, starting in junior high school. The curiously proper way I spoke, the unhip way I dressed, the excellent grades I earned, the white friends I hung out with from my neighborhood—to my black peers these were contemptible earmarks of my background growing up among whites. To the black kids, most of whom were poor and hailed from Seattle's inner city, I was something of a freak and quite ripe for ridicule, a black boy who couldn't dance, couldn't talk the dialect, strolled to class religiously with big tomes under his arm, always had money for lunch, and most suspicious of all, was well liked by the white teachers. For all these things I was, in the words of some, an "Uncle Tom." When several black toughs in my junior high first spat that expletive my way, my face burned hot with shame. But who was the real traitor and shame to our race, I wondered bitterly as I trudged home that day—the black person who tried to advance and change the white man's world or the one who never had the guts to try?

At Princeton I didn't feel a part of either the black or the white world really, and the people I counted as my friends on campus were similarly misfits of a sort—a secretly gay black art student from New Jersey, a lonely white physician's son from a small town in Iowa, and a poor Sephardic Jew from Seattle. My one pitiful attempt at hipness in college was to grow a huge Afro. At one point it encircled my head like an astronaut's helmet, with mounds and mounds of black curliness. But even in this effort my mixed racial ancestry proved inescapable. For whenever I put my head under the shower in my dorm, the big Afro melted, reconstituting itself into a thick, wet mass of limp, straight strings that hung down the back of my neck.

In general, I was so overwhelmed by the task of trying to succeed academically, shoulder to shoulder with what I presumed were the brightest young white minds in America, that my presence on campus amounted to little more than a spectral one. What kept me going was the fear of letting my family down, especially my mother. I often told myself that I simply couldn't fail because she had invested so much of her savings and hopes in my expensive education. And so I buried myself in books essentially from the time I arrived to the time I left, finding intellectual inspiration in the lives of Mao and Melville and Paul Robeson and relief from boredom in the marvelous movies from the 1930s and 1940s playing on New York City and Philadelphia television stations, which I often watched late at night on my rickety black-and-white set. I suspect I became just as knowledgeable about the works of John Ford, Frank Capra, and Howard Hawks as I was about Chinese political history, my submajor.

I graduated from Princeton with academic honors, but my thoughts and insecurities about race, prejudice, inferiority—and my elusive place in a society where there didn't seem to be too many people like me—haunted me during my isolating years there. To this day some of my fondest memories of college are the times late at night in my senior year when I freely roamed the campus in the tranquil darkness to scavenge for twigs, fallen branches, and other pieces of wood in order to make fires in the small brick fireplace in my single room at Dod Hall. I loved those late-night fires. In those moments I felt perfectly at peace in my aloneness, in control of my little world, and oddly content with my ascetic apartness from both whites and blacks. When my last class was finished that spring, 1977, I packed up and left Princeton for good, one week before commencement. I swore to myself that I would never return. In my class album there was no photograph of me nor any listing of activities. Only my major, political science, was mentioned. Otherwise, I was a faceless name in the records.

But life changed dramatically when I left. If nothing else, my college years had taught me that I could survive on my own in a forbidding environment if I had to, not unlike Natty Bumpo in the frontier wilderness, and that I could compete successfully with anyone if I put my mind to it. These qualities served me well when I was hired after graduation to be a summer intern reporter on the Metro Staff at the *Washington Post*, where I learned to write obituaries, cover the police beat, interview beauty queens, fire chiefs, strippers, derelicts—in short, learned all the ropes of life as a cub reporter. Inspired by the exploits of Bob Woodward and Carl Bernstein to take a shot at newspapering as a calling, I was one of fourteen interns that summer working in what clearly was a plum job for any young, ambitious writer, just three years after President Nixon's resignation and the *Post*'s journalistic triumphs during Watergate. In the *Post*'s eyes my internship application had displayed the "right" pedigree, beginning with my Ivy League education, which editor Ben Bradlee and the Graham family, who owned the paper, considered virtually essential for editorial hiring at the paper. The application had also included a couple of newspaper and magazine articles I had written about a three-week trip to China I had taken the previous summer with a group of writers and students—a temporary escape from

Princeton that proved exhilarating and certainly showed I had the kind of adventurous spirit on which journalism thrived.

But, I'm sure, most impressive to my employers was my race. It was just a decade after rioting had destroyed inner-city Washington in the wake of King's murder, and the *Post* remained eager to employ energetic, young black reporters who could help cover the largely black city and explain it in human terms to its largely white and very influential readership. Just nine years earlier President Johnson had convened a special panel to examine the causes of the inner-city riots in the 1960s. The National Advisory Commission on Civil Disorders, more commonly known as the Kerner Commission, warned in the conclusion of its 1968 report that America was moving still further, dangerously so, toward becoming two societies, black and white, separate and unequal, and it levied sharp criticism at the nation's white mainstream press for not reporting adequately or fairly on the problems of blacks and the poor. The commission urged American newspapers and broadcast media to employ more minorities to help convey to the public the full story behind the social and racial issues that had exploded so violently in the streets.

Racial integration, in short, was still a new phenomenon at America's newspapers, including the *Washington Post,* when I arrived in 1977, riding the wave of progress and transformation begun only a few years earlier. Indeed, in many ways the mid- and late 1970s set the stage for a golden era at the *Post,* giving rise to an extraordinarily gifted cadre of black journalists, all of whom I was proud to call my peers and contemporaries, all of us trained under fire in our idealistic youth in the crucible of the *Post* newsroom. How I admired the sharp wit and wisdom of columnist William Raspberry, the smarts and terrific writing style of New

Yorker Juan Williams, the folksy cool and streetwise city reporting of Louisiana-born Courtland Milloy.

It was a pioneering time that led later to seminal and provoca-
tive works by many of these black writers, books that richly
evoked the tenor, struggles, and victories of the age. Two works,
Jill Nelson's *Volunteer Slavery* and Nathan McCall's *Makes Me
Wanna Holler*, are bitter memoirs documenting their racial struggles within the very white corporate structure at the *Post* that embraced me and allowed me to flourish. A third autobiography,
Patrice Gaines's *Laughing in the Dark*, traces her remarkable rise
from poverty, drug use, and imprisonment to become an award-
winning feature writer on the big-city daily. Another black writer
whose skills were sharpened at the *Post* was James McBride, author of *The Color of Water*, a memoir tracing his relationship with
his white Jewish mother, his childhood in New York's housing
projects, and his family's unusual success. Still another personal
history, Keith B. Richburg's *Out of America*, recounts his experiences as my successor as the paper's Africa Bureau chief, a con-
troversial memoir whose damning and unmerciful rant against
African corruption and tribal wars aroused indignation among
many blacks in America. A sixth book, Eugene Robinson's *Coal to
Cream*, examines the differences in perceptions of race he encountered as a young black American coming of age in South
Carolina and later as the *Post*'s South America Bureau chief
based in Brazil. Another brilliant journalist trained on the *Post*'s
National Staff in the 1980s was Malcolm Gladwell, a biracial
Canadian with a flair for science writing who rose to be the
paper's New York correspondent before joining the *New Yorker*
and authoring *The Tipping Point*, a fascinating study of social epi-
demics. Still other volumes are groundbreaking works of jour-

nalism, including Leon Dash's *Rosa Lee: A Mother and Her Family in Urban America*, a Pulitzer Prize–winning series of stories about the hardships of a black woman's life in the South and Washington, D.C.'s ghetto, and two by Juan Williams—*Eyes on the Prize*, a history of the civil rights struggle, and *Thurgood Marshall: American Revolutionary*, his compelling biography of the black Supreme Court justice. Such books reflect not just the talent of the era's black journalists, but also the wide range of perspective among them.

My entrance into this journalistic brotherhood near its inception after the tumult of the late 1960s was a proud and exciting one, but it also was the source of my greatest secret at the *Post*, a secret I guarded closely when I was hired full-time in 1978 after earning a master's degree in journalism at Columbia University. This secret and all its irony made me smile inside, as if I were getting away with some monumental deception. I knew I had been hired partly because of my blackness, but the fact was that, as a product of white Seattle and Princeton, I likely comprehended little more about the lives of ordinary black people in America than the average young white reporter. In many ways I was as sheltered and ignorant as any of them. But I was certainly curious and hungry when I arrived. God, was I hungry to experience slices of American life that my wilderness years in Seattle and Princeton had told me little about. After four years in virtual hiding as a hermit behind Princeton's ivied walls, I sprang into the gritty world of urban America, much like a leopard freed from its cage, and eagerly used the *Washington Post*, just as the *Washington Post* certainly used me, to learn about life in a way that books and Princeton could never teach.

As a young reporter my intelligence, street smarts, and journalistic skill were tested often by my editors in the *Post* newsroom, a place that operated in a high-pressure style informally known as "creative tension." This phrase, coined by executive editor Ben Bradlee, described a method of newsroom management that essentially assumed that *Post* employees were at their most productive and creative if they were regularly made to feel somewhat tense or uneasy in their highly competitive jobs. Every day presented new tests for reporters and editors—new challenges to their security—and it was only the strongest and brightest, the top editors felt, who would thrive under such pressure and competition.

One day during my baptism of fire as an intern, in August 1977, Washington's brand-new subway system suffered a major breakdown after an underground flood. That afternoon I was immediately sent out to interview stranded commuters on Capitol Hill, and I returned hours later to write a feature story about their reactions. As I sat at my typewriter nervously pounding out a lead for my story, a cigarette dangling from my lips, I noticed my editor, Herbert Denton, stride back and forth between my desk and that of another summer intern reporter, a young man named Eduardo Cue. Denton, appointed just a couple of years earlier as the first black city editor in the *Post*'s history, stood silently behind me for several moments, eyeing my story as I typed it out, before inexplicably heading back to Eduardo's desk to do the same.

Finally, after about a half hour, Eduardo, a white Spaniard schooled in the United States, approached me with a crestfallen expression on his face: "Herb told me to fold my stuff into your story," Eduardo informed me. "He likes your piece better." Neither of us had known that Denton had sent us out separately to report and write the very same story that day. The test? To see whose reporting and writing skills measured up, whose story was best to print. It was my story that was published in full the next day, along with photos of the subway breakdown, with Eduardo's name second to mine in the joint byline. I thus passed, with flying colors, a typical but important test at the newspaper, proving my ability to report and write quickly and well—without even knowing I was being tested.

Although the system of "creative tension" at the *Post* often seemed little more than corporate cruelty, with each test of my journalistic promise, I somehow managed to survive and indeed to flourish. I truly enjoyed the frenzied pace and the constant intellectual stimulation my new profession offered, and most important, I saw myself increasingly as part of a larger moral and ethical enterprise that carried immense value in a democratic society.

I explored many sides of Washington in my early work as a journalist, from the daily travails of the black poor in the housing projects of Anacostia to the alienation of middle-class white youth in the Maryland suburbs. I soon found I was very good at asking questions, mainly because I was bursting with so many of them about practically everything: Why were so many people standing in unemployment lines every day? Where did they come from, and what were the stories of their lives? How did a family in such circumstances get by on so little each week? Where did a jobless derelict go for food by day and for shelter by night? How did a cop investigate a murder or a rape? How many victims were dying of gun violence in Washington each year, month, day, hour? Each question bred countless others, and with each answer I got and each compelling feature and news story I produced, I rose in the *Post* newsroom, gaining respect and admiration from my peers, local and national awards for my writing and reporting, and greater professional and personal confidence.

Fed up with feeling intimidated by white and black people as I had been in college, I found liberation and release in my new calling, blissfully throwing myself into a host of unusual investigative reporting projects with the full backing of my *Post* editors. They encouraged me to try to follow in the paths of Orwell, Kerouac, and Steinbeck, to use my curiosity to tell stories about the lives of ordinary people and the downtrodden. One winter I lived the life of a derelict in Baltimore and Washington, eating in soup kitchens, sleeping in flophouses, and panhandling for change with the down-and-out to write about the experiences of the homeless in a twelve-part front-page series. Another year I spent three months exploring Maryland's decrepit state prison system to write a long series of stories about inmate abuses and the need for institutional reform. Still another year I spent a summer month working undercover as a migrant tomato and cotton worker in the sweltering fields of North Carolina to expose corrupt practices in the rural labor system. How I loved exploring such worlds and ways of life so strange to me, loved the feeling of writing well about the stories I uncovered and the people I met, as if I were pinching the world on its fat behind to get its attention and shouting, "Take a look at this!" I loved seeing my byline printed above my discoveries, on the front page of the distinguished newspaper, to be read by millions. But perhaps most of all, I loved feeling the power of my words to do a little good in society, helping to spur reforms in rural labor in North Carolina, bringing new light to problems in the criminal justice system, and letting Americans see the plight of the faceless homeless in a way they perhaps hadn't considered before.

My assignments at the *Post* emboldened me, enabling me to transcend barriers within myself in many ways. If I had felt fearful, wary, and isolated as a student at Princeton, I felt fearless and engaged with the world as a reporter in Washington. A large part of the difference was that I found people at the *Post*, black and white, who believed in me—Herbert Denton, Charles Krause, Howard Simons, and David Maraniss chief among them—brilliant editors and writers who were generous in their teaching and guidance. And for the first time in my life I found a community of people like me (inside, at least)—young, eager, and ambitious reporters and writers, most of us bound as comrades not by our color or class background but by an overriding sense of shared professional mission, an integration of ideals and values. For some odd reason we believed in journalism and its power to inform and improve humanity. If I had wondered at Princeton what my place was in society as a cultural oddity, I found a powerful and creative one at the *Washington Post*. Apart from occasional incidents with racial overtones that I had to swallow for the sake of rising higher, like my confrontation with the small-minded editor who questioned my credibility on a story in the wake of the Janet Cooke scandal, I generally felt my racial unusualness was welcome at the *Post*, my talent encouraged, my potential greatly valued.

In time I was asked by top editors to join the National Staff, where I essentially was given free rein to travel the country in search of good stories. I especially loved writing about race relations in places as far-flung as Cairo, Illinois, and Rosebud, South Dakota, and about black coal miners in West Virginia, the homeless in Utah, and casino workers in Nevada. It was during that period of my career in the mid-1980s that I visited the University of Mississippi at Oxford, where I spent a week throwing myself into the life of the campus, interviewing teachers, administrators, and students of both races to gain an understanding of the progress of racial integration there. My long feature story about the university and the photographs I snapped there, which appeared on the front page of the *Post* about a week later, reflected the complex reality of race across America: while I was impressed by the progress of integration and the brilliant ambitions of the black students, I was also discouraged by the stark divisions between blacks and whites, from classroom to dining hall.

One of the most startling experiences during my visit occurred when a young journalist for the campus newspaper, the *Daily Mississippian*, phoned me in my hotel room to request an interview. He had heard that a *Washington Post* reporter was on campus to write about the university and its history, and he wanted to put together a short feature about my visit. I agreed to the interview and arranged to meet the student at a certain time and at a certain table in the cafeteria in the student union.

When I arrived at the appointed hour, I found the student at the table, his notepad at the ready. But as I took my seat and extended my hand, I noticed the young man, a freckle-faced sophomore with blond hair and blue eyes, slowly turn a bright crimson as he stared back at me. As he nervously proceeded to interview me, he stared closely at his pad and held his hand over his eyes like a visor, as if a searing light were shining in his face. The more he continued like that, stammering through his questions, the more obvious it became that he was shielding his eyes to avoid having to look at me.

Finally, after a few minutes, the student dropped his hand and said, "Look, I'm sorry. This is hard for me. I've never spoken to a black person like this."

I was surprised and for a minute thought he was kidding. But after a moment's silence I realized his torment was genuine, and I tried to put him at ease. "That's all right," I said. "Just talk to me like you'd talk to anybody else."

He was the son of a Hattiesburg, Mississippi, Cadillac car dealer, he told me. The only black people he had ever run across in his life were either domestics in his household or servants for his father. He had never spoken to a black person as an equal before—certainly not anyone who represented a superior station in life, as I did—and the experience was extraordinarily jarring for him. It was as if the only world he had ever known had been shattered right before his eyes in the cafeteria at Ole Miss.

As we continued the interview, I answered all the student's questions as plainly as I could, but inside I also experienced a strange epiphany of sorts. It's hard to describe it in words now, so many years later, but as I sat there I felt myself smiling inside, exulting over what seemed a private milestone in our long family history. "Attaway, Laura and Pearl," I heard myself saying inside my mind. "That one's for you."

For in a sense the incident signaled a small confirmation that we had indeed come a long way as a black family over the past century and a half since slavery and Reconstruction. And the fact that I found that affirmation in Mississippi, the heart of the South, the very region of America where it all had begun for us, was profoundly moving.

Mississippi. That state had represented so much to my family over the years. Mississippi was where my mother's paternal grandfather, Young Turner, was born a slave on a plantation near the town of Rodney. He fled north at the outbreak of the Civil War, served in a black Union Army regiment, and afterward settled in a small town called Lebanon in south-central Illinois, where he was taught to read and write by members of a sympathetic white family. In time Young Turner became not only a remarkably successful farmer and town leader but also one of the wealthiest men of any color in his region of the state. And like Laura, he valued education above all other gifts for his nine children, who included my grandfather Edward Clifford Turner. When the white leaders of Lebanon approached the successful former slave in 1892 to ask him to donate funds to help endow the local college, Young Turner replied that he would certainly do so, but for a price: that his second daughter be admitted to the racially segregated school. She was, and four years later, in 1896, after breaking the color barrier, Mamie Turner became the first black graduate of McKendree College and went on to a long career in teaching, like many other women in the Turner family.

Mississippi. The name alone evoked many memories and haunting visions as I continued to drive west that misty October day toward Vicksburg, for it was the source of some of the best and worst times in my family's past during segregation. Mississippi was where my father had sharpened his surgical skills in a rural black clinic in Mound Bayou in 1955 and 1956, a time that coincided with the some of the bloodiest struggles in the civil rights movement.

We were living then in Nashville, where my father was training in surgery at all-black Meharry Medical College. As part of this specialized training, each year's class of five or so young surgical students was required to provide care at Taborian Hospital in Mound Bayou, some 300 miles away. This twenty-bed clinic had been started in the 1930s with funding from a black fraternal organization. The small hospital in America's poorest Jim Crow state offered the only medical care available for black people within a 200-mile radius covering Mississippi and parts of Arkansas and northern Louisiana. Most of the patients were impoverished sharecropper families who were barred from the region's white hospitals.

The Mound Bayou program provided the Meharry surgical students with firsthand experience in the field. It had been started in 1947 by Matthew Walker, Meharry's dean of surgery, a legendary charismatic surgeon with bushy sideburns and a courtly manner, whom my father studied under and greatly admired. Dr. Walker's idea was to have his surgical residents spend six-month segments providing care at Mound Bayou.

So every few weeks during his six-month residency, my father kissed my mother good-bye on our front porch in Nashville after a two-day visit and made the five-hour drive south and west through Tennessee and the lush, lonely countryside of Mississippi in my family's Pontiac. Often he worried what he would do if he ever had a flat tire or ran out of gas and found himself at the mercy of the sullen, faceless, poor white men who drove the beat-up pickup trucks and ran the filling stations and deeply resented the push for black equality. In many ways Mississippi represented the front line of the battle over equal rights, a battle that was becoming increasingly bloody. Mississippi was where a black preacher, Gus Lee, had been killed in 1955 by suspected white gunmen angry over his attempts to register black sharecroppers to vote. It was where the state's NAACP leader, Medgar Evers, was similarly arousing passions among black people and drawing death threats from angry whites. And it was the state where fourteen-year-old Emmett Till had been murdered by white thugs in 1955 for the crime of winking and saying, "Thanks, baby," to a white female store clerk. As I drove through Mississippi, heading through the rolling green fields toward the Mississippi River, I tried to imagine my father's intense feelings more than forty years earlier as he made his regular journey through the state. He used to say he felt almost haunted on those trips, the feeling lifting only when he made it to Mound Bayou, a historically all-black town where he was on duty twenty-four hours a day, working and sleeping at the medical clinic and treating every surgical emergency that came his way.

He was on duty there the night of November 26, 1955, when a black civil rights activist named Gus Courts was rushed into the clinic at about 10:30 P.M., having suffered serious gunshot wounds to his stomach and left arm. A grocer in the central Mississippi town of Belzoni, eighty miles south of Mound Bayou, Courts headed the local NAACP chapter and was leading a drive to register blacks to vote. He had been standing with his wife at his cash register when a car with two white men stopped out front. Shots rang out from an open window of the car and struck him after shattering the store's front window. Friends immediately helped Courts into a car and rushed him as quickly as they could to my father's operating table, nearly two hours away and across two Mississippi counties. En route, as Courts bled profusely in the back seat, they passed two hospitals reserved for whites only.

My father was awakened from his bed in the clinic and immediately went to work. He realized that he would have to quickly and deftly open up the patient's stomach, find and extract the bits of metal, and begin patching the holes in the intestines if the patient were to survive. For more than four hours that night, into the predawn hours, he labored with his glistening instruments and gloved hands, cutting through the patient's insides all the way to the abdominal cavity, feeling for the shotgun pellets, then doing his best to repair the holes and stop the leaks of blood and other internal fluids. He did the same for the patient's arm, which had suffered extensive nerve damage. It wasn't until after my father had finished stitching the patient up, had satisfied himself that the man would not go into shock from the severe loss of blood, and was convinced that the victim would survive the shooting, that he found out who his patient was and the circumstances of the attack.

The next day Associated Press and *New York Times* reporters sped to Mound Bayou to interview my father about the operation and the shooting, which represented another milestone in the unfolding struggle over black rights. The story was carried in newspapers around America, as well as *Jet* magazine, which published a series of photos of Courts with my father in his hospital room.

In addition, my father was interviewed by FBI agents sent from Memphis to investigate the shooting. He showed them the shotgun pellets he had extracted from Courts's arm and stomach but was told to keep them. For weeks he kept the pellets in his wallet, expecting to hand them over to the authorities whenever they called for them. But they never did. And Courts's assailants, like those of so many other black martyrs in the South, were never captured.

Courts survived. He moved to Chicago with his family to make a new life far away from the horrors of his native Mississippi and two years later traveled to Washington, D.C., to give Congress one of the first firsthand accounts of the growing bloodshed in the South being suffered by civil rights workers. I found his testimony in a leather-bound edition of the *U.S. Congressional Record* for September 1957 in my library at Berkeley, two floors below the library office where I had procured the *Tensas Gazette* on microfilm. Part of it reads:

> I was born in Mississippi, my parents and grandparents before me. We helped to make Mississippi rich and prosperous. Now, just like those Hungarian refugees from Russian oppression, you see before you an American refugee from Mississippi terror. I have had to leave my grocery business, my trucking business, my home and everything. My wife and I and thousands of us Negroes have had to run away. . . . We are the American refugees from the terror in the South, all because we wanted to vote.

Journalist Carl Rowan once wrote that when he was covering the civil rights movement in the South, he asked Courts why he, an ordinary small-town grocer in rural Mississippi, elected to put himself in such terrible danger in the first place. Courts told him, "Young man, you wouldn't understand. I just wanted to be able to say that I voted once before I died."

My father told me that he tried to contact Courts while on a visit to Chicago some years after the shooting, but by then Courts had become somewhat reclusive in his exile from Mississippi and declined to see him. He said Courts died in the early 1960s, without having the satisfaction of seeing President Johnson sign into law the Voting Rights Act of 1965, guaranteeing the ballot to every citizen regardless of race.

As I drove through Mississippi that quiet Sunday morning, I tried to envision what life must have been like for my father and mother in the South during segregation, for I could remember them only as they were during the era of racial integration in faraway Seattle many years later. I was just over two years old when we left Nashville in 1956, and my only memories of racial segregation were very faint. I vaguely recalled traveling with my family in our two-door Pontiac on dusty southern roads and my mother keeping a big glass Mason jar on the floor between her feet in the front seat. Since we couldn't use public restrooms while traveling on the highways in the South because of Jim Crow, my big brothers, Bobby and Wayne, and I had to pee in the Mason jar, which once held pickles and still smelled like them. Pissing into an old pickle jar at fifty miles an hour over bumpy roads wasn't an easy trick, and sometimes, despite their best efforts, my brothers would miss and Mom and Dad would get sore. But that was about all I could remember about those days. I had a hazy impression of warm Dixie wind coursing through the car windows, of my father's strong brown hands grasping the steering wheel, of that infamous pickle jar. From my childhood vantage point in the Pacific Northwest, it seemed as if there had been a long, dark, nightmare period in my parents' past, one I couldn't remember and would never know, one my mother often summed up for people in Seattle by saying simply, "We wanted to get as far away from the South as we could back then, and we certainly did."

But it was more complex than that, certainly in my father's case. One of my fondest memories of growing up was of the many times I joined him on his house calls to visit his patients in Seattle, a regular occurrence in our first years there in the late 1950s and early 1960s, when he was working long hours to make himself known and to establish his general practice among the city's black residents. This was long before the days of managed health care, at a time when medicine truly was *personal*. It was in many ways the prime of my father's life, as he pushed himself to succeed as a young black physician in Seattle. He was the most dashing and highly skilled man I knew, and I was proud to be his son. I thought he would be young and strong forever.

Many evenings after dinner Dad would make house calls in Seattle's Central Area or stop at the various hospitals on the city's "Pill Hill" section downtown, overlooking Puget Sound, to look in on patients he had operated on. I remember sitting in the front seat of our car as we traveled around the rain-slicked streets of the hilly green city, my short legs hanging over the edge, hearing the clatter of the windshield wipers as I rubbed my hands across the mottled surface of my father's black leather medical bag resting on the seat between us. When we stopped at a stranger's house, I would remain in the car, filling in drawings in my coloring books or watching the rain splatter and pool and race in rivulets down the windshield. I never saw my father treat his patients, but I nevertheless felt like I was helping him out in some small way, even if just hanging out in the car.

In the early days house calls were the meat and potatoes of my father's practice. During his baptism in medicine in North Carolina, just after he finished medical school in 1944, he had often delivered babies at odd hours of the night in rundown sharecropper shacks in the tobacco town he grew up in, Winston-Salem. When he migrated to Seattle after finishing his surgical training in 1956, he continued offering this sort of personalized care. He was a compassionate physician, especially to the poorest of his clients. Once he called my mother from the office to say he had just visited an elderly cancer patient at her apartment in a rundown section of the Central Area and told her the freezing winter weather would kill her before the cancer did. "Go downtown and buy an electric blanket for her, will you?" he asked, giv-

ing my mother the address. And my mother did, immediately—
she often performed such deeds on a moment's notice in support
of my father's work.

As a child I knew little about what exactly my father did to
make people well, but I knew it was important work and that his
patients were always remarkably thankful for his visits and very
respectful to him. I watched these strangers shake my father's
hand reverently and look into his eyes with admiration and gratitude when they said good-bye to him on their front steps, often
walking him to the door of his car. I invariably felt delight whenever Dad finally hopped back into the car with his medical bag in
hand and said, "Okay, Neilly, let's go to the hospital now," or
"Okay, Neilly, back home."

He was born in 1920 and raised in the shadow of the tobacco
factories in Winston-Salem, the only son of a black physician also
named John Robert Henry. His father was a thin, light-skinned,
courtly man who, as a member of a very small stratum of black
professionals, was something of a town leader. My father thus
grew up around medicine. The brick family house on East Sixth
Street was three stories tall, with the upper floor reserved for living quarters and the downstairs used exclusively by my grandfather as a medical office. At nearly all hours of the day during my
father's childhood, the ground floor was filled with patients suffering everything from broken bones or the flu, to mumps,
measles, or chicken pox, to tuberculosis or cancer.

As a boy, my father cleaned the medical office, washed his father's instruments, and folded and stocked the linens. What he
didn't enjoy for long periods during his boyhood, though, was a
mother. Irma Neal Henry, my grandmother, was an adventurous
young woman, a liberated soul way ahead of her time, who left

her husband and family on many occasions to travel far and wide. She visited the Soviet Union in the 1920s to see firsthand what life was like in a revolutionary society where she had heard that all people, including black people, were recognized as equals. (According to my father, she returned later saying it wasn't true at all and that Russia was much too cold.)

Often, as a boy, my father would accompany John Sr. in a horse-and-buggy to make house calls on patients in the Carolina countryside—much as I accompanied Dad in the car on his house calls forty years later in Seattle. They would usually return home bearing wild game or fresh vegetables as payment for my grandfather's services.

John Sr. was admiringly known as "Cap" by my father, a shortening of the word "Captain," and as "Harry" to others in Winston-Salem who knew and worked closely with him. He loved to smoke Cuban cigars and recite poetry by Whitman and Poe, and he liked nothing better than to sit in a chair on his front porch on hot and humid summer evenings, with his legs propped up on a post, and watch the traffic go by on East Sixth Street. A devout Methodist, he believed in moderation in everything, especially politics and race relations in his conservative southern city, and was keenly aware of the tenuous nature of black existence under the ever-present heel of white oppression in the South. The aphorisms my grandfather often recited reflected his attitude toward provocation and conflict:

Thoughts unexpressed may sometimes fall back dead,
But God Himself can't help them once they are said.

Boys flying kites haul in their white-winged birds.
But you cannot do that when you're flying words.

While my father similarly believed in moderation and nonviolence when it came to race relations, he developed an edge to his beliefs as a young man to go along with his desire to push the limits imposed by racism. He came of age at a time in the first half of the twentieth century when there were not many opportunities for young black men. He could have become a Pullman porter or a waiter or a civil servant or some other kind of service worker, as did many other black men who desired something better than manual labor. But he preferred a recognized profession like dentistry or medicine, as his father had, largely because he wanted respect from people.

That was always the most important thing in his life. *Respect.* One summer during his college years he worked as a baggage handler at Chicago's Union Station, toting suitcases, footlockers, and hat boxes for crowds of white travelers. Loading baggage wasn't the hardest part of the job, he told me. The toughest part was the arrogant and imperious way white people often treated him. "Hey, boy!" they liked to shout. "This way, boy!" "Grab a bag, boy!" Far more than money or other earthly gain, my father wanted the respect of others. He became a doctor because he enjoyed it, to be sure. Saving patients' lives on his operating table with his two gloved hands was certainly a satisfying calling. But he also felt a priceless sense of personal dignity and racial pride whenever people, especially white people, had to address him as "Doctor."

Respect came in both big and small ways. I remember once when I was kid he went to great pains to show me the proper way of paying for things after seeing me toss a crumpled dollar bill on the counter of a drugstore, where I was buying some soda and candy. "Like this," he told me, handing over a dollar folded neatly down the center. "Don't ever crumple money like that. Shows you've got no upbringing, that you don't think much about the person you're giving it to. Show respect for people."

And he certainly felt it was equally important to demand respect back. Whenever my white school pals visited me to play in our house on Lake Shore Drive, I knew to remind them even before they entered the house that they should be sure to address my father as "Dr. Henry," not "Mister." (He would have let me know about it if they didn't.)

My father was meticulous about many things, a result, no doubt, of both his profession and his upbringing. The suits and ties he wore always appeared neatly pressed, his shirts fresh from the cleaners, his leather shoes shiny. Upon arriving at his office in the morning, he would take off his jacket and immediately replace it with a starched and pressed white physician's jacket with "Dr. Henry" stitched in red at the pocket. His grooming habits were just as neat, his hands and nails perfectly clean at all times. He combed his thin, curly hair straight back from his forehead and, to keep it in place, would often slick a special white lotion on it that my older brother Bobby used to laughingly call "Stay Back." Frequently on call for medical emergencies, my father carried an electronic beeper with him at all times. In his suit jacket pocket he kept a small black leather-bound notebook in which he would jot down daily reminders—"See Sikes," "Beer," "New office stationery." Over the years his little black notebook turned smooth and glossy from use.

My father's disciplined personality helped to give our family life a conservative tone, one that extended in many ways to his children, perhaps me especially. The rise of Muhammad Ali in the 1960s, for instance, presented me with a dilemma. While I admired Ali's skill in the ring, I had also been taught as a boy in my father's household to detest braggarts and the conceited and to esteem humility in all things. Quiet acts of excellence always meant more than mere empty words, I was told, even if one could back the words up. Jim Brown, Willie Mays, Elgin Baylor— those were my kind of heroes.

In the face of this personal dilemma over Ali's fiery rise, I managed to find a compromise: I rooted happily for the loudmouthed champ whenever he fought white guys, no matter how obnoxious and disgraceful his behavior out of the ring, because it was important in my mind, always, that black defeat white. But when Ali fought a black contender, I usually rooted hard for his opponent, who invariably showed much more humility in the face of struggle. I figure I was probably the only black kid in America pulling in vain for quiet and dignified black fighters like Floyd Patterson and Jimmy Ellis to knock the champ down to size.

Such conservatism also influenced our household outlook on political and social change. During the civil rights movement we were squarely in the nonviolent camp of Martin Luther King, Jr., Julian Bond, and Ralph Abernathy and wary of angry provocateurs like Stokely Carmichael, Malcolm X, and H. Rap Brown. The latter were hotheads and anarchists whose political style seemed to threaten to overturn with bullets and firebombs everything we valued, including the hard-won integrationist gains that our folks had struggled and fought for through so many generations. Our ancestors had worked for centuries to claim their share of the American dream, and we were not about to accept regression after finally joining the middle class. To white America our household may have seemed fairly radical. But to black

America we were comparatively conservative in our goals and outlook.

As a young man, my father was thin but tightly muscled. He loved to play tennis and had won a number of black amateur tennis tournaments in his native North Carolina. His skin and eyes were brown, and he wore a mustache throughout his adult life, which he liked to keep pencil thin across the top of his lip, as his favorite singer, Billy Eckstine, and the suave movie actor Errol Flynn did.

As his children, we had to be sure to answer the telephone at home with a clear, pleasant "Hello?" because, as my father often reminded us, we never knew who might be on the other end—a patient in distress, another physician, the hospital calling on an emergency. The greeting was critical, he said, if only to tell the caller that this was a house where the caller was welcome and the residents concerned. There simply was no room for moodiness or discourtesy on my father's telephone line.

Impressions were important, my father emphasized, but impressions meant nothing if they were not backed up by the substance of skills and deeds. That was critical. You had to *prove* yourself worthy of the respect you demanded from others.

At twenty-one, when he finished all-black St. Augustine's College in North Carolina in 1941, my father, with his father's backing, went off to Meharry Medical College in Nashville, an esteemed and renowned institution that had educated many decades of black physicians. If you were black and wanted to be a physician in the United States in the years before about 1950, Meharry was surely the place to be, a shining jewel in the crown of black education in America. In fact, Howard University's all-black medical school in Washington, D.C., and Meharry were almost the only places to learn medicine, since aspiring black physicians, with few exceptions, were not admitted to other U.S. medical schools before the advances of the civil rights movement. As late as 1976, fully half of all black physicians working in America had been educated at Meharry.

The school was named after five Irish brothers from Indiana who donated $30,000 to endow the school in 1875. The endowment represented the fulfillment of a promise one of the brothers, Samuel Meharry, had made after a kind black family had rescued him and given him shelter in 1826 when the salt cart he was traveling in tumbled off a country road in the Ohio Valley and became mired in a swamp. According to legend, Meharry vowed to do something one day for the race of the people who were so compassionate and generous to him. The medical school endowment was his gift.

My father finished on the dean's list in his 1944 class of fifty-nine at Meharry, and in short order he married my mother, the pretty daughter of an upstanding St. Louis family, and my older brothers, Bobby and Wayne, were born. But after returning to Winston-Salem to work with his father in the small-town practice, he soon stagnated and yearned to branch out on his own. Not only into his own practice but into a specialty—surgery, the most exciting and challenging branch of medicine in his era.

The Korean conflict provided my father with a fortuitous ticket out of North Carolina. Realizing he was about to be drafted anyway, my father volunteered for the military in 1951. After completing his training in Texas, he promptly went overseas to work as a U.S. Army physician in a Military Ambulance Service Hospital unit. He was posted not in Korea but in

Heidelberg, Germany, where my mother, Bobby, and Wayne accompanied him and where I was soon conceived. Afterward he returned to Meharry to study surgery in 1954, the year I was born.

It was during their two years in Nashville between 1954 and 1956 that my parents decided to make a break from the South. Their experiences in the newly integrated U.S. military, living and socializing with white service families and enjoying the comforts attached to my father's rank as captain, had exposed them to the benefits of equal opportunity for the first time in their lives. My father in particular was keenly aware of the limits of opportunity—and respect—he could ever find among white people in the South.

This bitter reality had been brought home to him in many ways under Jim Crow, and sometimes his joys and his inner rage were bound together precisely because of racism—in much the same way as I experienced in Seattle a generation later. For example, the night before he became a father for the first time in 1947, he had taken my mother and Fredda in his new car to a movie in Winston-Salem. Afterward, as they were getting into his long black Pontiac, a white woman in an adjacent car stuck her head out the window and exclaimed, "Boy, whose car is that you drivin'?"

My father was infuriated. "Mine," he muttered. "Whose car is that *you're* driving?"

But the damage was done, the insult swallowed. All the way home on what should have been one of the happiest nights of his life, my mother recalled, he fumed, trembling and cursing under his breath, enraged at the disrespect the white woman had shown him. Years later it wasn't my brother's birth he recalled so distinctly, but the earlier incident in the parking lot of the Carolina Theater, behind the Robert E. Lee Hotel.

My father knew racism imposed strict limits on his life and potential in the South and that no matter how skilled he became in medicine and surgery, no matter how great the deeds he accomplished, he would always be in the eyes of many suspicious white people just a black boy with a shiny car. But, after his military experience in Germany, he recognized that life could be much better elsewhere, that black people got a fairer shake in other places. He had visited big northern cities like New York and Philadelphia before and discovered that life in other parts of America wasn't as pervasively harsh for blacks as white people made it for our family in the South. Not that he ever felt the North was the Promised Land or anything close to it. It was just that he could do a little more as a black man in the North. He could ride streetcars and buses, for one thing, and sit wherever he damn well pleased. He could freely try on shoes and hats in department stores without having some white clerk point him to the door or call the cops on him. He could go to picture shows and museums and use whatever public men's room he wanted. And he could vote in elections, a right not granted to millions of blacks in the South.

When he completed his surgical training in Nashville in 1956, my father moved us to Seattle, largely because it was one of few cities in America at that time with hospitals willing to accept a black surgeon on staff. It was a bold move under any circumstance. My father was just thirty-six years old and had already accomplished a lot, to be sure, especially for a young black man in America's early postwar years. But it was our new house, the house he and my mother decided to build in 1960 right in the heart of an affluent white neighborhood to gain equal access to the best public schools for us, which turned out to be the most important achievement of all for him, he later told me. For it signified more than anything else his empowerment and progress as a man from the segregated, oppressive society he had always known to something else, something better and more just, something that had always been denied him before because of white racism.

It did not come easy. The costs he paid for the "giant leap" to the white middle class may have been hidden, but they were real. When our white neighbors on Lake Shore Drive banded together in the months before our move to offer us $100,000 not to move in—a huge sum of money in 1960—my mother suggested to him that if those white people were willing to go to such extremes to keep us out, they might also be willing to go to terrible extremes to make our lives hell once we moved in.

"Maybe this isn't so good for the kids, John," she remembered confessing to him in a moment of deep anxiety and doubt.

But my father simply answered, "It's principle. You don't bend on principle," no matter how much money the white man dangles in front of you. That was not the way to earn respect.

Instead, several nights after dinner in the weeks before our move from the black world to the white, my father got in our family car and drove out to the new neighborhood to visit a few of our prospective white neighbors in person, knocking on the front door of several stately houses on Lake Shore Drive to extend his hand, introduce himself, and try to allay their fears. A few of our new neighbors were Jewish, including a dentist and a physician, both of whom had joined in the opposition to us, a fact that especially troubled and disappointed my mother. Indeed, when my family was living in Germany in the mid-1950s, they had visited the remains of Hitler's concentration camps and sensed the horrors suffered by Europe's Jews during World War II. If any people should know about prejudice and injustice and be able to sympathize with the aspirations of minorities, my mother felt, surely Jewish people should.

But my father got little satisfaction when he visited our white neighbors on those cool autumn nights after dinner—only fear and empty words about declining property values. Exasperated, he went downtown to the head office of the John L. Scott Realty Company, the biggest real estate brokerage in the city's south end. John L. Scott himself had been very active in organizing our neighbors' opposition to us, once he heard that black people had somehow, by some trick, purchased property in his territory. My father said he met Scott at his office to try to understand more about him, to find out why he and all the white people were against us. He remembered asking the white realtor, "Why are you doing this? Do you even know any Negroes? How can you do this when you don't even know us?"

"This is business. It's about what's best for us and what's best for you in the long run," Scott replied. "And I do know Negroes, Dr. Henry. I like Negroes a great deal. That fellow downstairs shining shoes in the lobby. His name's Sam. He's one of my best pals."

My father left Scott's office shortly afterward, knowing there would be no getting through to any of them, no matter how hard he tried, no matter how much he reasoned. We would simply move in when our house was finished and take whatever came.

Years later as an adult, whenever I thought about my father's experiences back then, I wondered how he ever managed to balance within himself all the conflict and torment he must have felt about our move and about white people. He once told me that the rainy day we moved into our new house—December 1, 1960, less than three weeks before his fortieth birthday—was the proudest day of his life, far prouder even than his graduation from medical school or even his first day working as a surgeon on the medical staffs of the white hospitals in Seattle.

"Because of everything we went through," he explained to me. "Because of what it meant. Because it was bigger than us."

He meant, I think, that our move was historic and deeply symbolic of a new era in America in which capable black people everywhere were simply *expected* to make such stands for equality and racial progress. To make a stand for the next generation.

The house was my father's stand.

But, for that experience, he had to endure a great deal of hurt, just as he did so many times growing up in the South. And as with so many things about my father, I never understood exactly how he did it. How he overcame. How he dealt with all those hurts, fitted them inside his soul. He was a quiet, often moody, melancholic, and guarded sort of man. Certainly he carried himself with an outward sense of purpose, pride, style, and conviction, but he repressed many demons deep inside him. Beneath the skin he kept tightly contained a box of pain, sorrow, and rage whose depth none of us, even my mother, ever really knew. The strongest emotion we ever saw my father express was anger, which erupted most harshly during the times he beat me or my brothers in our basement. The punishments were fairly regularly inflicted on our bare buttocks for transgressions large and small.

"Get my belt," he'd snap in a seething tone, quickly concluding all discussion about the boyhood wrong I had committed. Whereupon I would have to trudge to the clothes closet in his bedroom, select a leather belt from its door rack, and meet him downstairs. Wordlessly I would hand the belt over to him, lower my pants and underwear, and bend away from him at the waist. The basement would erupt then with the sounds of his furious voice, the slap of leather on flesh, and my shrieks of pain.

Don't you ever talk back to your mother that way!

Whap!

I won't, Daddy, I won't!

Whap!

Do you hear me?

Yes, Daddy, yes, Daddy, yes!

Whap!

Ever!

The beatings were excruciating, the pain sometimes lasting into the next day and the emotional repercussions lingering far longer. Bobby suffered his last beating at Dad's hand at age sixteen and afterward reflected for hours, amid angry tears, on how much those lashings told him about what slavery must have been like, when masters whipped slaves like mules.

But even in those terrible moments my father's rage was remarkably brief and tightly controlled. Swiftly he returned his inner fire to its box inside his soul, almost as soon as he unleashed the final lash. Today experts on child development consider corporal punishment of all forms abusive, and they may not be far wrong. But such punishment was the only way my father knew how to correct our behavior, and at that time it certainly was not an uncommon method in many homes, black or white.

My father concealed his hurts and sadnesses just as completely as his anger. My mother once told me that the only time she ever saw him weep was late one night in their first year of marriage, in 1947, when they were living in Winston-Salem, and he learned that one of his patients had died. He had worked so hard to save the patient, she recalled, and he was absolutely inconsolable with grief as he lay in bed beside her.

Now, many years later, with Mississippi's history flashing through my mind and its lush scenery flowing by my car windows in a blur of greens and browns, I was traveling due west through the state toward the Warren County Court House. I hoped to find clues to our old family puzzle there, to find the white Beaumonts whose blood we shared from so long ago. But remarkably, as I traveled, I realized my ruminations were focusing not on the white branch of our family tree, but on the black.

It was shortly after 3 P.M. when I arrived on the outskirts of Vicksburg, where I had appointments with courthouse officials and researchers scheduled for early the next morning, a Monday. Realizing that I had a couple of hours of Sunday afternoon daylight left, I immediately decided to press farther on in my journey. I turned at Vicksburg and headed due south through a forest of green hanging kudzu vines on a sleepy two-lane highway called the Natchez Trace, near the Mississippi River, to the city of Natchez, fifty miles away.

It was a fairly quick trip, for I found myself approaching the city about an hour later. Located high on a grassy bluff overlooking the Mississippi River, Natchez was a storied old town noted for its cool summer breezes and antebellum mansions. It also possessed a historic cemetery in a prime, majestic location high above the river. Throughout the nineteenth century this cemetery had provided an eternal resting place for the genteel white residents of Delta towns for miles around. I knew that A.J.

Beaumont and his widow, Mary Ann, were among them. I wanted to find their graves.

I slowed to enter the city. Amid a clumsy collection of jarring road signs directing visitors to the city's gaming casinos jammed on the riverfront (Natchez is now known far more for its gambling enterprises than its antebellum gentility), I spotted a small white sign with a historic landmark symbol informing me that the city cemetery was just north along the river. I traveled along a city street lined with beautiful mansions shaded by majestic magnolia trees, some of the houses featuring grand whitewashed porticos and tall poles flying Mississippi's red, white, and blue state flag. The street soon wound its way into a far less prosperous neighborhood dotted with ramshackle and abandoned houses. A little beyond this neighborhood, I found the cemetery on the right-hand side of the road, on a beautiful plateau opposite the river to the west.

Framed by low stone walls and iron fencing, the cemetery was a rolling expanse of trim green grass dotted with trees and sprinkled with what seemed like thousands of headstones. It was divided into numerous sections, and I drove slowly through the first section on the right-hand side nearest the front gate, trying to glimpse the dates of death and last names engraved on the headstones, hoping to find a date somewhere near 1901, when Arthur Beaumont died, or a preponderance of surnames beginning with B. Of course, as I quickly realized, to my private embarrassment, people don't die in chronological or alphabetical order. I would have to hike on foot through those many confusing sections of headstones to locate the area with the graves from Beaumont's time.

I parked my car and set out through the magnolias, my sandaled feet making crunching sounds in the twigs and grass. The afternoon air had turned muggy and misty, and within a few minutes beads of sweat began to collect on my brow and neck as I walked slowly amid the dead. I was alone in the cemetery save for the cicadas buzzing in the closely trimmed grass, the songbirds chirping in the treetops, and a half dozen or so dark-clad attendants at a burial on a far edge of the graveyard, seemingly a mile way.

Several of the cemetery's sections featured truly ornate iron fencing turned brown and rust-red by age. I spent more than a half hour roaming in one of those sections. Dating to the mid-nineteenth century, it presented a vast tableau of marble headstones and granite markers, some of them massive monuments topped by beautifully sculpted angels and Virgin Marys.

I continued wandering through the groves of magnolias from one old section to another. I found an old, small Jewish section and a Roman Catholic one. Scattered throughout the graveyard were numerous headstones featuring the engraved weather-worn letters "CSA," denoting that the interred was a Confederate veteran of the Civil War. Repeatedly, I ran across headstones engraved with surnames—Watson, Bondurant, Garrett, Newell— I recognized from my hours and hours of microfilm research in the old *Tensas Gazette* newspapers. These were Arthur Beaumont's friends and contemporaries during his life in St. Joseph, and their names were mentioned alongside his in numerous articles about the town's white society in the late nineteenth century.

As I rambled up and down the graveyard's knolls, I came across the cemetery office, a small two-room building with leaded-glass windows perched on the edge of a single-lane road coursing through the property. Near the door a sign read "1914 Shelter House." The building was closed, its windows and door locked tight. But near the door was a big metal bell with a long cord attached. "Ring for Superintendent" read the small hand-printed sign beside it.

I pulled hard on the cord several times, and the loud clangs of the bell echoed through the graveyard in the warm, muggy, early evening air. I waited. I took a seat on a granite wall to gather my breath, suddenly thinking for a moment what a wickedly fine as-signment a graveyard search might make for my journalism stu-dents at Berkeley some day.

> You need to locate one grave out of thousands in an old ceme-tery. You have the name of the deceased and the dates of birth and death, but that's all. You have no other guide or reference to assist you. Find it. Deadline: 5 P.M.

I laughed softly to myself.

Several more minutes passed. No one came.

I had only a few minutes left before it would be too dark to continue, and I felt tired and sore from all the hiking, climbing, and searching after a long day's drive. Perhaps I should come back another day, I thought.

I rose and began to walk slowly to the other side of the ceme-tery office, where I found a pleasant little hollow near the front gate. It seemed the most tranquil section in the entire cemetery, a level expanse of green about two hundred yards square in a prime location close to the river, bordered by an old wrought-iron fence. A dark metal sign and historical marker near the fence described the section as "1st Zurhellen Addition," one of the old-est in the cemetery. Another sign close by read:

> Natchez City Cemetery—Established in 1822 on a 10-acre tract, the cemetery grew into a park notable for its variety of

19th century iron and marble work. People from all walks of life are buried in the cemetery.

I decided to wander through that section of the graveyard on the way back to my car. I strolled slowly between the rows of headstones, my eyes glancing at the names etched into each one. Many of the graves dated back to before the turn of the century. I came across one reading "MCGEE" in big letters amid the graves of a dozen or so family members—Nathan, Irene, Sarah. Among these but slightly apart, I spotted a small headstone reading, "Mammy—Henrietta Clark—1820–1908."

I walked on.

Then, on a monument barely ten feet beyond that one, I saw the letters "BEAU . . ." out of the corner of one eye. I stopped in my tracks, instantly feeling a familiar tingle in my spine, the same sensation of alert I had felt whenever I ran across those letters during my microfilm research in Davis and Berkeley.

I stepped closer and read all the letters in bold uppercase: "BEAUMONT."

The name was engraved near the top of a six-foot-tall marble obelisk. My eyes wandered to other words engraved higher on the obelisk in a half circle above the surname. "On Thy Cross I Lean," they read.

I lowered my eyes to a level beneath the name "Beaumont" and found these words:

In Memory of My Beloved Husband, Arthur J. Beaumont, Died
    April 30, 1901, Aged 62 years.
As a Husband Devoted
As a Father Affectionate
As a Friend Ever Kind and True.

I jotted the words down in my notebook and tried to capture the headstone's appearance in a line drawing. The monument seemed impressive, slightly taller than me, not as grand or elaborate as some in the graveyard, but certainly more distinguished than many. Like most of the other headstones in the cemetery, it faced east, in the direction of sunrise.

I felt profound satisfaction in that moment, along with a sense of relief that prompted a lengthy and audible sigh. "So there you are, A.J.," I told myself in vindication as I gazed at the headstone of the white man whose photograph and letter to Pearl had filled me with so many hours of torment and wonder. Here was the last resting place of the English immigrant and Confederate veteran whose life had been the focus of so much of my reflection and ambivalent rumination in recent years. If I found out nothing more about him or the whereabouts of his white descendants, I knew that at least I had the satisfaction of that moment, of finding his grave that way, just one out of thousands in the old southern cemetery.

Then I glanced at the monument next to Beaumont's, that of his widow. It was much more modest, about half as tall, smaller in size, and in granite. It read on its face:

In Memoriam
Mary A. Beaumont, May 2, 1859, June 15, 1914.
In Heaven.

Part of the short headstone was oddly in the shape of a tree trunk, with the words "Woodsmen Circle" and the likeness of a hammer and ax carved into its side. I had no idea what those words meant. I jotted them down and drew a picture of the monument in my notebook while making a mental note to research what the Woodsmen Circle was. I ran my hand over the head-stone, feeling the rough, mottled surfaces where time had left its marks.

I couldn't tell when anyone had visited the site last. There were no flowers, not even dead ones. I did notice atop Mary Ann's grave an ancient, badly weathered, and discolored stone flower urn resting upside down. I reached over to right it, but when I did a horde of red fire ants charged out. I quickly stepped back.

The two graves were the only ones in the plot. No other Beaumont family members were interred there.

I had driven 502 miles from Atlanta to find the cemetery that day, Sunday, October 12. I had discovered the graves right at sunset, about 6:30 P.M. It was an eerily beautiful scene, utterly quiet and still.

As I gazed at the sun setting in a blaze of orange and violet over the Mississippi River to the west, I reflected not just on the Beaumonts, their white descendants, and the task still ahead of me in the courthouse at Vicksburg. I also contemplated the many paths our black family had taken all over America in the years since A.J. and Laura loved in the 1870s. And as I waited to watch the sun brilliantly flame out of sight, I thought not so much about the dead white couple at my feet as about Laura, Pearl, Fredda, and Mary, my mother. Especially my mother.

We had traveled so far from the South since that time long ago.

CHAPTER FOUR

Jim Crow's Shadow

My mother hated the South at the time I was born. She hated the constant struggle of simply trying to endure and raise a young family under the pervasive oppression of segregation. It was bad enough that my father was absent from our home in Nashville for days and weeks at a time in the years between 1954 and 1956, that he often traveled somewhere deep in Mississippi, filling her with loneliness and dread. She had almost grown used to that.

In fact, on the cold, snowy night I was born, January 28, 1954, in Nashville's "colored" hospital, my father was on surgical duty in Mound Bayou and she was alone. Years later, when I was growing up in Seattle, she loved to talk about that night, filling the story with vividly dramatic detail. "A comedy of errors from the start!" she'd begin, recalling how she was alone in our house on Hawkins Street when the labor pains started coming on strong.

She put my brothers, Bobby and Wayne, in the care of a housekeeper, then waddled outside to our car and drove herself to Hubbard Hospital, Meharry's teaching facility, gripping the wheel of the stick-shift car as it made its way through the slush and snow. "Then," she would go on, her eyes growing wide with excitement, "as soon as I got there, the nurse told me I had to wait. Can you believe it? They told me I couldn't deliver."

The nervous and inexperienced nurse informed her that her obstetrician, Dr. Carr Trehern, a Meharry teacher, was attending an Arthur Rubinstein piano concert across town and that it would take a while for him to rush back to the delivery room. "So the nurse pointed me to a bed," my mother would continue, "and she said, 'Just lie down right here, Mrs. Henry. And whatever you do, make sure you keep your legs together *real* tight.'"

My mother would start laughing then, her bright eyes narrowing, her straight white teeth glowing, recalling how she did her best to keep me inside her despite the pain, demonstrating with her tan-colored hands the way she grabbed her belly tight. When Dr. Trehern finally rushed in, she would conclude, she squeezed me out in no time flat.

"The nurse wrapped you in a blanket and handed you to me. And you just sort of lay there on top of me late into the night with your eyes wide open, looking at me like the 'feetis' sang' that ever lived," my mother would say, as she slipped into her old St. Louis drawl, magically transforming words like "sweetest thing."

She was thirty-one years old that year, the mother now of three little boys, working full-time as a librarian at Fisk University to support us and my father in his surgical training. Her life was nothing if not a whirl of obligations. She was, like many black women in America's long history, a "working mother" long before white feminism claimed and celebrated the term. Adding to her busy-ness was the tension she felt over my father's absences and the sheer terror of the times. The racial strife breaking out across the South made it seem to her as if we were living in the middle of a war zone. Boycotts. Firebombings. Lynchings. She didn't want to see our family hurt and was particularly fearful that her kids might become fodder in the coming struggle in Nashville over court-ordered desegregation of the public schools, which promised to be bloody.

The pressure she felt in those years was always keenest whenever she got word of a new gain or setback in the movement for equal rights. In her job at the Fisk University library, she worked once as a researcher for a noted black sociologist, Charles S. Johnson, who was also the president of the university. Dr. Johnson was an expert on race relations, had written many sociological studies of the black South, and spent a lot of time giving lectures around the country and interviews on the radio. Working for him was often like being a witness to history, my mother said. She especially remembered May 17, 1954, a warm spring day four months after I was born, when the U.S. Supreme Court announced its momentous decision outlawing racial segregation in the public schools. She felt thrilled to field telephone calls that day from reporters at newspapers around the country seeking comments from Dr. Johnson. And she vividly remembered the cheers that erupted all over the black campus as the news spread among the Fisk University students, faculty, and staff who were listening to the radio bulletins. Fisk was located right across the street from Meharry, and the *Brown* decision soon set off a spontaneous celebration on those hallowed corners of black Nashville.

But at the same time she rejoiced, my mother felt terrified. Even then, in the back of her mind, she knew that my brothers and I were among the ones who ultimately would be in the middle of all the rage and fury when the transition at the public schools in Nashville came. And she knew that many white people in Nashville would not go along with such radical change without a violent fight.

Within two years her worst fears were realized when white extremists threatened to bomb Nashville's public schools and published fiery petitions in the city's newspapers calling for white people in the state to stand together to fight racial integration. The following example was published in the *Nashville Banner* on March 5, 1956:

> RALLY TENNESSEANS!
>
> Something CAN Be Done!
>
> Stand with Virginia, the Carolinas, Alabama, Georgia, Mississippi and our other sister states of the South in the fight to preserve our constitutional rights, including the right to maintain a fair and just separation of the races in our schools and parks.
>
> Let It Never Be Said That Tennessee Weakly Surrendered!

One day as the Montgomery bus boycott unfolded in December 1955, my mother's stress openly erupted while she was at work. She was listening to a radio in the library with a friend, Alva Johnson, as an announcer broadcast news about a clash between the black boycotters and the white police. Her friend pumped her fist in the air in solidarity with the protesters, repeatedly interjecting, "Give it to 'em, just give it 'em! This is great!" as she heard the news.

"I don't think this is great at all, Alva," my mother shot back in rage. "You can sit there and say all this because your husband is right across the street. Do you know where John is? He's in

Mississippi, where all this stuff is going on. I'm not happy about this at all."

"Why, Mary!" her friend replied, rendered nearly speechless by the anger in my mother's voice. "You should be ashamed of yourself."

"You send your husband down there while those white people are shooting folks," my mother answered bitterly, "and then tell me how you feel about it."

White people. White people and the old system of inequality were the bane of my mother's existence in 1956, the source of nearly every sorrow. She hated everything about the personal degradations she had to endure in our everyday life in Nashville, where we were barred from most restaurants and public parks and relegated to the back "colored" seats of public transports and the decrepit "colored" public restrooms. Most of all she hurt deep inside witnessing us, the next generation, having to suffer under the same burdens endured by so many previous generations in our family.

She had known Jim Crow very well all her life, from the moment she was born in Peoples Hospital in St. Louis, a private black hospital established in 1903 to serve the city's African American population under segregation. So it wasn't that the system was new to her. It was just that the Jim Crow that she had known in St. Louis, a cosmopolitan city at the crossroads of North and South, where Laura and Pearl had moved to establish the family in the 1890s, was a more genteel form of racial separatism than the oppressive kind that characterized the Deep South.

In the St. Louis of my mother's happy childhood, there was a lot that a black girl could do. She and her friends could freely attend cultural events like the municipal opera, exhibits at the art museum, and musical concerts at Forest Park. She could ride the St. Louis streetcars wherever she wanted, along with everybody else. Racial segregation was a comparatively discreet form of evil in which the city's restaurants, movie theaters, and other amenities were rigidly separate but many other civic offerings, including the public libraries, museums, and restrooms, were not.

Her segregated schools were all quite good, and her teachers among the best and brightest of their generation of black Americans, for few other professions and opportunities in society were open to them. And these teachers were nothing if not demanding in pushing my mother and her contemporaries toward achievement.

Nevertheless, the hypocrisy of American life was ingrained in her mind from the time she was a child, so much so that she, like many young black people, often looked at the racist society with a sarcastic humor. My mother remembered the way she and her black classmates at Sumner High in St. Louis used to recite the Pledge of Allegiance every morning: "I pledge allegiance to the rag of the United States of America," they would say, holding their hands over their hearts. "And to the Republic for which it stands, one nation, under God, indivisible, with liberty and justice for all," they would conclude, making sure to mutter "them white folks" as they took their seats.

My mother ran into the real Jim Crow for the first time at age twenty-two, when she left St. Louis to attend library school at Atlanta University, in the very heart of the South. The shoe stores, department stores, buses, restrooms, drinking fountains— everything was segregated, even the beloved libraries where she had found such peace and happiness in her childhood. Life among black people in the South was pervasively insulting and bleak.

Connecting St. Louis with the South were the trains that she traveled back and forth to attend school, and it was on these trains that she often encountered the starkest contrast between her native Midwest and the South. The routine for black people was always the same, no matter which railroad she took—the Southern, the Norfolk and Western, or the Nashville, Chattanooga, and St. Louis. The Ohio River represented the racial demarcation, the Mason-Dixon line. North of this line black passengers enjoyed equal treatment on America's railroads. South of it they entered hell. When the train crossed the Ohio River from Cincinnati into Paducah, Kentucky, the conductor went up and down the aisles making sure all the black people had headed up front to the "colored" cars. These invariably were the most decrepit cars on the train and were usually located just behind the coal car that supplied the fuel.

My mother carried a bottle of rubbing alcohol in her purse to wipe the coal soot off her face. For more than thirty hours on these rattling rides, she held her bowel movements and urine in check, so she wouldn't have to use the train's unattended and unkempt "colored" lavatory, which usually overflowed with trash, chicken bones, fish bones, and sewage. By the time she arrived at her destination she was nearly always sick with fever and nausea, vomiting out of one end and having diarrhea out the other, a Jim Crow disease that could last for days.

Traveling by rail in the shadow of Jim Crow during the 1940s was like going to war for my mother. When, on a starlit night in 1944, an old high school friend named Clarence Jefferson handed her a "White–Colored" sign that he had unscrewed from a Jim Crow train before shipping off to war as a GI in the Pacific, she kept the gift close to her soul, her equivalent of a Purple Heart for the struggle that was still going on at home.

Once in 1945, when she arrived home in St. Louis for the Christmas break from her job at Bennett College in Greensboro, North Carolina, she lay hot and feverish in bed for days after the Jim Crow train ride. At this point her mother, Fredda, insisted she do something. That she fight the system. The granddaughter of the English immigrant A.J. Beaumont and the daughter of the light-skinned Pearl, Fredda had so much white blood in her that most strangers would have sworn she was white. She had straight brown hair, light hazel-colored eyes, and fair skin, so fair that no one ever bothered her or even thought twice about her when she broke the color line to shop at department stores or shoe stores on her visits to my mother in the South.

When, as a child, my mother accompanied Fredda on trips to downtown St. Louis, where Fredda would pay the family's bills, she never failed to notice the way the white clerks at the gas, electric, and telephone offices would look up in shock upon seeing her and her mother together. The two visions didn't seem to go together. Why was this white woman with this little black child? Such puzzled reactions by white strangers constituted some of my mother's earliest and most vivid memories.

Indeed, Fredda or her own mother, Pearl, could easily have passed over to the other side and lived as a white woman, married a white man, raised a white family, and disappeared into white America leaving hardly a trace, as many very light-skinned black people did for centuries to get a fairer shot in American society. But, though they appeared white outside, both Fredda and Pearl were ebony black inside. Pearl would never have left the world of her darker-skinned mother, Laura, and Fredda felt the same. She had always known somehow, from her earliest years growing up in her grandma Laura's boardinghouse in St. Louis, that there was no happiness or love for her on the other side of the color line.

And love was all that mattered. *Love.* That's what the Bible said, didn't it? Passing outwardly as something she was not, forsaking all that she loved just to live a little better, was out of the question. And when in 1918, at age twenty-three, Fredda met the handsome, amiable, dark-skinned man of her dreams, Edward Clifford Turner, a postman who came from a big and happy black farming family in Lebanon, Illinois, she knew her life's path was set.

Once when my mother was about fifteen, she asked her mother if she had ever considered living as white, even for an instant. "No, never," her mother replied. "I always knew I'd rather live my life as a middle-class colored woman than a poor white any day."

And that's what Fredda did. Throughout her adult life A.J. Beaumont's granddaughter never moved from her beloved Ville, even as it rapidly decayed in the 1960s and 1970s, as so many of America's inner-city neighborhoods did with the exodus of the black middle class to the suburbs. Into her eighties Fredda insisted on walking and traveling by bus in the increasingly mean, abandoned streets of the Ville to go to the grocery store and run errands downtown. On more than one occasion she encountered tough black youths who didn't know a thing about her and spat and cursed at her, calling her a "honky" and an "old white bitch." The degeneration of her beloved Ville was the greatest sadness of my grandmother's long life.

It was in the Ville in 1945 that Fredda devised a plan for my mother to trick Jim Crow. Angry and tired of seeing her daughter suffer constantly from her train travel, Fredda urged her to masquerade as a white woman on the southern railroads, securing better accommodations and treatment in the White Only cars.

"You've got to act like you *belong* there. It's your attitude," my grandmother admonished my mother, whose thicker, wavy hair and tan-colored skin made her more noticeably black than either Fredda or Pearl. Fredda sat my mother before the bedroom mirror and proceeded to dab face powder all over her face and arms, then pulled a hat down low over her head to cover her hair.

"Oh, Mama, this'll never work," my mother protested.

"It will *too* work," Fredda answered, her voice filled with indignation. "But you've got to act like you belong there, do you hear? It's your attitude. You just sit in your seat and you stare straight ahead and don't you let those white people bother you. They won't make you move."

So my mother tried it, more to mollify Fredda than for any other reason. On her trip back south she remained in the White Only car. By the time the train crossed into Kentucky heading south into Dixie, it was the middle of the night and my mother found herself dead asleep on the shoulder of a white man sitting beside her. He was asleep as well.

But then the conductor came along checking to see that all the white and black people were in their right places on the train. He lifted my mother's hat to see her powdered face, then shoved his index finger into her shoulder. "Forward," the white man ordered. "Forward," to the Jim Crow car.

"I did exactly what you said," my mother later wrote Fredda after she arrived back in Greensboro in January 1946, sick with Jim Crow fever once more. "I sat in that car and acted like I belonged.

I really did. I had on the white powder and I was even asleep on the shoulder of a white man. But it didn't do a bit of good."

My mother said she vowed she would never again try to pass as something she was not. But now, ten years later, she was watching her own children grow up under the same oppression, the same racial meanness, the "same ol' shit," as she put it when she was feeling her most discouraged and depressed.

What made it worse was that she knew damned well that life could be much better. She had glimpsed a bit of the "other side" of the mountain in American society just a few years earlier in Germany, between 1951 and 1953, when my father served in the U.S. Army. Equality was enforced by law in the newly integrated U.S. armed forces, and my parents had thrived under a system in which white enlisted men crisply saluted my father as "Captain," a white soldier escorted my brother Bobby to school each morning, and my mother was respectfully addressed as "Mrs. Henry" and "Madam" wherever she went. My father found himself working side by side with white surgeons and nurses. For the first time in their lives they felt *free* from the constraints of segregation.

It was especially fantastic to be stationed in Heidelberg, a city rich in intellectual and cultural history, home of Europe's oldest university, built in 1386. Set in the valley of the Neckar River and surrounded by thick forests, the picturesque eight-hundred-year-old city had been the birthplace of German Romanticism and an inspiration to centuries of great thinkers and writers, Hegel and Goethe among them. Mark Twain, too, had rhapsodized about Heidelberg in his 1880 book, *A Tramp Abroad,* calling the enchanting city "the last possibility of the beautiful." Twain had traveled across Europe on a Grand Tour to find release from a protracted case of writer's block he was suffering during his creation of *The Adventures of Huckleberry Finn*, the classic American novel of race, youth, and life on the Mississippi. The year of his visit was 1878, one year after the freed slave Laura gave birth to Pearl.

Despite Heidelberg's role as a center of fascist "brown shirt" support for Adolf Hitler, the city had been spared bombing by the Allies during World War II. Just a few years removed from the war, and three-quarters of a century after Twain, my mother and father found inspiration of a different kind. My mother gushed about the liberties they discovered in Europe in numerous letters to her family in St. Louis. In late June 1952 she wrote to Fredda:

> *We went to one small Austrian club one night and John and I were sitting at the table alone while Alice and Foster were dancing. And get this: A white fellow came over to our table and said in all sincerity—out of the clear blue sky—"God, am I glad to see you people. I just got over here today from the States and it does my heart good to see somebody from home—and to see you here doing the things you should be able to do back there." He emoted for about ten minutes and I became convinced that he sure must have been homesick, to carry on that way. John had on civvies, but the white guy said right away, "You're in the medical corps, aren't you? I can tell." He was from Minnesota and asked where we were from. We said North Carolina, and he said, "God, what a hell of a place to be from!"*
>
> *That white man never would have approached us like that in the States. Can you imagine? But here, in Heidelberg and across Europe, we are suddenly Americans.*

Yet back in Nashville just two years later, life was as hard as ever. My mother was "Girlie" and "Missy" once again to all the white shopkeepers, and all of us were relegated to a second-class citizenship. Meantime, my father was struggling to find a place for himself as a trained black surgeon in an America that was far from ready to accept one. He agreed with my mother that they needed to find somewhere far from the South for our family to live. Unlike so many black people caught in the maw of terror and change in the region, we were fortunate to possess the means and opportunity to escape. But to where?

My father's specialty was abdominal surgery, a skill he sharpened at the rural clinic in Mound Bayou and under steady fire at Hubbard Hospital's busy emergency room in Nashville, where he tended to shooting, knifing, and car accident victims, gaining the sort of priceless medical training only an inner-city hospital could provide. The plan my parents soon decided on was that once he finished his training in 1956, we would try to settle somewhere in the Midwest or farther east, between her family in St. Louis and his in Winston-Salem. My parents wanted to stake out a new place for us but didn't want to settle too far from the people they loved.

Most important, they hoped to find somewhere in America that offered good public schools, livable neighborhoods, and especially an accepting atmosphere for a young black surgeon to practice his skill. The prospective city and its medical community would have to possess a high degree of racial tolerance, since a black surgeon was a rarity in America then. Indeed, according to census data, 4,026 black physicians were practicing medicine in the United States in 1950, less than two percent of the nation's total. While I could find no available breakdown of these statistics into medical specialties such as surgery, the numbers were clearly quite small. Meharry's postgraduate surgical training program was begun only in 1941, and the first board-certified black surgeon to be trained under director Dr. Matthew Walker finished the program in 1948. According to Meharry records, my father was just the sixteenth surgeon to finish the school's still-fledgling residency program. When he completed his training in 1956, he was among the first fifty black surgeons in American history to graduate from one of the two surgical residency programs affiliated with black medical schools and accredited by the American Medical Association and the American Board of Surgery. (Howard University Medical College's surgical program, begun in 1935, was the other.)

My father's biggest dream was to pioneer, to put his skills and training to work in a topnotch hospital in the mainstream of American medicine, to pursue a dream often expressed by a trailblazing black surgeon of his era, the renowned blood plasma researcher Dr. Charles Drew—to take advantage of the new age of "equal" opportunity and set new standards of black possibility. As my father once told me years later, he wanted "to see what I was made of." The problem was that few places in America seemed to possess all the civic qualities my parents were looking for. It was one thing for the government and the courts to begin to outlaw racial segregation in schools, public transportation, and other areas, but it was another for civil and professional societies—white people themselves—to bend with the new ways.

Just as Jackie Robinson had found it hard to gain acceptance from many of his white peers in his chosen profession when major league baseball integrated in 1947, my father found very few hospitals in the Midwest ready or willing to take on a black surgeon in 1956. In some ways my father and other black surgeons may have faced greater difficulties in integrating mainstream medicine than Robinson did in baseball. My father and his black contemporaries were not, for the most part, blessed with the help of a white visionary like Branch Rickey, someone who possessed the desire or the power to force the issue of racial integration and acceptance on his white peers. In fact, the American Medical Association—the preeminent professional organization in the United States—historically barred black physicians from membership in many state and local branches, particularly in the South. Since membership was required by most hospitals for surgical and other hospital privileges, black physicians were effectively kept out of these hospitals until 1968, when the AMA finally voted to amend its constitution to bar racial discrimination at both the local and the national level.

So, in 1956, despite his excellent and fully accredited surgical training at Meharry and his U.S. Army medical experience, my father was either denied surgical privileges outright or actively discouraged from seeking them at white-run hospitals throughout the Midwest because he was black. He and my mother traveled that year to Louisville, Cincinnati, Lima, Indianapolis, Omaha, and many other places in search of a place to call home, but at each hospital the message was essentially the same: "Whites Only."

The reasons had far more to do with fear, ignorance, and bigotry than with science, of course. The system did not want the hands of black doctors healing the bodies of white people. "White society was scared to death in particular of the idea of a black doctor treating white women," explained my uncle, Dr. Frank Demby, a 1957 graduate of Meharry and retired longtime medical director of Napa State Hospital in California, one of the largest public hospitals in America. "It's that simple. That's why they didn't want any of us in their hospitals. It was the same old racial stereotype, the same old fears about sex, the same old racist stuff that guided America all along."

"In those days, in the 1950s, some of America's bigger cities— Washington, New York, Chicago—were beginning to see black surgeons obtain hospital privileges for the first time," noted Dr. William E. Matori, professor of surgery and director of continuing medical education at Howard University Medical School, when I called to ask him about the difficulties black pioneers faced in medicine in the postwar era. Matori was a contributor to a remarkable two-volume history of black surgeons entitled *A Century of Black Surgeons: The U.S.A. Experience*, published in 1987, in which my father is listed. "But if you were starting out somewhere new, in a place that hadn't really seen a black surgeon before," Matori continued, "you absolutely had to have the support and acceptance of your white fellow surgeons. And most of these white people who were approached just feared the reaction of their other colleagues. It's like the white man who says, 'I'd love to have you over to dinner, but you know the neighbors would object.' That was the real hurdle we all had to face."

Without a hospital to operate in and without the support of the white medical community, my father couldn't practice his skill in the places he and my mother wanted to live. They realized they would need to expand the scope of their search greatly.

And then, in March 1956, something else happened, something wretched and terrifying that made their search for peace and opportunity in America even more of a pressing and desperate concern.

I was sick with an earache on the cool March night that it happened, a two-year-old toddler lying fast asleep on the bed next to my mother in our house on Hawkins Street in Nashville.

It was late on a Friday night, my mother recalled. My parents had gone to the movies with another black couple earlier at a "colored" theater and afterward invited the friends over to the house for drinks. Then, as often happened in those days during my father's surgical training at Meharry, the telephone rang. It was a nurse at Hubbard Hospital's emergency room. There had been a shooting, and the hospital needed my father in the operating room.

"Will you be long, John?" my mother remembered asking him.

"I don't think so," he said, pulling on his jacket.

"I'll wait up for you, then."

My father hurried off, and the visitors said good-bye too. My mother checked on my brothers, who were sleeping in their bedroom near hers in our single-story house, then got into bed with me to read a magazine.

The house was still.

Half an hour after my father's departure, she heard a squeak in the hallway outside her bedroom, a sound she recognized as a footstep in a particular place on the wooden floorboards. Thinking it was my brother, she called out, "Bobby?" but got no response. Then she heard the squeak again. Before she could make another sound, a stranger appeared in the doorway and quickly approached the bed with a foot-long knife in his hand.

"Don't you say a word," snarled the intruder, a tall, dark-skinned black man with a bushy head of hair, cursing at my mother as he placed the knife first against her throat, then against my back as I slept beneath the blanket.

She stayed as still as she could.

"Please don't hurt my baby," she said to the man. "Please

don't hurt my baby. . . ." Over and over during the next long minutes, she repeated the words like a religious incantation, "Please don't hurt my baby," as he kept the knife on my back and attacked her.

When the man was finished, he slowly backed away from the bed and pulled up his trousers, still clutching the long-handled knife in his hand. He demanded her money and grabbed the few coins that spilled from my mother's purse after she managed to hand it to him. A moment later he turned his wild-eyed glare on her again. "Don't you open up your mouth, bitch," he said, cursing at her again before disappearing into the night just as suddenly as he had appeared.

My mother listened for one second. Five seconds. Ten, she recalled. Then she got up and reached for her bathrobe on the chair next to the bed. She pulled it on, held it closed tightly with her hands, and dashed on her tiptoes into the living room. She flicked on the ceiling light switch. The attacker was gone.

She could hear herself breathing each breath, loudly and deeply. She locked the front door latch, ran through the kitchen to make sure the back door was locked, then raced to Bobby and Wayne's bedroom.

How did he get in? The doors had all been locked, she knew.

She checked to make sure the boys, nine and six, were safe and still fast asleep in their beds. Then she noticed their bedroom window was wide open, wider than it had ever been, as the cool air of the Nashville night filled the room. She pushed the window down, locked it tight, and returned to the living room, where she picked up the telephone and slumped on the couch.

Tears ran in hot streaks down her face. She wiped her eyes with her trembling hands. She struggled to stop shaking. Her legs, her arms, her hands, nearly every part of her seemed to quiver without control.

She picked up the receiver and dialed o for the operator. "Please, can you give me the police?" she remembered saying through muffled sobs.

She heard several clicks on the line, then the sound of ringing. Then a connection. She took a deep breath. "I want to report . . . a crime," my mother heard herself saying into the phone, still overcome by the eerie sense of separation in time and space she first felt when the attacker tore away her nightgown. She felt as if her mind had somehow separated from her body and that they were now two completely different and disconnected things.

"What sort of crime?" a voice asked her.

"It's . . . a rape," she remembered stammering. "I've been raped."

She heard the white police operator's voice grow excited. Rape was the sort of crime that many women in 1956 hesitated to report because of stigma and fear. The policeman said he would have someone at our house right away.

My mother took a few more deep breaths, then reached to switch on the lamp on the stand beside her. Then she got up and went around the house flicking on lights everywhere, in the dining room, the hallways, and the kitchen, killing every speck of darkness she could find.

She then called my father at the black hospital where he was chief resident surgeon, the same hospital where she had given birth to me on the snowy night two years earlier. It was located a mile northwest of Tennessee's state capital downtown, not too far from our house on Hawkins Street, which was located barely a block from Twelfth Street, in the heart of the city's ghetto.

Most black people lived in this part of the city because of racial segregation, and Twelfth Street was a commercial hub everyone had to live with, a sometimes dangerous street after dark.

My mother began crying again as she waited for my father to come on the line and couldn't stop when he picked up the phone moments later in Hubbard Hospital's emergency room. She told him what had happened through her sobs. He said he would return home immediately.

The rest of the night was a blur to her. First the Nashville police arrived in a flash of red and white lights that lit up the neighborhood. White detectives with thick southern accents tried to reassure her as they pressed her for information. My mother didn't know if she was making any sense. The words just came tumbling out as if she had no control over them. The next hour was almost like a fantasy, a weird nightmare with one strange scene blending into another, little of it comprehensible to her.

"I was lying in the bed with my baby . . . I was reading . . . I heard a noise . . . I saw a man . . . he had a knife . . . he came to the bed . . . he put it against my neck . . . then he put it against my baby's back . . . then . . . ."

"Did he hurt the child? Did he hit you or cut you with the knife?"

She shook her head no. She answered all their questions, and the lead detective grew especially concerned upon learning that her husband, a surgeon, was away working at the hospital when the attack occurred.

"A man out doing good for his people in the dead of night, and this happens," the white man said. "Don't you worry, Mrs. Henry. We're going to find this man."

My father soon arrived. He wrapped my mother in his arms as

the police finished checking the house, inside and out, for evidence. After the police were done, my father called a fellow physician at Meharry who lived in our neighborhood, and he soon arrived to examine my mother. He checked her thoroughly and reassured her that she was okay. He also told my mother and father not to worry, that he would perform an abortion if she was pregnant.

And my mother began to weep uncontrollably anew.

"You're the third victim I've seen in the last two weeks," my father's colleague said. "But you're the only one who reported it to the police."

Late that night my father ran a hot bath for my mother, and after taking me out of their bed and placing me in my crib, he took the bedclothes and threw them in the trash. He telephoned Fredda in St. Louis, told her what had happened, and asked her to please come to Nashville as soon as she could. Then he changed the sheets, turned out all the lights in the house, and held my mother closely in his arms as she quivered and sobbed through the night.

For weeks afterward my mother and father struggled to cope with the rape. My mother couldn't sleep without all the lights on in the house and often went to bed fully clothed. She shook uncontrollably for weeks. The Nashville police frequently visited her at work in the library at Fisk to show her mug shots of suspects, none of whom resembled the man who had attacked her.

The more she thought it about, though, the more she thought it might be best, in a perverse sort of way, if the man simply got away and never had to face the justice system. She knew that if they did catch him, the white cops would hurt him, and that if he was found guilty, the court system could kill him. She didn't want that on her conscience. And she felt deep down that the man needed help, mental help of some kind, more than he needed to be punished. In time she began to wish that the police would just leave her alone. She wished she could just pick up her life and start somewhere else.

But my father's behavior troubled her just as much. He didn't trust the white Nashville police to do what needed to be done, and in the weeks after the rape he tried to seek justice himself. He bought a gun and spent hours searching Twelfth Street for the suspect, my mother recalled. Three times he brought strangers to our house at the point of his gun, each time asking my mother if this was the man. Each time she answered no and pleaded with him to stop trying to take the law into his own hands.

Not long afterward she received a call from Dr. Matthew Walker, my father's surgical idol and the mentor to many generations of black American surgeons at Meharry. He was checking to see how she was doing and wondered if there was anything he could do for her. My mother told Dr. Walker she was doing okay but was terribly worried about my father. "Please tell him not to try to hunt for this man," she said.

My father stopped his search soon after.

Time passed. Wounds began to heal—or at least to hurt somewhat less. And my parents' search for a new life somewhere far away from Jim Crow and the harsh despair of Nashville continued.

Frustrated by the discrimination he kept encountering at midwestern hospitals, my father decided to look farther west. My parents had heard wonderful things about the Far West from a white army colleague, a warrant officer from Minnesota, whom they had met in Germany in 1951. The white officer and his wife used to rhapsodize especially about the beauty of the Pacific Northwest, describing the rivers, the mountains, the fishing. It sounded so clean, fresh, and different that the images stuck in my parents' minds when they returned to the States.

That summer, in 1956, my parents dropped my brothers and me off at our grandparents' house in the Ville in St. Louis and, following the path of Lewis and Clark, headed across the Mississippi River and the Great Plains states on a long expedition west, with plans to visit Denver, San Francisco, Los Angeles, Portland, and Seattle. It was Seattle that my mother and father visited first, and they never went any farther. My father drove our old cream- and orange-colored Oldsmobile up and over the Cascade Mountains, across the Lake Washington Floating Bridge to the sparkling city by Puget Sound, and they were astonished by what they saw. The scene that spread before them was so idyllic, so blessed with clear air, freshwater lakes, tall pines, Douglas firs, and majestic snowcapped horizons, that it reminded them of Stockholm, of Salzburg, and especially of Heidelberg, where they had enjoyed a taste of freedom and equality for the first time in their lives as black Americans.

Like Heidelberg, Seattle was a small, peaceful, and provincial city back then, but one populated by many different kinds of people, Scandinavians, Italians, American Indians, Chinese, Japanese, and a small but growing number of blacks—1.7 percent of the population in 1950. Many of the newer residents had come to Seattle for work during the war years. To my parents the city certainly seemed, on its face at least, much more tolerant of human differences than the South ever could be because it was so diverse.

My father interviewed at all the hospitals in and around Seattle's First Hill medical district—"Pill Hill," people in Seattle still call it. After passing the Washington state medical and surgical board examinations, he found to his surprise that he was quickly invited to join the surgical staff at Doctor's, the Sisters of Providence, and St. Francis Cabrini hospitals.

The small but growing city—whose population expanded nearly 20 percent from 467,591 in 1950 to 557,087 in 1960—needed good surgeons, and it apparently didn't matter what color the surgeons came in. Or, at least, no one had thought to explicitly exclude nonwhites from the city's medical community, since there were only a handful of nonwhite physicians in the entire state anyway. Of Washington's 2,754 licensed physicians practicing medicine in 1950, just three were listed in census data as "Negro" and ten as "other nonwhite."

My parents stayed at a lovely place, the Sorrento Hotel, high atop Madison Hill near the hospitals overlooking the city, and for both it was a wonderful experience simply to register at the front desk and not have to worry about being turned away because of their race. One night, while my mother and father admired the view of Elliott Bay at sunset from their hotel room window, watching the ferry boats cross back and forth from Bainbridge Island, they realized almost simultaneously that the city possessed practically everything they could ask for.

"Why don't we just stay, John?" my mother remembered asking softly.

Dad took only a moment to reply: Why not?

So it was that in July 1956 my parents decided that Seattle was where we would live. My mother traveled by rail back to St. Louis to pick up my brothers and me from the old house in the

Ville, having meantime arranged to have our furniture and household goods, including the beloved china dinnerware she had purchased in Germany, shipped to Seattle from Nashville. Soon we all boarded a westbound Great Northern Pullman to join my father in the Pacific Northwest for good.

My father had arrived in Seattle at about the same time as a Meharry classmate from Louisiana named Philip V. Lavizzo, the father of the girl who would become my first sweetheart fifteen years later. Together that July, Dad and Dr. Lavizzo became the first black general surgeons in the history of Seattle, and the city, so far away from everything we had ever known, became our new hometown.

During all the years I was growing up in Seattle between 1956 and 1972, my parents never mentioned the sexual assault on my mother. Not once. They certainly never discussed it in front of us, their children, if they did mention it at all to each other. I guess they figured there was no reason to talk about it, given all the other bewildering things going on in our family's life as we came of age during the vexing era of racial integration.

As far as I, my brothers, and my sister, Sharon (born in Seattle in 1959, three years after my mother's rape), knew, a stranger had once tried to break into our house a long time ago on a cool March night in Nashville when I was a baby, but that was it. A burglar. A thief. A "bad guy," just like all the bad guys Eliot Ness and Matt Dillon were trying to catch each week on our black-and-white television in the 1960s. But the bad guy didn't get a thing from us. He was foiled somehow. Right had prevailed. That's what we always thought.

To us, the attempted break-in was just a factual event in our family history. My brothers, sister, and I knew it had happened, but we figured that it wasn't especially important, though it did produce certain repercussions in our daily lives. My oldest brother, Bobby, who was nine when it happened, vividly remembered the burly Nashville policemen who came to dust for fingerprints on his bedroom windowsill the next day—the first white people he had ever seen in our house. He also recalled seeing a worker erect iron bars on all of our windows soon thereafter.

The break-in led to a new addition to our family, a gentle-tempered boxer who moved with us to Seattle later that year. We named him Sang because he seemed just "the feetis' sang" to Mom. Another result of the break-in was that we had to avoid playing anywhere near Dad's clothes closet, for Dad had a gun in there somewhere. And the break-in was why we all had to make sure to shut and lock the doors and windows tight each night on Lake Shore Drive, why my mother always felt uneasy, perhaps more so than we figured was warranted, if my father had to leave her alone in the house at night.

From the time I was a little kid, I knew that my mother and father had migrated to the Pacific Northwest from the Deep South to make a better life for us, to get as far away from the evils of Jim Crow and institutionalized bigotry as they could. I knew that that very quest had fueled much of our family's spirit, providing its lifeblood in the second half of the twentieth century. What I didn't know until many years later—what none of my siblings knew—was that Nashville had held even greater evils for my mother and father, evils that were deeply personal and painful.

It wasn't until the mid-1980s, when all of us were grown, out of the house, and leading our own lives in different parts of America, that my mother revealed what really happened that night in Nashville. By then I guess she had come to peace with it herself. She was retiring from her twenty-six-year career as a public school librarian in Seattle, proud that her four children were happy and independent, and keen on tying up the loose ends in her life.

My mother had always been open and honest about most things in our family and didn't like keeping secrets from us. The rape was the biggest secret of her life, and I guess she felt that letting us all know about it then, so many years later, would help fill in some pictures from our childhood for us and complete her own sense of healing.

I was thirty-one years old, living and working as a reporter in Washington, D.C., when my mother, on a visit from Seattle in 1985, told me almost offhandedly about the attack. We had gone for a walk near Dupont Circle one afternoon when she noticed the iron burglar bars over windows in the row houses on Nineteenth Street Northwest, near my apartment. She said they reminded her of the bars that were put up over the windows of our house on Hawkins Street in Nashville the year Dad was finishing his surgical training at Meharry.

"For that guy who tried to get in," I said.

She paused a moment and slowed her gait before speaking again. "He did get in, Neil. We never told you kids, but he did get in," she said. "He raped me. He held a knife on your back while you were sleeping next to me and he raped me."

I felt my breathing stop as I heard her words. I remember feeling as if I were frozen in place and sick inside, as if time and life and the earth had suddenly stood still. All I could stammer was "What?" and then question followed question after question.

We went to a coffeehouse and she told me the whole story, very calmly and matter-of-factly, from beginning to end, noting the attack was even covered in the Nashville newspapers. Rapes weren't often reported to the police in those days, and the rape of a black surgeon's wife had seemed especially newsworthy.

During that visit, she and I took the subway one morning to the Library of Congress to try to find the Nashville newspaper articles on microfilm. The library's periodical holdings, located in an office building across Independence Avenue from the Capitol, included microfilms of nearly every day's issue of nearly every newspaper in America, dating back to the eighteenth century. My mother wasn't sure of the exact date of the attack but knew it had to be near St. Patrick's Day. She had always associated St. Patrick's Day with her nightmare, she told me.

So we searched the March 1956 issues of the *Nashville Tennessean* and the *Nashville Banner* that morning, and within minutes we came upon the week of St. Patrick's Day in the reels of microfilm. My mother's face radiated anxious curiosity as we looked through the news pages, scanning each story in the columns of type. She discovered the article first. Suddenly, pointing to a small item on page 2 in the March 19 issue of the *Nashville Tennessean*, she exclaimed, "There! *There* it is, Neil."

The article was surrounded by larger news stories about the smashing of Joseph Stalin statuary in the Soviet Union, the acceptance of the first black students at the University of Texas, and a debate by southern newspaper editors over the pace of racial integration. Headlined "Attack Reported by Doctor's Wife," it read simply:

The wife of a Negro physician reported to police that she was raped in her bedroom shortly after midnight yesterday by a tall, bushy-haired man who threatened her with a knife.

The Negro attacker entered the South Nashville home after removing a storm window, according to Sgt. Carney Patterson of the city police department.

He slipped through a bedroom where two small sons were sleeping to enter the woman's room, Patterson said. The doctor was on call when the attack occurred. A third child was sleeping in the room with the woman, police said.

"Why didn't you ever tell us?" I said after reading the article slowly, over and over, on the microfilm reader. "Why didn't you let us know?"

"You all didn't need to know. For goodness' sake, what purpose would it have served to tell you?" she answered softly. "My word, you were having challenges enough when you were growing up. You didn't need to know about that."

For many minutes I couldn't speak. I felt tears welling in my eyes. I stumbled over my words. "How did you ever get over it?" I asked. "How did you cope?"

"You probably never get over it, honey," she replied after a pause, her brown chin resting in her hand as she sat back in the chair, her dark curly hair sprinkled with gray, her eyes reflecting a soft serenity. "I guess I haven't still. It's only been in the last year or two that I've started to feel safe again, and it's been, what? Nearly thirty years now."

She said it could have been a lot worse, all things considered. The crime wasn't murder, after all. The attacker didn't beat her or stab me with the knife. We were alive. We had survived it. And wasn't that the most important thing? Then, as she read the article again, she suddenly chuckled slightly and turned to me with an inexplicable smile on her face, a smile that seemed so out of place.

"You know what was really funny? It sure wasn't funny then, but I find it hilarious now," she said. "This ugly man, when he's finished, he climbs off me and he says, 'Give me your money.' So I go get my purse on a chair next to the bed, and there's practically nothing in there, just coins. I've got no cash at all. So I tell him, 'Can I write you a check?' Can you believe it? I mean, how *dumb!* I said, 'Can I write you a check?'"

And then, right there in the main reading room of the Library of Congress, my mother put her palm over her heart and started laughing so hard that tears came to her dark brown eyes. It was the same beautiful laugh I remembered from my childhood whenever she heard a good joke from one of her friends or a funny story from one of our crazy days at school with the white kids—a laugh that was so full and infectious. Soon I found myself starting to laugh with her, purely by reflex. We laughed and laughed for several minutes together like that, releasing ourselves to the irony and strange liberation of the moment. As I gazed at my mother next to me, I felt more respect for her than I had ever felt for any human being.

A couple of years later I summoned enough nerve to ask my father about the rape. We were having coffee together one morning in Seattle, where I was visiting on vacation. "Who told you about that?" he asked with a start, his eyes filled with fire, only nodding slightly and looking away when I told him that Mom had.

My father was never very forthcoming about his emotions or reflective by nature, and he certainly found it difficult, visibly so, even to think about the attack when I mentioned it to him. After a long pause he sighed and glanced out a living room window. For a moment I thought he wouldn't answer at all. But then he started to speak in a voice so soft I had to edge closer to hear him. He told me that for a long time, even after we had moved to Seattle, he would find himself taking a second look at strangers he ran across who even remotely resembled the man my mother had described to the police. Somehow, in the back of his mind, he feared that the rapist had followed us to Seattle.

It was crazy, he told me. There was never any reason to suspect that the rapist had followed us or to suspect anyone in Seattle, but suspect these strangers he did, especially the aimless, rough, unemployed black men he ran across in the city's Central Area slum. He couldn't get over the maddening mental picture of a stranger casing our house in Nashville that night, witnessing him leave for the hospital, and then committing the assault while we were unguarded. He told me he was obsessed with the rape for years and only began to get over it when he saw how my mother, determined to get on with life, had slowly gotten over it, had stopped being so afraid—at least outwardly. "She was very strong," he said as he sipped his coffee with a sad and distant look in his eyes. "That's the only reason we managed to make it. She was just incredibly strong."

As I listened to my father that morning and remembered my mother's words, I realized how impossible it would be for anyone to ever get over such a thing completely. How could you? Like most hurts in our family, this one, too, had been buried, swallowed, pushed somewhere deep within, probably in the same place where the racial hurts went. That was our longtime method of emotional survival, after all. The hurts had to be stowed away somewhere if my mother and father were to get on with the struggle, raise their children, and survive the various challenges society presented every day of their lives. There were more important things to do than obsess about the past. It was over. Done.

In the years that followed, I often thought about my mother's rape by the black man in Nashville, turning her nightmare over and over in my mind and trying, in retrospect, to make it fit into the emotional fabric of our family life and my childhood. I realized the repercussions were many and powerful, not least of which was its role in shaping my brothers' and my attitudes toward a central challenge in our lives—growing up as black males in a racist society.

"Thugs," I vividly remember my mother muttering during my childhood in Seattle. "Jackson Street *thugs*," she'd say under her breath with venomous scorn as she drove us in our station wagon through the city's impoverished Central Area and International District, glancing balefully at the jobless black hustlers and idlers spilling out of bars and hobnobbing on drizzly cold street corners. I realized years later, in hindsight, that it was at such times, when she pointed out bitterly how empty and desperate life was for the vast majority of black men in our society, that life's choices were made painfully and graphically clear to us. Those choices, always quite clear in our mother's mind, and my father's, were doubtlessly greatly sharpened by the Nashville assault.

We could choose to skip school, fritter away opportunities, and escape into drugs, alcohol, or sexual conquest, like the black "bums" we passed in the inner city. We could choose to fill our insides with rage, self-loathing, and resentment about society and the hurts black people suffered and seek release in vengeance.

We could choose to end up in jail or jobless, dead at an early age or strung out in a gutter somewhere on any number of Jackson Streets in America, like so many millions of our kind. We could easily choose all that.

Or we could do better, my mother implicitly told us. We could turn the fire on itself and defeat the infernal demons. We could reach inside ourselves somewhere and rise above the base stereotypes and pitifully low expectations society placed on black men. We could strive to replicate in our lives the perseverance and vision of the people who came before us—Frederick Douglass, Sojourner Truth, Jackie Robinson, Martin Luther King, Jr. We could take advantage of the rare opportunities they worked to give us and pursue what we wanted in life despite our country's abysmal expectations.

We could do it. If we chose.

We could turn the fire on itself.

Or we could succumb to the depression and rage that every black person in America must feel at various points in life, regardless of background or class or skin tone. We could sink inexorably toward the nadir.

One or the other.

That was it, really. That was the ultimate truism about black opportunity that shaped our childhood during integration in Seattle. Whether it was really *true* didn't matter. It was this chilling observation about black existence in America that we were compelled to take in from our middle-class vantage. The stark reality seemed to be that there was precious little gray area, few other options, no middle ground of forgiving ambiguity or room for error for people like us. There never had been. There was no time to pause, to let up the fight, no chance to drop one's guard.

That was the clearest reality in a society that feared, despised, disrespected, and distrusted so many of us and harbored such low expectations of us. For black men in American society, there was essentially no middle ground—certainly not in A.J. Beaumont's time, not in my grandfather's or father's time, and likely not in mine.

As I contemplated the repercussions of the attack on my mother so many years later, I reviewed all that I had been taught about race in America. It was true, on the one hand, that my mother and father had sought escape from the South because they felt deeply menaced by white racism. But it was also true that they had felt menaced by the incomparable desperateness and self-loathing of black existence there. Indeed, I realized, by transplanting themselves as far away from the South as they could get, to largely white Seattle, my parents were seeking escape from *black people* in a certain sense—or, to put it more precisely, from a pathological "element" festering in the black South. That was the word my urbane, St. Louis–bred mother often used. "That *element*," she told me many years later, with bitterness and resentment in her voice—an amoral, criminal element bred by the sick system of entrenched black poverty, ignorance, hopelessness, and alienation that white racism had created and perpetuated, one represented graphically, she felt, by the wild-eyed black man who had raped her.

The most chilling irony, of course, was that it was the very fear of the nightmare she had experienced that simmered at the heart of white racism in America. The stereotypical vision deeply ingrained in the mind of white America was of a black male sexual predator on the loose, *unchained*, attacking a defenseless woman in her home in the night. That singular fear had helped fuel so many laws oppressing black people and given rise to Jim Crow separatism. That demented fear had sparked thousands of gruesome lynchings and other insane acts of mob terror and violence. And yet that racist nightmare—so evil, so insidiously harmful, and so false—had nonetheless materialized for my mother that night in Nashville, with certainly lasting emotional and psychological consequences.

My mother's attacker was never captured. My father believed the Nashville police did not do everything possible to find him— "she was a black woman," was all he said, his voice not disguising the disgust and resentment he still felt for white southern cops. My mother, however, disagreed, at least as far as that investigation went. She said the white policemen were remarkably kind to her—kinder than she had ever suspected white southern policemen could be to black people—and persisted for weeks in showing her mug shots of suspects. The lead detective especially was outraged that something like that could happen to the wife of a "colored" man who, he kept saying to her over and over, was trying to do so much good for his people.

At one point, curious to know how the police had conducted their investigation, I tried to get a copy of the official police report about the attack. But the Nashville authorities told me all such "minor" records from the 1950s had been destroyed years ago and never put on film. The criminal investigation was simply marked unsolved sometime in the 1960s, a police official told me over the phone, and left open, likely for eternity.

In nearly every child's life there comes a time when he can't help feeling sharp defiance and hostility toward his parents, no matter how loving they are. Pent-up feelings from childhood get somehow jumbled up with the affection and respect. I certainly

went through a period like that after I left Seattle to begin my
own path in life in the late 1970s, feeling a sharp, lingering resentment toward my mother and father over the unnecessary
hurts and strains they each had inflicted upon me and my siblings
when we were growing up. I despised my father for the whip-
pings he had given me and my brothers; I remembered the psychological terror those attacks had created, the pain and the tears
we sometimes went to sleep with. I despised the emotional pressures both my parents had exerted on me to excel in my white
schools, recalling the disappointment so obvious in my mother's
expressive eyes and so devastating to me whenever I fell short at
anything. I hated the bitter memory of the bandaged splint I
wore on my finger in junior high school after she had beaten
me in a rage with a clothes brush and fractured the finger one
Sunday morning when I refused to attend church with her. I
loathed the old pathology about race she harbored, the one she
had grown up with in St. Louis, the destructive ideas handed
down and absorbed by me and shared by millions in our culture,
which favored "good" hair and "light" skin over everything black.

But as I grew older and began to contend with life on my own
terms, I, like most grown children, came to see my mother and
father not simply as my parents but as humans with understandable frailties, flaws, and vulnerabilities as well as strengths. I
couldn't fairly blame them for my demons anymore, because
God knew they had plenty of their own. It was odd, but as their
brown faces wrinkled and their hair turned silvery gray, I saw
them as a microcosm of their entire generation of idealistic and
ambitious black Americans whose often anonymous struggles
and accomplishments nonetheless loomed large throughout
many sectors of our society. No matter where I traveled in
America for my newspaper, I began to see my parents every-

where in the dignified faces of strangers, of old and retired black professionals, looking back on lives lived through the daunting challenges of their age, yet lived fully and so humanly.

My mother and father took as articles of faith such basic things as racial integration and equal opportunity and the other great promises of their era. They believed so strongly that they cleared a trail from the South to the Pacific Northwest to see them come true, overcoming myriad racial and personal hurdles they found in their way. Such hurdles exacted a toll on them emotionally. They were, after all, human, and all humans are flawed. But when I thought about it at age forty-three, amazed by all that they had struggled with and overcome by the time they were forty-three, I wasn't sure if I could have done the same. I wasn't sure if I could have summoned the same emotional resolve, the same sturdiness of character, to see it through. I wasn't sure many people could have done that, given the same obstacles, hurts, and challenges to their souls.

But I was sure of a few things. I knew the results of their endurance. My parents stayed together through the toughest of times in our childhood during integration in Seattle and lived to see the day when their four children and seven grandchildren could take advantage of the openings in mainstream American society they and millions of others helped create. I knew that in 1997, forty-one years after my father migrated from Nashville to begin his practice in Seattle as a general surgeon, there were forty-seven black physicians listed with the King County Medical Society in Seattle, including experts in specialties spanning dermatology, urology, obstetrics and gynecology, ophthalmology, psychiatry, and surgery. And I knew that restrictive race covenants in residential neighborhoods, like the ones my parents were the first to fight in Seattle's south end in 1960, had largely been consigned to the ash heap of American history. And this was mainly because of my parents' ambitions and those of other, equally anonymous black parents of their era who had the courage to test the new laws of equal opportunity in their personal and professional lives.

Early on the morning of Monday, October 13, the day after I found the graves of A.J. and Mary Ann Beaumont in Natchez, I drove my rental car to the Old Warren County Court House in Vicksburg, my mind filled with our history, my heart pounding with anticipation. The day had finally arrived when I felt sure I would be able to find answers to all my questions about our family's racial past, about the white branch of our tree—answers that had eluded me for so many years.

I parked the car on a quiet side street. It was a drizzly, muggy morning on the banks of the Mississippi River, and as I walked along the stone path leading to the courthouse, I felt myself gradually coming to an understanding about my emotional struggles over race and my genealogical project. It was still an intellectual exercise for me, surely. I still badly wanted to satisfy my curiosity. I wanted to find my distant white cousins, to hear their family's story from the other side of the color barrier, and to compare their struggles over the past century to ours in order to draw a more complete portrait of our shared history.

But as I reflected on my mother's and father's lives, I also began to sense in a strange but unconscious way that in all my searching I also wanted to recognize what they and so many others had tried to do, to pay a small tribute to them, to reaffirm that despite the tough obstacles that still exist in American society, their generation's values of equality and struggle survive.

I didn't know what was ahead of me. I didn't know what kind of white people I would discover in my distant kin, if I could find them. I didn't know what changes America's racial progression and regression had brought to the Beaumonts' lives since the day in 1877 that our blood was joined by Laura, the former slave, and A.J., the white immigrant. But I felt an unusual clarity and strange tranquillity inside me that morning, a feeling that put into deeper perspective the old anger and disappointments over race and prejudice that my early middle age had brought out so sharply in the years after my daughter was born. For it grew clear in my mind that our family, too, had scaled a ways up the mountain that Martin Luther King, Jr., once dreamed of so vividly. And while the stark truth remained that none of us in America would ever be over the jagged peaks of racism, ignorance, and inequality until all of us were over them, I was nonetheless awed by the distance our black family had managed to travel.

My old rage was still there, somewhere inside. I supposed it would always be there, as long as I contemplated that my daughter would inevitably encounter some of the same racial hurts and struggles in her lifetime that we all had, throughout our family's time in America. I guess I was beginning to accept the inner fire as part of my being, as a fire that was not necessarily harmful if I could learn to control it, to harness it somehow, and use it to clarify things in my head. But I also felt a sense of confirmation, as only the South could imbue in me so deeply, that our long family journey from slavery had been worth it. And I had faith that my private project, too, would prove worthwhile somehow, that the common humanity my black ancestors had always tried to believe in despite the barriers of prejudice would see the search through to a meaningful end.

PART TWO

Discovery

CHAPTER FIVE

The Chase

The Warren County Court House was a magnificent old stone structure rising from a steep hill in downtown Vicksburg, overlooking the Mississippi River. From every mildewed corner, the building seemed to throb with history. Guarded by Civil War–era artillery pieces on its front and sides, it featured Greco-Roman granite columns supporting a pyramid-shaped roof and an imposing bell tower replete with clocks on all four sides.

During the Civil War the courthouse was a focal point in the siege of Vicksburg between 1862 and 1863, when the building stood as a defiant symbol of one of the last great stands of the Confederacy. Surrounded by advancing Union troops, Vicksburg's rebel defenders held out for many agonizing months before the army led by Ulysses S. Grant finally prevailed and returned the Stars and Stripes to the top of the courthouse bell tower.

For my family, too, the building held history. According to Louisiana military history, my great-great-grandfather's artillery unit, the Cameron Battery, had fought Grant near this very place in defense of Vicksburg before being forced into retreat. Now, 135 years later, I was about to embark on a different kind of siege of this building. I felt certain that somewhere in its records, in the old ledgers, deeds, and microfilms cramming its ancient shelves, were clues to the whereabouts of A.J. Beaumont's white descendants.

I entered the courthouse at 8 A.M. from the drizzle outside and immediately found myself at the entrance to a small museum just inside the front door. The museum was dedicated to the Civil War, the siege of Vicksburg, and the building's storied past. I took a peek inside, where I saw glass cases filled with battle flags, muskets, pistols, and bugles. Several displays featured faded military uniforms and articles of period clothing, including a pair of tattered trousers once worn by a "plantation mammy." The walls, smelling sweetly of old pine, displayed brittle newspapers from the Civil War era and yellowing antebellum posters advertising auctions of slaves and land.

I wandered through the museum and soon found the room I was looking for, the office of Gordon Cotton, the archivist and curator of the Old Warren County Court House museum and library. I had spoken to him on the phone several times from my house in California in preparation for my visit and had been amused by his name the first time I heard him utter it in a drawl as smooth as velvet. I wondered what the Mississippi librarian looked like.

I knocked lightly on the open door and saw inside a pale, gray-haired man in his fifties seated at a delightfully cluttered wooden desk. The office was actually a small library filled from floor to ceiling with old leather-bound books, rare maps, and other ancient documents and tomes perched on wooden shelves anchored against the walls.

"You must be the fella from California," drawled the man, dressed in faded jeans and a plain plaid shirt, as he rose from his chair with a big smile. "Professor Henry?"

"It's a pleasure to meet you, Mr. Cotton," I said, shaking his extended hand. He invited me to take a seat at a table near his desk and offered me a cup of coffee. His office was a wonderful place, filled with the smells of fresh coffee and the sweet aroma of old books and ancient wooden floor planks.

"So you're doin' some investigatin'?" he asked as he took a seat at the table across from me.

As I told him the old story about Laura and Arthur and my long search for the Beaumonts, I found myself liking the historian instantly. His eyes reflected a bright twinkle that conveyed not just a quick wit but a genuine interest in what I was telling him, and when he spoke, it was with a smooth, gentle, and very likable Mississippi drawl that reminded me of the Civil War historian Shelby Foote.

"And you've got documents too," he commented, smiling as he glanced at the photos of A.J. Beaumont, his 1901 obituary, and the letter he wrote to Pearl acknowledging the mixed-race woman as his daughter. "Remarkable. Extraordinary," he muttered softly. "We see a lot of folks come through here trying to research their heritage, but not a lot of them have the kind of material you do. You're lucky."

"Well, yes and no," I answered. "I'm stuck in the year 1914. I know the Beaumont family was living in Vicksburg then, but that's as far as I've taken the trail."

I told the historian offhandedly about my visit to the Natchez city cemetery the day before, where I found the Beaumont graves. Suddenly I remembered the odd inscription on Mary Ann Beaumont's headstone—"Woodsmen Circle"—and I asked Cotton what it meant.

"Oh, that was a burial society in the old days," he answered. "You see, a lot of people paid dues to burial societies to ensure they were buried proper when they died. The Woodsmen Circle essentially guaranteed that its members would have headstones and proper funerals. Bereavement societies have always been very big in the South, for white people and black."

Cotton then rose from his creaky wooden chair and sauntered across the wood plank floor to a wall full of books on shelves behind his desk. There he reached up for one thin book among many similar ones, each protected by a white plastic cover closed with Velcro strips.

"These are the Vicksburg city directories from the period you're interested in. Telephones were pretty new back then, and the directories only began in 1905. They list pretty much everyone in town, even if they didn't have a phone."

He opened the plastic case and gently placed the 1914 directory on the table. Its pages were fragile and yellow with age. He carefully opened it up to the B's and stopped at page 128. He turned the book to me, and I ran my finger down the page to the name Beaumont.

"That's them, isn't it?" he asked.

I nodded in fascination, staring at the listing: "Beaumont, Arthur W." This was the sole surviving son of Arthur J. Beaumont. The listing also showed his wife's name, Anna, in parentheses and described him as a "foreman" for the Gotthelf Coal Company. The family's address was 728 Dabney in Vicksburg.

The listing also pointed out that Mary Ann Beaumont, Arthur W.'s mother, lived at the same address; she was described as "(wid Arthur J)."

"What's the Gotthelf Coal Company?" I asked, curious why the only son of a prosperous nineteenth-century cotton grower and plantation supplies merchant in Louisiana would be laboring as a coal worker in Mississippi barely more than a decade after his father's death.

"The Gotthelfs were one of our prominent Jewish families in the old days," Cotton explained. "That company was the big supplier of coal in town for many years. We don't have so many Jews in Vicksburg anymore. We used to have quite a few. But they all moved away to the bigger cities as the century moved on."

Cotton returned the volume to the shelf and came back with the issue of 1918, four years later. The listings showed the Beaumonts residing at the same address. But in the 1919 volume the Beaumont name did not appear. Cotton grabbed 1920, 1921, 1922, 1925, and 1929. No Beaumonts. I felt my heart sinking again as I scanned the telephone directories. The family seemed to have vanished again.

"Maybe there's something in the Fisher Funeral Home records," Cotton told me, reaching into another bookshelf for a large leather-bound tome. "Fisher was the big funeral home for many years in Vicksburg. These records go all the way back to 1854. If you had a little bit of money back then and died in Vicksburg, chances are Fisher put you in the ground."

He opened the old ledger and scanned the B's, turning the book toward me moments later, opened to page 10. It showed the record for the June 15, 1914, funeral of Mary Ann Beaumont, Arthur's widow:

Age 57. One black broadcloth casket and box, $140.00;
Embalming remains $25.00; Ladies burial robe $15.00;
Telephoning to Natchez 40 cents; Candles and hack to
train $3.00—$183.40.

I made photocopies of all the information I found in the directories and the funeral ledger before Cotton escorted me back
down the Old Court House steps and across the street to the
"New" Warren County Court House, which was built in 1935.
There he introduced me to clerks who would help me investigate
the probate, property, marriage, and other civil records in hopes
of finding more clues to the white family's history in the city.

But I was feeling stumped again, my head filling with doubt.
Every bit of information about the Beaumonts that I found with
Cotton was leading not to answers about the old riddle but to
more and more baffling questions. Where did the family go in
1918? Why was Beaumont's son working for a coal company?
Why did Mary Ann Beaumont feel the need to purchase burial
insurance after laying her prosperous husband in the ground in
Natchez and gracing his grave with such a distinguished marker?
What had happened to the immigrant's business, his plantation,
his fortune in St. Joseph?

I rapidly scrolled through probate records on microfilm,
searching for the case of Mary Ann Beaumont, hoping to find a
will of some kind that would have had to be registered with the
court. I found her probate record, case number 5680. It contained more than twenty-five documents, all photographed on
microfilm, each recording minor and perfunctory actions over
about a year's span.

"In the matter of the estate of M.A. Beaumont," read the first page of the record, dated June 15, 1914, written in the court clerk's flourished cursive handwriting. The documents revealed that Beaumont's widow died without a will, that her estate totaled $394.76, all of it in cash at a local bank, and that her son, Arthur Wilford Beaumont, was her only heir.

There were also records naming Arthur W. Beaumont the administrator of the estate. One document showed that most of the money in the bank went to pay for hospital fees at the Vicksburg sanitarium, where the widow had spent a month before her death, and for funeral and court costs. The document also showed that her headstone was provided by the Woodsmen Circle. The last document in the probate record was dated September 21, 1915, and in it the court abruptly expressed satisfaction that the Beaumont estate was administered properly.

I struggled to comprehend what I was seeing as I pressed the copy button on the court's microfilm reader to retrieve paper copies of the documents. The white family, whose lives by all appearance and description had seemed so prosperous and comfortable before the century's turn, appeared virtually penniless barely a decade and a half after A.J. Beaumont's death.

As I studied the documents in my hands, I couldn't help reflecting on my family's history during the same period. In 1915, the year the last document in Mary Ann Beaumont's probate record was being recorded by her son at the courthouse in Vicksburg, my grandmother Fredda—the granddaughter in St. Louis whom A.J. Beaumont never knew—was nineteen years old, deliriously happy, and being wooed by the beautiful black man of her dreams, postman Clifford Turner, a son of the distinguished ex-slave Young Turner in Illinois. My mother would be born eight years later. Also in 1915 my grandfather John

Robert Henry, Sr., was in medical school in North Carolina and about to begin his practice in Winston-Salem. He would meet Irma Neal in 1918, and my father would be born two years later.

I realized that my black family's foundation was being solidified and its unlikely rise in this century commencing at the same time that the white Beaumonts seemed to be in full descent, leaving hardly a trace in Mississippi. This was not the way I had expected the story, the saga of two American families, to unfold. It was not the kind of story that conventional wisdom and stereotypes about race in our country would ever tell. What were the records trying to say to me?

I had two more places to look for clues in the New Court House. I raced upstairs to a second-floor office containing marriage and divorce records, believing I might be able to find something about Arthur W. Beaumont or his children. A clerk escorted me into a small back room filled with bookshelves and large red leather-bound ledgers dating from the 1830s. Unlike the information in other departments, the marriage records were not on microfilm or microfiche. The records were originals, exquisitely written by hand in the red volumes. Until as late as 1970, the records separated all Warren County citizens into "white" and "colored" categories. The red volumes on the shelves read "Marriage Record White" or "Marriage Record Colored" for every year and were separated by race on adjoining shelves.

The clerk, a young brown-haired white woman, shyly asked me in a soft southern accent, "Is your party white or black?"

"White," I answered. "I'm looking for a white family."

"Okay, you'll find the years you want right here, Mr. Henry," she said, pointing to a shelf with red ledgers starting in 1915. "I'm sorry about that question. We have to ask, though."

I told her not to worry, that I understood. But I also made a mental note to spend a class session at Berkeley teaching my journalism students about the peculiarly fascinating things they could expect to encounter if they ever found themselves having to navigate county court records in a state like Mississippi.

I spent close to an hour in the book-crammed library, scanning all the white marriage and divorce records for Warren County between 1915 and 1949, but didn't find anything useful. I then returned to the first floor to hunt among the property records. The listings for the years 1915 to 1920 showed that the Beaumont house at 728 Dabney, which had been built in 1904, was owned by a man named Katzenmeyer. It was among several houses he owned on the block. The Beaumonts apparently were renters during the years they lived in Vicksburg.

My trail had turned cold as ice. It was close to 4 P.M. when I finished searching in the courthouse, and I was filled with far more questions than when I had started. Gordon Cotton sensed my confusion and disappointment when I returned to his office to thank him and say good-bye.

"No luck, huh?" the genial historian asked as he extended his hand to shake mine.

"I moved it up to 1918," I said. "But then the family simply vanished on me again."

Cotton nodded and clucked in sympathy. "Well, I'm sorry to hear that," he said. "I know how disappointed you must feel, especially after coming all this way."

He walked me to the courthouse door and looked briefly at

the darkening sky before saying good-bye. A storm was coming. "You never know, Mr. Henry," he encouraged me. "One thing we've learned around here is that skeletons have a way of rattlin' their bones when you least expect it. Keep the faith."

I had spent a full day at the courthouses in Vicksburg, from 8 A.M. until closing. As I drove all the way back to Atlanta on Interstate 20, retracing my path through Mississippi, Alabama, and Georgia in the driving rainstorm that began shortly after I left Vicksburg, I wondered what my next move would be. I was disappointed that I hadn't discovered as much as I had hoped, but intrigued by the nuggets of information I had mined. I realized the white family could have gone anywhere in America, but I didn't know where or how to search for them next. Through the rain, wind, and thunder I drove, racking my mind for possible new directions to explore.

"Four years. All this way, and all I was able to do was pull the story forward to 1918," I told Letitia over the telephone when I arrived back in my hotel room in Atlanta late that night. "They could have gone anywhere."

Letitia sighed and tried her best to boost my spirits. "Well, it sure sounds intriguing, doesn't it? I mean, this family went from the landed gentry to the lower working class in just a few years? That's pretty amazing."

"Seems so, but it's all so hazy, Tish. I mean, anything could have happened to them. There was a huge flu epidemic in 1918. It killed thousands of people in America. Maybe they just vanished. Maybe I'll never find out."

Letitia put Zoë on the phone then. My daughter immediately told me about her day in kindergarten—riding a tricycle, jumping rope, eating crackers, and singing songs. Within minutes I felt better just hearing her voice. Moments later we all said good-bye and I fell asleep instantly, exhausted by the discoveries and new puzzles of the day.

Early the next morning I attended the graduate and professional school fair sponsored by the city's historically black schools, which was the official purpose of my trip. I met scores of bright black students there and tried to recruit some into our journalism program at Berkeley. Late in the day I encountered an inspiring young woman who told me she hailed from a small town called Tifton in Georgia. She was graduating soon from Clark-Atlanta University, and I managed to excite her about the idea of coming west. The daughter of two schoolteachers, she was smart, committed to a career in journalism, and boasted a terrific academic record. She had a real spark in her eyes, and I knew she could be a fine addition to our program.

The young woman applied to our school of journalism and was accepted a few months later, our first-ever admission from one of Atlanta's historically black schools. I was thrilled. That Sherri was an honors graduate of the same black school my mother had attended for her library degree in the 1940s under the shadow of Jim Crow deepened my sense of elation.

My trip also turned out to be critically valuable for my genealogical research. I didn't know how critical until after I returned to California, where I soon visited a temple of the Church of Jesus Christ of Latter-Day Saints in Woodland, the county seat near our home. The Mormon Church operates family history centers at many of its temples, including the one in Woodland, where private citizens can conduct genealogical research using a host of valuable databases on microfiche and compact discs. These databases provide all kinds of census extracts and information from original birth, death, marriage, and military records from local jurisdictions across the country and around the world.

The Woodland center, located in a basement office near the church on the edge of a tomato field, also has U.S. Social Security indexes listing every deceased American citizen who ever registered with Social Security—from 1936, when Social Security was established, to 1995, when the indexes were issued. These compact discs contain hundreds of thousands of names and detail where each person resided at the time of his or her death.

I had been to the Woodland center many times before, hunting unsuccessfully for Arthur W. Beaumont's name in all of the files. Apparently, he either died before Social Security legislation was enacted or never applied after it was. But now, after my trip to the courthouse in Vicksburg, I had a new name to look up— his wife, Anna Beaumont, who was listed in the 1914 Vicksburg telephone directory with her husband.

I searched the Social Security index and discovered eight different Anna Beaumonts with dates of birth ranging from 1889 to 1926. Among the places these Anna Beaumonts died were Maryland, Texas, Indiana, and Illinois. One, though, was born in 1894 in Mississippi and died in Louisiana in March 1976. I thought she could be the right one and pressed a button on the computer to find the zip code of her place of death. It was listed as 71360, which encompassed nineteen jurisdictions in Rapides Parish in central Louisiana, near the town of Alexandria.

Later that afternoon at our house in Davis, while my daughter played with her friend Rachel amid the red and yellow roses

in our backyard, I called central Louisiana telephone information
to find out the name of the daily newspaper in Alexandria. The
operator told me the paper was called the *Alexandria Town Talk*
and gave me the number. I phoned the city editor to find out
more about the newspaper. She told me it was 120 years old, the
only daily in central Louisiana, and that the obituaries it published were very extensive and reliable, covering much of that
part of the state.

The next morning at Berkeley I put in a request at the main library to see yet another small-town southern newspaper on microfilm, the *Alexandria Town Talk*, for the months of March and
April 1976. Then I waited.

Shortly after the New Year, 1998, nearly two months later,
the microfilms finally arrived on interlibrary loan from Louisiana
State University. I picked them up at Doe Library on campus and
immediately raced downstairs to a microfilm reader in the basement to see if one of the films contained an obituary for Anna
Beaumont. I scrolled through the first roll of microfilm, turning
the metal knob on the side of the reader with my left hand,
checking each page in March 1976. I went slowly through the
first five days of the month. The news pages were filled with happenings in the presidential primary season, featuring photographs of Ronald Reagan, Jimmy Carter, and Howard Baker,
while the sports pages brimmed with news about the NCAA basketball tournament. I scrolled on through the microfilm, hunting, searching.

Then, on page A5 in the March 6 issue, among listings of the
recently deceased in Rapides Parish, I found it. The obituary
flashed before me like lightning in the night.

MRS. BEAUMONT

Mrs. Anna V. Beaumont, 81, of Pineville died at 7 a.m. today
in her residence. A native of New Orleans, she was a former
resident of New Iberia and was the widow of Arthur W.
Beaumont. . . .

It was her. My breathing quickened. I read on.

The obituary listed Anna Beaumont's memberships in numerous Catholic charity organizations, noted the time and place
of her burial in Pineville, and then listed her survivors, including
four daughters.

Four daughters.

I felt my heart pounding in my chest now. In a matter of seconds I had brought the white family forward in time all the way
to 1976, a leap of fifty-eight years. This was the white branch of
my family's ancestral tree coming to life before my eyes. But
the bigger question remained: Were any of the four Beaumont
daughters still living in 1998?

According to the obituary, the sisters all lived in Louisiana and
had assumed their husbands' surnames—Guggenheimer, Himel,
Guirard, and Decoux. Later that night at my computer at home
in Davis, I found three of their exact full names, addresses, and
phone numbers in an Internet telephone directory. The next
morning I mailed a letter to each of these three sisters explaining
who I was, my relationship to them, and my research. I also sent
them copies of documents, including A.J. Beaumont's 1901 obituary and his photograph.

I waited anxiously day after day, wondering what the white
families would think of my letter. Every time the phone rang, I
expected to pick it up and hear a Beaumont on the other end of

the line. But as each day passed and my anxiety mounted, I realized I could take only so much uncertainty for so long. When I didn't receive a reply by phone or letter after one week, I telephoned the Himel residence in Pineville. A housekeeper answered. I asked to speak to Mrs. Himel, but the voice replied that Mrs. Himel had died the year before. I felt my heart sink.

I told the voice I was searching for any of the Beaumont sisters and asked her if she or anyone else in the household knew of their whereabouts. The housekeeper replied that only two of the Beaumont sisters were still living and that one was suffering terribly from Alzheimer's.

"But Rita's still around," the voice said.

"Rita?"

"Yes, would you like her number?"

I answered yes, realizing that Rita was the one sister whose name I couldn't find in the Internet telephone directory, Mrs. Rita B. Guirard.

The housekeeper gave me her current name, Rita Beaumont Pharis, along with her telephone number and address in Pineville.

I debated the issue for hours in my mind, looking at it from every conceivable angle as if it were a prism refracting rays of light. I was unsure how to approach the white woman. In the end I decided to make my first contact by letter, not by telephone. I couldn't just call a white stranger out of the blue and introduce myself as a long-lost black cousin whose ties to the white family went back to the plantation era. That would have been just too nutty, too outlandish, too abrupt.

No, I decided that I would have to do it in writing. I would explain our historical saga, all of it, in a page or two. I would try to craft my request to meet her and to hear her family's story so that she would understand and not feel threatened in any way. I knew I had to play it as straight and as sincerely as I could, one human being to another. I would include copies of Beaumont's photograph and his 1901 obituary with the letter. Then I decided to tell her I would phone her after she received the letter and documents. I didn't want to have to wait, hoping for her to call or write me.

I sat down at our computer to type the letter. It took only a few minutes to write, the adrenaline rushing in a torrent through my fingertips to the keyboard.

February 6, 1998

Dear Mrs. Pharis:

I am a professor of journalism at the University of California at Berkeley. For a number of years, as part of a personal writing project, I have been searching for the descendants of a man named Arthur J. Beaumont, an English immigrant who settled in St. Joseph, Louisiana, in the 19th century.

Mr. Beaumont, a longtime merchant and cotton grower in Tensas Parish, died in 1901 and was buried in the historic Natchez City Cemetery. His obituary, published in the Tensas Gazette *in May 1901, is enclosed.*

I have been searching for Mr. Beaumont's modern descendants in order to write a study about my family and his over the last century in America, for our families are very distantly related.

In the 1870s, before he married, Mr. Beaumont had a relationship with a freed slave woman which resulted in a child. The woman and her child subsequently moved to St. Louis in the 1890s, where they remained the rest of their lives. These two women, Laura Brumley and Pearl Brumley, were my great-great-grandmother and great-grandmother.

Throughout these many years Mr. Beaumont's obituary, his photograph, and a handwritten letter he wrote in 1901 before he died, in which he acknowledged he was the father of the black woman's child, have been handed down as keepsakes in our family.

The study I am writing is largely about my family's experiences during this century, including the story of my great-great-grand-mother after she moved to St. Louis. It also is about my mother and my father, a pioneering surgeon in Seattle, and my own expe-riences as a journalist in America and overseas. For many years I was a newspaper writer for the Washington Post *and* News-week *magazine before entering the teaching profession five years ago.*

I have been able to locate you largely through research I have conducted at libraries, courthouses, and census offices.

I know this letter must sound astonishing to you. Believe me, I am quite astonished myself, not least of all because I have been able to locate you.

As I say, I am a researcher and writer and want nothing more than to talk to you about the Beaumont family for my study. I would love to talk to you about your memories of your mother and father and your own experiences over this century. There are absolutely no legal or financial implications to this request. . . .

I will follow this letter up with a telephone call and will be glad to answer any questions you might have about me or my work. It would be an honor to meet you if you would consent to my visiting you in Louisiana at some point in the future.

I printed the letter on a sheet of my official university sta-tionery. Then I signed my name with a ballpoint pen at the bot-tom and decided to send the packet of material via express mail, which I knew usually took just two days for delivery. I went to the post office with Zoë on that windy winter day and held her in my arms as I paid the $4.39 fee. Zoë asked the clerk to stamp her hand, as she always did whenever we visited the Davis post office on routine occasions, the purplish "First Class" stamp of ink staying on the back of her hand for days.

Then I waited nervously again, unable to eat or sleep much, my stomach knotting with each passing hour. I knew I was close to solving the puzzle. But how would the white woman and her family react?

One day passed. Two days. Three. I hoped to hear something from her first, before I had to call. But I heard nothing.

Late on the third day, Monday, February 9, I couldn't stand it any longer. I was baby-sitting my daughter that afternoon while Letitia was teaching her class on African politics at the Naval Postgraduate School in Monterey. Zoë and her pal Alex were playing a pretend game in her room, both of them dressed up in princess costumes—Zoë as Pocahontas, Alex as Cinderella.

"Zoë, I'll be on the phone for a few minutes, okay? You guys play here quietly and let me talk."

"Okay, Daddy," she said.

I retreated to my bedroom, picked up the telephone, dialed the number for Rita Pharis's house in Pineville, then sat down at my desk with my pencil and a yellow notepad in hand. My gaze fell on Letitia's roses outside our window as the call went through.

The phone rang once, twice, three times. I inhaled deeply to calm my nerves. For an instant I pondered whether I should leave a message if an answering machine picked up. But then the ringing stopped. The receiver had been picked up. I heard a moment of silence, then a woman's voice.

"Hello?"

I felt a sick nervousness in my stomach, very much like the

kind I always got before my lectures and other public speaking events.

"Mrs. Pharis?" I said.

"This is Mrs. Pharis."

"Mrs. Pharis, this is Neil Henry. I'm a professor at the University of California."

"Yes," the voice answered. It sounded a bit guarded, distant.

"I was wondering if you got a package of material I sent you. You should have gotten it over the weekend."

"No, I haven't gotten any package," the voice answered, the sound of a lush southern accent more obvious to me in this longer sentence.

A moment of silence followed. I was speechless. Now what? The scene I had so feared, the one I had tried so hard to avoid, was now unfolding inexorably before me like a nightmare. I realized I would have to explain everything by voice to the strange white woman listening in puzzlement on the other end of the line.

Where would I begin? I felt panic for a second, but then I took a deep breath and told myself to get to work.

Concentrate. Keep her on the line. Be professional. Explain what you want and fast.

"I'm sorry about that," I said. "Let me try to explain, Mrs. Pharis. I'm a teacher and I'm doing research for a book that your family might have something to do with. What I mean to say. . . ."

Tell it straight. Don't confuse her.

"Our families are very distantly related, Mrs. Pharis. For a number of years I have been searching for the descendants of a man named Arthur Beaumont. . . ."

"That was my daddy!" she interrupted. Her voice sounded intrigued then, her tone a bit stronger, firmer.

Keep going. Get to the point. Tell her about Laura and Pearl, but do it smoothly, clearly, succinctly.

"Yes, I thought it was," I said. "Your father's father was named Arthur Beaumont too, I believe. And a long time ago, you see, back in the 1870s, your grandfather had a relationship with a freed slave woman that resulted in a child. And that child and her mother were my great-great-grandmother and great-grandmother."

"I see, yes," she said.

Keep going.

"What I've been doing is researching and writing about my family history, Mrs. Pharis. And I was hoping I could include in this story some information about your family."

"Well, you see I'm the youngest of my sisters," she answered then, coughing slightly but seeming not in the least put off by my request. The tone of her voice was even, strong. "Goodness, my sisters could have really helped you if they were still living. . . ."

She paused.

Let her keep going.

"You see, the others are gone now. Except for one. And she's got Alzheimer's."

"Is that Mrs. Decoux?"

"No, she's passed. Mrs. Guggenheimer is the sick one."

"Well, that's sort of how I found you, Mrs. Pharis. With their names. You see, I sent letters to three of the four sisters I found in a 1976 obituary of your mother. And I called the Himel residence on Friday and got your name and address and number. That's how I found you."

"Yes, I had a different name back then when Mama died."

"Right, it was Guir . . ."

"Guirard, yes."

"And you know, I think that's why it's been so difficult for me finding all of you, because the Beaumont name hasn't lived on."

"Right, my mother and daddy only had girls."

"I have so many questions I don't know where to start."

Start with the easy ones. Don't scare her off.

"Look, I was wondering about something," I said. "Your father and mother at one point lived in Vicksburg back in the 1910s."

"Yes, that's right."

"And your father worked for a coal company. . . ."

"I thought it was a steel plant. . . ."

"Well, telephone directories back in the 1910s list him as the foreman of a coal company. Do you know why the family moved from Vicksburg to central Louisiana?"

"No, they didn't move here. They moved to New Orleans. They spent most of their lives in New Orleans."

"Oh, I see. And what did your father do there?"

"Oh, a lot of things," she said. Her voice was sounding freer, unguarded. "He was self-employed for a while. Then he got disabled in a car accident. . . ."

"Your mother was involved in a lot of things according to her obituary. Catholic organizations and the like. . . ."

"Oh yeah, she was a real pepper pot."

"Can you tell me when your father died?"

"Let's see, I was seventeen when he passed. Which means that would have been in 1947."

I did a quick calculation in my head as I listened to her. She was born in 1930, which made her just sixty-eight years old, seven years younger than my mother—her unknown second cousin. The two women, one white, the other black, were a generation apart in the family tree but as close in age as siblings.

A part of me had always wondered if the Beaumont I found would be too old to remember much of the family story. Instead, to my amazement, I was discovering that Rita Beaumont Pharis was much younger than I ever could have expected or hoped.

"Mrs. Pharis, in this packet of material I sent you, there's an obituary of your father's father from the *Tensas Gazette* in 1901. . . ."

"Oh my goodness!" She sounded thrilled and started to chuckle.

"Yes," I continued, "it's been in my family all these years. And it talks a bit about the origins of your family in England. It mentions that the Beaumonts are descended from a long line of British military men. Did your folks talk much about this family history?"

"Oh, well, my Daddy did. He wrote a book about it."

"A book?" I exclaimed, feeling a jolt in my stomach. "What was the title?"

"Well, it was just a book he put together on his own. It wasn't published or anything like that. It's lying around here somewhere. I've given most of these things to my daughter. She's got all kinds of family papers. She's even got a photo of the house Daddy grew up in, in St. Joseph."

"Really!"

"Yes, indeed. Maybe we can collect this stuff for you."

Elation!

"That would be outstanding, Mrs. Pharis," I answered.

But I knew I still had to ask the most important question while

I had her on the line, the one that had been burning inside me all these years whenever I thought about the white family, *this* one white family out of the millions in America.

"Mrs. Pharis, I was wondering, did anybody in your family ever talk about your grandfather's relationship with a freed slave? Was anything like that ever discussed in your family when you were growing up?"

"Well, not that exactly," she answered after a pause. "It was not talked about openly. But my mother did for a very long time correspond with a child of my grandfather whom she cared about very much. We always understood her to be an Indian woman, though. That was the story we had always understood, you see—that my granddaddy Beaumont had had an affair with an Indian that produced this child."

"An Indian? Where did she live, do you know?"

"I think it was California, but I'm not sure. Her name was Pearl."

I felt a lump in my throat.

"Pearl," I said. "That was my great-grandmother's name."

"Yes? What was her last name?" she asked.

"Well, that's a good question. I believe she went by Beaumont for a while. . . ."

"No, that wasn't it. I would have remembered that."

"She also went by Hall. Pearl Hall. She was married a few times."

"No, that's not what I recall."

"She was also known by Brumley. That was her mother's name, Laura Brumley. She was born a slave on a plantation in St. Joseph."

"Brumley!" Rita Pharis exclaimed. "That was it. Brumley. Yes, my mother and Aunt Pearl corresponded all the way into the 1940s. I do remember that. I never met her, but we always knew her as Aunt Pearl, the half sister of my daddy."

"Oh my!"

My heart raced. I doubted that anyone in my family was aware of this information, of how hard Pearl had tried throughout her life to maintain contact with her white family, despite her white father's rejection of her, of how many overtures she had made and of how she had largely kept these overtures secret from her black loved ones, knowing they would feel ashamed of the connection and disapprove. Black was black and white was white, with no room in a racist country for middle hues. In that instant of revelation, as I listened to Rita on the phone, I marveled at how Pearl must have struggled in the 1920s and 1930s, with such evident loneliness, to navigate her own course along the color line—all in an effort to keep meaningful ties to both her white and her black families and to nurture those ties somehow, despite the monumental countervailing pressures of a racist society and culture.

"Mrs. Pharis, you say your mother talked about Pearl a great deal and kept in touch with her. Did any of that correspondence happen to be handed down? Did it survive the years?"

"Oh, no. I'm pretty sure not."

"Did your father ever talk about her?"

"Oh no, not at all," she said, chuckling.

"Why, do you think?"

"Well, you know, in those days it was just not talked about. People considered those kinds of things best kept swept under the rug, you understand, those relationships between the races. My mother was the kind of person who was very understanding and welcoming because she knew what it was like to be something of an outcast. She was poor and came from an Italian immigrant family in New Orleans. She was the one who kept in touch with Aunt Pearl. She was the one who loved her.

"But my daddy," she continued, "goodness, he would never have talked about such a thing, that his daddy had had an affair outside marriage, even if it was before he married. Especially if it was to someone who wasn't white. We are a very southern family in that way. The old way. . . ."

Her voice trailed off.

"But somebody in your family did recognize her. You say your mother kept in touch with Pearl," I said.

"Yes," she replied, "but Aunt Pearl was always an Indian to us. That's how she was described. And I suppose that's why it was understandable or partly acceptable."

"I wonder why," I said before thinking, puzzled. "Why was she described as an Indian?"

"Well," Rita Pharis said after a short pause, measuring her words. She coughed slightly. "I don't mean this in the wrong way, Mr. Henry. I hope you understand. But as far as my family was concerned, knowing my daddy and how he felt about race, well—better Indian than black."

I sighed, suddenly feeling stupid. Extraordinarily, terrifically stupid. Of course. That's exactly what a white southerner would want his people to believe, I thought. To a white southern man was there anything lower on the scale of humanity than a black woman? Was there anything more abhorrent to a white man than having to admit to a loving relationship with a black woman and to siring a mixed-race child with her? *Of course not.* Better Indian than black.

I contained my emotions and a few moments later thanked Mrs. Pharis for her time. I told her I'd call again in a few days after she had gotten my packet of documents. I mentioned I would very much like to visit her in Louisiana at some point, to meet her in person and talk to her about her family history.

She was quiet for a moment. She then told me she had been very sick lately, with nerve problems in her legs and back, and was under heavy medication. But she didn't reject the idea out of hand. "Let's just wait and see," she said hesitantly.

I decided not to push it and simply said good-bye. But I ached with anxiety as I hung up. I wanted so much to meet her and her family in person, to see what they looked like and how they lived in Louisiana, and to hear how they felt about so many things in American life.

I knew I was close to realizing my goal and was inexpressibly hopeful. Yet at the same time I knew that the white family could easily close themselves off to me, leaving me in a painful intellectual quandary from which there might never be an escape. Much of my dream rested on what Rita Pharis and her family would decide after reading my letter.

I waited a few days to give the white family a chance to receive and digest my letter. All the while I went about my normal routines at home and at school almost in a total daze. Several times during that period Letitia just hugged me tight without saying a word, to bolster me more than anything else. I was so excited and yet a mess of worry and confusion.

A few days later, after delivering a morning lecture to the ninety undergraduates in the "Mass Media and Society" course I teach each spring at Berkeley, I was sitting at the desk in my office when I decided to make a second call to Pineville. It was about noon Pacific time, two hours later in Louisiana. I dialed Rita Pharis's number, then took a deep breath as I sat back in my chair gazing at the sunlight dancing on my daughter's finger-paint pictures on the wall alongside a photo of Letitia smiling and holding Zoë.

She picked up after several rings, saying, "Hello?"

"Mrs. Pharis. It's Neil Henry in California again."

And then, as if by magic, a huge weight was suddenly lifted off my shoulders, for I instantly detected in her voice not distance or guardedness anymore but a brightness and cheerfulness upon hearing mine. She immediately told me that she had gotten my package and that she and her daughter were simply enthralled with it, especially the photo of her grandfather, Arthur Beaumont, and his obituary from the *Tensas Gazette*.

"It's just so thrilling to know we have a cousin we didn't know about," she said, her southern accent clear and her voice warm and delighted. "Especially on my father's side of the family."

I was puzzled by her use of the word "cousin" at first, so much so that for a moment I wondered whom she was referring to. Then she used it again—"My daughter Bobette's little boy wants to know if his new cousin likes Batman," she said with a chuckle—and it was only then that I realized she was talking about me. *I* was the cousin.

I realized that the door to the white family was opening. I was eager and satisfied, yet at the same time I felt a vague new worry about what I was getting into with these white strangers in a small town in central Louisiana. What sort of connection was I making? What sort of connection did I really want to make? What sort of connection were they expecting?

But I held those thoughts in abeyance, for I was so excited by what I was discovering. I was finally striking gold, the mother lode, in my long search. And I felt a sense of vindication and a renewed connection to Laura and Pearl—two women I never knew but whose lives had loomed so large in our family history.

"We're digging out all kinds of things for you around my house. And also my sister's house. We'll have them all here for you whenever you can make it out."

"Great, Mrs. Pharis. That's terrific."

"Call me Rita," she said good-naturedly.

I then decided to ask her a few more out of the endless questions I had for her about her family. Most important, I wanted to get an inkling about her family's quality of life. What did everyone do for a living? How well did they live? I told her that my family had moved all over the country since Laura left Louisiana back in the 1890s. I asked her if her people had stayed in Louisiana all those years.

She replied, "You know, I was thinking about that very thing myself just this morning, Neil. Mama always used to say she felt so wealthy inside her heart, knowing that all of her people—all the people she loved—were in the same part of the same state we always came from.

"We've never left Louisiana," she went on, "or done anything that anybody would consider great, I guess. I mean, there aren't any doctors or lawyers or writers in our family. Nothing like yours, I mean. We've had to get through some pretty hard times, to tell you the truth. We're just simple, ordinary people," she said. "But that's fine, too."

A moment later I asked again if I could visit her and her family. She said she'd like that very much but wanted to leave it up to her forty-one-year-old daughter, Bobette Coughlin, to decide when was best.

"She'll get in touch with you soon, Neil," she said. "I know she will."

When I hung up moments later, with energy and excitement coursing through me, I stepped outside my building to take a brisk walk on campus in the bright sunlight of that February day. I was thrilled, filled with the same sensation of discovery I had often felt in my journalistic work in Africa, in Washington, D.C., and so many other places whenever I believed I had a good story to tell and was about to sit down to write it.

As I paced toward the Campanile, the tall clock tower that stands over campus like a sentinel, I tried to fit the 150-year-old story of our two families together in my mind and felt bewildered by the unlikeliness of it all. On one side of our extended family tree was a white American family living an archetypal immigrant's dream during the era of Reconstruction and on to the turn of century, enjoying a prosperous way of life built on white supremacy and the plantation system. On the other was a tiny black family— a former slave and her child—possessing little but a dream at the start of the same era, an era oppressive to millions of black Americans. Yet during the century and a quarter that followed, the black family steadily climbed upward to somehow realize many of its dreams, with careers in medicine, engineering, education, and journalism, despite the obstacles of American racism. At the same time the far more advantaged white family seemed to suffer a mysterious and devastating fall after the patriarch's death in 1901—a decline I first began to glean in the courthouse records in Vicksburg and now badly wanted to find out more about.

I felt stunned and surprisingly elated by the paradox. Who could have predicted such a thing, given the stereotypes about race and low expectations for black people that have defined life in America? What would staunch believers in black inferiority have to say about these apparently contrasting black and white family stories?

Several days later, on February 22, I received an e-mail message from Rita's daughter:

Dear Neil:

  Hi. My name is Bobette Coughlin. My mother is Rita Pharis. We were very pleased to hear from you. Your letter was very interesting. We are gathering information that I hope you can use. It is Mardi Gras time here in La. My son and I caught a parade in Lafayette and caught many Mardi Gras beads and trinkets. It was a beautiful day and great fun. We are looking forward to hearing from you in the future. Wishing you all the best . . .

I replied to her by e-mail and told her a little bit about my life in return, pointing out that I was a parent too, of a five-year-old girl. Then she answered with a second e-mail, telling me she had recently taken a new job as a speech pathologist and that she hoped my visit could be scheduled around her unusual work hours.

A few days later I telephoned her in Pineville to arrange the visit. She had a soft southern accent, just like her mother's, though her voice wasn't husky like Rita's.

We agreed on a date during my spring break from classes at Berkeley—the first weekend after St. Patrick's Day, Saturday, March 21.

"Hope you like seafood gumbo," Rita told me over the phone with a giggle later that same day. "It's our specialty 'round here."

"I love it. My mother cooked it from the time I was a kid."

"Well, good. We look forward to meeting you, Neil. My sister's daughter and her husband will be here—they're driving all the way up from New Orleans—and the husband of another sister too.

"We've got a lot of things to show you," Rita added shortly before we said good-bye. "A few surprises too."

CHAPTER SIX

"Welcome to the Family"

Named after the lush stands of pine that have grown in the fertile brown earth of central Louisiana almost since the beginning of time, Pineville is a sleepy southern town of about five thousand people on the banks of the famed Red River, which cuts a diagonal swath across the state from its entering point on the border with Texas to the Gulf of Mexico. The very tranquillity of this quiet hamlet belies the region's often troubled political and racial history.

During the Civil War numerous skirmishes and battles took place in this vicinity, including the burning of the stately Rapides Parish seat of Alexandria, just across the river, in 1863 by retreating federal troops. Later, this area became key to the rise of Huey Long, the populist Louisiana leader and champion of poor whites whose appeal to old southern values and conservative racial traditions resonated throughout the region in the 1930s. More than half a century later, Long, along with Ronald Reagan,

remained a hero and beloved icon to most of the white population in central Louisiana.

Today, Pineville is perhaps most noted around Louisiana as
the home of a state mental institution. Bordered by beautiful
green forests growing along the banks of the rust-colored river
drifting gently by, it is, like most towns in America, a place where
most black people live on one side and most whites on the other.

To get to Pineville, I flew from Sacramento to Dallas, then made
a connection to a thirty-six-seat propeller plane for the two-hour
flight 240 miles southeast to Alexandria, the airport closest to
Rita's house. As the plane soared high above the terrain, which
gradually changed in color from the browns and reds of north
Texas to the luxuriant greens and rust colors of central
Louisiana, I tried to imagine what it must have been like to sink
deep roots in one small region of America, this region, for more
than 150 years, as the white Beaumont family had ever since A.J.
Beaumont first arrived there from England.

I also thought about my years of research and how close to the
white family, geographically, I had often been all along.

Natchez, where I had found the graves of Arthur and Mary
Ann Beaumont five months earlier, was barely sixty miles east of
Pineville. Vicksburg, where I had discovered several important
clues in my search at the Warren County Court House, was one
hundred miles to the northeast. Mound Bayou, where my father
had saved the life of civil rights activist Gus Courts in 1955, was
just 225 miles away.

I had been so close to the Beaumonts, I realized. Yet so many
worlds apart.

I rented a car as soon as I landed at Alexandria's small commuter airport and checked into a Holiday Inn in town. I hadn't thought it necessary to call ahead from California to reserve a room, figuring Alexandria would not be especially popular as a destination for tourists. But the hotel clerk told me there was a state basketball tournament going on, along with a convention of the United Daughters of the Confederacy, and all the hotel rooms in Alexandria had been booked for months. "We got a cancellation just a few minutes ago," she said; "otherwise you would have been out of luck, Mr. Henry."

I found my room and immediately telephoned Rita after tossing my bag onto the bed. I took notes as she gave me directions to her house on Tudor Street in Pineville, which was located directly across the Red River from Alexandria.

After hanging up, I got back in my car, found the main artery connecting the two cities, MacArthur Boulevard, and soon crossed the Red River on an old iron bridge to Pineville. This road soon took me past a Louisiana state park with historical markers pointing out sites where Confederate troops had built artillery defenses on the Red River more than 135 years ago. Rita had told me her house was located on a short tree-lined street less than a mile from the state park, set among about a dozen other similarly styled, small, single-story homes built in the 1970s. Her neighborhood, which I soon found, seemed a humble, unostentatious enclave of working-class and retired whites.

It was a warm, overcast afternoon. Several front doors on the block were open to let in the spring air, brimming with the season's new life. Sweet smells of honeysuckle filled the air as I drove slowly down the street, looking for number 130. One white man in overalls was cutting his grass with a push mower. At the curb in front of another house, an elderly white-haired man was bidding good-bye to a younger man and woman. Birds swooped and chirped overhead, and white butterflies floated amid hedges of azalea.

Rita's home was at the end of the block, a modest two-bedroom house with a short flight of stairs leading to a small porch. After making a U-turn on the quiet street to park in front of it, I turned the ignition off, got out of the car with my satchel on my shoulder, and walked up a short cement path through a well-clipped lawn to the porch. The porch was framed by beautiful blossoms of tiny white and yellow bridesweed flowers. On my right, out of the corner of an eye, I noticed a white couple working in their yard next door. The man looked up at me briefly, quizzically. I nodded my head slightly in greeting, then turned to the door.

The screen door was shut, but the front door to the house was wide open, revealing a darkened blur of furniture in the front room and bright sunlight from a lace-curtained window in the kitchen in the rear. I knocked lightly on the screen door, the sound of wood on wood echoing lightly but surely inside. In one hand I cradled a bottle of red California wine for Rita, in the other a San Francisco 49ers T-shirt for her nine-year-old grandson, Patrick Coughlin.

I waited, my ears listening for a sound, my eyes peeled for the opening of the screen door. I took a deep breath, hearing only the birds singing softly in the treetops and the clipping sounds of the neighbors working in their yard. Then, seconds later I heard a low cough and the sound of footsteps padding along the floor inside, growing louder and closer. I noticed the outline of a figure approaching. A hand—a white hand lightly speckled with age spots—pushed the handle of the screen door.

As the door opened, my eyes fell upon the face of a smiling slender white woman with short, wavy dark hair sprinkled with flecks of gray. She was dressed in plain slacks and a warm beige sweater embroidered with red, purple, and green flowers. Around her neck hung a pair of bifocal eyeglasses on a gold chain.

"Hello, Neil," Rita said in the husky yet dulcet southern accent I recognized from the phone, her smile growing wider as her eyes found mine. "Come on in."

She kept the door open for me to enter, and I suddenly found myself tripping over my words. I was so nervous. I told her I had so much to show her from the documents and photographs I carried in my satchel.

"Me too. But let me do this first," she said. She stepped closer, then and folded her arms gently around me. I found myself returning her hug. "Welcome," she said.

Years of keepsakes filled her living room, which was furnished in early American–style pieces of solid wooden furniture. It was a very comfortable room with a well-worn carpet on the floor. Portraits and ceramic figurines of angels and Virgin Marys decorated the walls and bookshelves, testimony to her family's Roman Catholic faith.

As I followed Rita to her bright kitchen in the rear of the house, I found myself remembering all the times I had imagined this scene, this very moment, when I finally met the white Beaumont descendant in person. I had always envisioned the descendant as a white man, not a woman, for some inexplicable reason. I also had imagined family pictures filling the walls, including photos of the English immigrant and Confederate war veteran, Arthur Beaumont. But as I passed through Rita's living room, I noticed only one prominent photo, set atop a large console television set sitting in a corner. It was a black-and-white portrait dating from the 1930s, of Rita's beloved sisters—the granddaughters of Arthur Beaumont. Taken in the prime of their Louisiana youth, it showed them smiling gaily into the camera.

As we entered the kitchen, I was enveloped by the warm aroma of tomato sauce, seafood, and gumbo filé. Rita apologized for the smell of tobacco also lingering in the house. "I smoke," she confessed with a slight blush. I replied that I didn't mind in the least.

We then sat at a small kitchen table to share our treasures, our words spilling over themselves and our old keepsakes—photos, documents, letters—mixing together on the tabletop amid the salt and pepper shakers, spices, and a big tray of napkins. Things happened so fast and we spoke so quickly that it was hard to keep track in my notes, which I scribbled furiously in my notebook.

I pulled out my photos of A.J. Beaumont and my copy of the letter he wrote to Pearl in 1901. In addition, I pulled out a family tree I had sketched in pencil on the airplane from Dallas showing our relationship to the Beaumonts, along with photos of my family, including Laura, Pearl, Fredda, my mother, and Zoë.

Rita seemed fascinated by the photos, examining them closely through her bifocals, and instantly identified the former slave Laura as Pearl's mother without my telling her who she was.

"How did you know?" I asked her.

"I don't know," Rita said, nearly as stunned as I was. "Something inside me just said that must be Aunt Pearl's mother." Then, pointing at the photos, her bifocals perched on her nose, she instructed me, "Look—doesn't it look like they could be taken for Indians if you were told they were?"

"I suppose," I said. "I never thought about it."

Indeed, I hadn't. Laura to me had always been the beloved matriarch who had established our family's foundations in St. Louis so long ago, the woman who had raised Pearl on her own after leaving Beaumont behind. That's what I saw whenever I glanced at her photo, which had hung on the brick wall in our living room throughout my childhood in Seattle.

But to the Beaumonts, Laura had been little more than the mysterious, nameless, faceless "Indian woman" in Arthur Beaumont's past. The contrast was staggering when I thought about it. I had never considered race as a way to identify either Laura or Pearl. But for the white family all these years, race evidently was the only identifying mark.

Then Rita, opening a folder containing a pile of documents, showed me old photos from Arthur J. Beaumont's life in the late nineteenth century, when the family enjoyed its finest days in America. Among them was a large black-and-white picture of the two-story office of his flourishing plantation supply firm on Plank Road in St. Joseph. It seemed a bustling, thriving business in the old photograph, with numerous workers, black and white, posed out front.

Another photo showed Beaumont, his wife, Mary Ann, and his young boy, Arthur W., standing with a bicycle in front of a rambling country house featuring intricate wood latticework, one of two houses and plantations Arthur J. Beaumont farmed, Rita said. I instantly recalled the short 1894 account about Arthur W.'s ninth birthday, which I had found in my microfilm research of the *Tensas Gazette* nearly a year earlier.

> MASTER ARTHUR BEAUMONT entertained his young friends on
> Monday night at a charming birthday party, which was largely
> attended and highly enjoyed by the young folks.

Seeing the picture before me now of nine-year-old Arthur W. and his parents gave me visual evidence of the family's lifestyle that the newspaper had hinted at so tantalizingly in words. This and the other photos seemed to mirror a comfortable, genteel way of life befitting a rags-to-riches English immigrant's story, as he and his family enjoyed his twilight years amid all the trappings of the Gilded Age in a typical small town in the American South.

"What happened, Rita?" I asked as I examined the old photos carefully. "The family seemed to be doing so well. What happened after that?"

"Well, they were. They truly were," she answered in her husky voice, softened by the gentle southern accent, a cigarette perched in her fingers, her eyes gazing at the photo of her grandfather's plantation. We both were sipping from cups of coffee.

"What can I say? My daddy always used to talk about how wonderful those years in St. Joseph were when he was a boy. But then, after Grandpa Beaumont died, things just went to pot. The story is that the boll weevil destroyed everything we had," Rita explained, referring to the insect pestilence that swept up from Mexico and wiped out thousands of cotton farms in the South, beginning at the turn of the twentieth century.

Of course, I thought to myself. The boll weevil! That explained everything. For the scourge did indeed change a way of life for millions of people, black and white, ruining the fortunes of many and ending the tight economic hold "King Cotton" had had on the South for decades. The devastation wrought by the voracious plant-eating beetle cut across the cotton states of Texas, Louisiana, Mississippi, Alabama, Georgia, and South Carolina like a scythe, prompting many farmers to diversify into other crops, such as peanuts. The scourge also spurred the northern migration of millions of suddenly unneeded black sharecroppers whose lives in the South's labor-intensive plantation system had revolved around cotton for generations. In A.J. Beaumont's beloved Tensas Parish in Louisiana, the population as a whole fell nearly 30 percent between 1900 and 1920, from 19,070 to 12,085.

For our bifurcated family, too, the boll weevil scourge surely had had a lasting effect. For the white Beaumonts, it resulted in the destruction of everything that the immigrant Arthur Beaumont had built over his half century in America, barely a few years after his death. For my black family, although the pestilence may not have triggered Laura's decision to leave Louisiana, she benefited from the burgeoning black migration to the North. It probably helped fill the rooming house that she ran for years in St. Louis for black workers and travelers, the house in which my grandmother Fredda was raised.

"It was certainly the boll weevil, but alcohol played a part too, I suspect," Rita continued. "You see, my daddy wasn't trained to do anything with his life except inherit what his daddy had built and to enjoy it. And when that fell apart, when the plantations fell away—well, there was little left except the memories. Dust and memories. It was all gone."

In *Trouble in Mind: Black Southerners in the Age of Jim Crow*, historian Leon F. Litwack notes that black sharecroppers and farmers, who suffered from the ravages of the boll weevil every bit as much as white plantation owners, nonetheless felt a grudging respect, even admiration, for the insect, not least because of its extraordinary ability to "render white men powerless [and] exert controls over white men," as blacks could not. Litwack quotes Mahalia Jackson as saying, "They were a proud and selfish people, those plantation owners and I believe . . . that God finally sent the boll weevil to humble them. . . . Thanks to the boll weevil, a lot of those thieving plantation people died out, too."

Still, for the black man, the bug's rapaciousness was in the end "no match" for the white man's, Litwack claims, and he cites the words of a black farmer, Ned Cobb: "What the boll weevil can do to me ain't half so bad to what a white man might do. I can go to my field and shake a poison dust on my crop and the boll weevil will sail away. But how can I sling a man off my back?" It was an era in which many poor blacks saw righteous justice in a natural disaster that crippled the white man as surely as the white man had crippled blacks through so many generations.

I watched as Rita rose from her chair to stir a pot of rice on the stove, and I realized I was liking her more and more as the minutes swept by. It was funny, but I had imagined for a long time that if I ever got the chance to meet a white Beaumont descendant in the flesh like this, somewhere at the end of my long search, I would feel the old resentment rise up deep inside me—feelings rooted in old hurts my family and I had endured at the hands of white people for so many years. I imagined myself focusing this bitterness on the descendant, the white cousin, I found.

But that wasn't happening with Rita at all. Far from it. With each passing moment I was finding myself drawn closer to her, appreciating her extraordinary candor about her life and her family's saga—along with the treasures she had unearthed for me—in a way that seemed to transcend our contrasting color and histories. It's difficult to explain. Perhaps impossible. But I stopped feeling so much like a black man sitting as a guest in her kitchen and stopped seeing her so much as a white woman acting as host.

We were just two people, two human beings linked by blood long ago and by a racial history peculiar to America, who were meeting in her small house in a small southern town on a spring afternoon simply to talk about it.

Rita carried herself with ease and physical grace. Her soft brown eyes reflected a genuine warmth as they looked into mine whenever she spoke, and her face was lined with wrinkles that spoke of dignity more than age. She laughed easily as she described her life to me that afternoon and evening, flashing a delightful, radiant smile and letting loose a low, infectious chuckle, usually punctuated by the words "What can I say?" Yet she also had a vague sadness deep in her eyes that never really went away.

The smells of crab and roux and steamed rice, familiar from my childhood in Seattle, filled the kitchen as Rita prepared dinner for the family gathering several hours away while we shared our stories. We were to be joined by Rita's niece, Carolyn Layne, and Carolyn's husband, Jack, who were driving to Pineville from New Orleans, five hours away, to meet me. Also coming were Rita's daughter, Bobette; Bobette's husband, Robert Coughlin, who was a special education teacher ; and their nine-year-old son, Patrick—they lived nearby in Pineville. One other family member was going to join us at the table: the elderly widower of one of Rita's sisters, Newton Himel, who also lived in Pineville. Like most residents of central Louisiana, he had worked in the oil and gas industry all his life.

Rita had asked me to come to the house early so we could talk and share our treasures before dinner. And as she spoke, I began to realize that much of the story she had to tell me was punctuated by sorrow. Ask most people about the major turning points in their lives, and invariably they mention some of life's traditional transitions—happy ones like marriage and the birth of a child or terrible ones like the death of a loved one. For Rita, there had been too many turns of the latter kind, particularly in recent years.

These were difficult days for her, she told me as she sat back in her kitchen chair, an apron tied around her waist. Within the last several years she had lost her three older sisters to death and disease. Rita had also been widowed twice and told me she never really got over the first time, in 1975. That was the year her young husband, an electrical worker named Alfred Patrick Guirard, succumbed to brain cancer after an agonizing seven-year battle. His fight against cancer sent the family into a turbulent fall that not only severely tested their economic well-being but also shattered Rita's long-held faith in the Roman Catholic Church, which she found less than supportive or sympathetic.

The disaffection she described to me eerily resembled my mother's feelings in 1968 when her Episcopal church in Seattle failed her in her hour of spiritual need in the wake of Martin Luther King's assassination. Indeed, it was in the same year, 1968, that Rita, who had been married for seventeen years to a man she loved deeply, found herself suddenly having to work full-time in a low-paying job at the Central Louisiana Electric Company to support her family while caring for her incapacitated husband and raising their eleven-year-old daughter, Bobette. Tears glistened in Rita's eyes as she described the loss of her second husband and of her sisters within the last two years. In recent months, Rita said, the losses had become overwhelming and she began to suffer panic attacks. Her doctor put her on antidepressants, the first time she had needed medication of any kind.

"It's not been easy," she concluded softly, looking toward the bright sunlight outside her kitchen window, her words trailing off. She dragged on her cigarette until it glowed red on its end.

A moment later I heard the porch screen door open and turned to see a stout young boy and a bespectacled woman with reddish blond hair and piercing eyes stride into the kitchen. "This is Bobette," Rita announced, sounding brighter, "and that's my grandson, Patrick."

Bobette smiled as she took my hand in hers. "It's wonderful to meet you," she said. As a welcoming gift, she handed me a T-shirt reading "Louisiana," and I gave Patrick the 49ers shirt I had brought from California. Bobette then kissed her mother's cheek and took a seat at the table with us, while Patrick was given permission to watch television in the living room. For a moment there was an awkward silence.

"It's been a very hard time for my mother, for a very long time," Bobette finally remarked. (A speech pathologist at a local nursing home, Bobette had worked to put herself through college in the 1970s and 1980s after her father's long illness and death, earning a master's degree from Louisiana Tech.) "She hasn't been feeling well, physically or emotionally—have you, Mom? We've gone through so many sad things in our lives lately, but your call to Mama, just out of the blue like that—it was the best thing that's happened to her in a really long time."

"The whole thing has been a blessing," Rita's daughter added, glancing and smiling at her mother again. "Just a wonderful surprise."

I had always wondered what emotions I would feel upon meeting the Beaumonts in person. Would I rage at my white cousins? Would I cry? Would I dare to confide? But as I sat at Rita's kitchen table listening to Bobette, I realized how little I had ever thought about the effect I might have on the white family. Bobette, whose French name was a tribute to her father's Cajun heritage, told me over and over that my call had immensely bolstered and renewed Rita's spirits, which had fallen desperately low after her sisters' recent deaths.

My long search was leading me to places I never could have expected. Among the many surprises that day, my sympathy for Rita, the closest living blood link to A.J. Beaumont, was one of the biggest surprises of all.

She had been a mistake. A terrible mistake. An "oops" of providence, she told me. A child born in 1930 during the darkest days of the Great Depression to a thirty-seven-year-old poor white mother who could ill afford another mouth to feed. The last granddaughter of A.J., Rita Mary Beaumont entered the world in New Orleans, long after his death, with three older sisters, the youngest of whom was thirteen years her senior.

The family had fallen far and fast. So much so that another baby was simply the last thing in the world Anna Ventura Beaumont wanted or needed. It was bad enough that Anna was poor. What was worse was that, at the time of Rita's birth, she was in the throes of a final separation from her incapacitated and sickly husband, Arthur Wilford Beaumont, after nineteen years of heartache, betrayal, and alcohol abuse.

When Anna Beaumont found out she was pregnant with her fourth daughter, she cried and cried for weeks. As a devout Roman Catholic, however, she would take responsibility for her new child, doing the best she could. She would carry on in the face of adversity as she always had, from the time she was a poor immigrant girl from northern Italy known as Anna Sophie Ventura, whose parents, Joseph and Crucifixia, had struggled mightily to adapt to the new world after their arrival in New Orleans at the turn of the century.

That's how Rita had entered the world sixty-eight years ago, she told me, as we sat with Bobette at the kitchen table, our keepsakes in a clutter in its center. And as Rita talked about her childhood in New Orleans and elsewhere in Louisiana, I couldn't help comparing it to my mother's, growing up in St. Louis. For they were contemporaries—one a white woman, one a black woman, related by blood but with two very different stories to tell.

Rita's childhood in Louisiana was colored by her mother Anna's strength, grit, and constant tears. It was a childhood crippled by poverty and a torn family. By contrast, my mother, born in 1923, enjoyed a wonderfully happy childhood in St. Louis, buoyed by a loving and close family life and a steady source of income, even through the harshest days of the Depression, thanks to her father's job at the U.S. Post Office.

"Mama used to tell me that she just cried and cried for weeks after I was born," Rita recalled. "So that kind of set the tone for my upbringing. I never was very close to my daddy, and I probably felt for him much of the same sort of resentment that Mama did. She felt terribly betrayed by Daddy. But I loved my mother."

"And when I think about it," she continued, "Mama is probably the only reason we're able to meet today. She believed deeply in family, you know. Nothing was more important than family, no matter what our circumstances."

Anna met Arthur Wilford Beaumont in 1910, according to Rita. Anna was fifteen then and suffering almost nightly beatings by her father, Joseph. Desperate to escape her father's terror, Anna was willing to do practically anything, including marrying the young Beaumont, who had first come to her house in New

Orleans to woo her older sister but had fallen in love with Anna instead.

Arthur W. Beaumont was twenty-five then, a pale, willowy man who told Anna that his family hailed from northern Louisiana, from St. Joseph in Tensas Parish. He said he was the lone descendant of a very distinguished family that had once owned a great deal and often talked about the splendor of his family's past, especially on his father's side. He claimed his family roots were sunk deeply in England, where his male ancestors had valiantly served the monarchy in the Battle of Waterloo.

"Daddy believed really deeply in those things, in bloodlines and the old southern ways," Rita said. She then pulled out a manuscript her father had written in 1941, a few years before his death in 1947. She had made me a bound copy of the original, which I opened and began to read as Rita returned to the stove to put the dinner together.

The manuscript was written in Beaumont's elegant and flowing script. He had titled these eighty-eight pages of family history "The Family of Beaumont, Memory Genus."

"He had beautiful handwriting, didn't he?" Rita said, turning from the stove. "You can tell that he was an educated man."

"Yes," I said, shaking my head in amazement. His handwriting seemed perfect—so beautiful and precise it reminded me of the cursive alphabet on the posters pinned above the blackboards in my elementary school in Seattle.

Arthur W. Beaumont dedicated his book, which included numerous quotations from scripture, Shakespeare, Kipling, Longfellow, and other great literary figures, to his daughters to "help them through life." "I trust that as they travel along the avenue of years that this history and the verses and sayings in this

Rita Mary Beaumont at eighteen, in 1948 in Louisiana. Born during the Great Depression, this white granddaughter of A.J. Beaumont grew up in poverty in a single-parent household. She was fortified, however, by the love of her mother, Anna Ventura Beaumont, and her three older sisters. Photo courtesy Rita Beaumont Guirard Pharis.

Rita Beaumont Guirard with her first husband, Alfred Guirard, and their daughter, Bobette, in 1959. Photo courtesy Rita Beaumont Guirard Pharis.

Anna Ventura Beaumont (1894–1976) at sixty-six, in 1960 in Louisiana. The wife of Arthur W. Beaumont and the daughter of an Italian immigrant, she believed that "family was family," no matter the bloodline, and stayed in touch with the nonwhite "Aunt Pearl" against the wishes of her bigoted husband. Photo courtesy Rita Beaumont Guirard Pharis.

Arthur W. Beaumont (1885–1947), the white son of
Arthur J. Beaumont, at four, ca. 1889. He was raised
to be a "gentleman," to lead a life of privileged ease
and prosperity. When the family holdings were
destroyed during the boll weevil plague at the turn
of the century, however, he spent the remainder of
his life longing for all that was lost, including the
structure of white supremacy. Photo courtesy
Rita Beaumont Guirard Pharis.

Arthur J. Beaumont, progenitor of a dual racial legacy in America, near the end of his life, at sixty, ca. 1899. Photo courtesy Mary Turner Henry.

A.J. Beaumont's plantation supply store and saloon, with workers out front, in St. Joseph, Louisiana, ca. 1889. Photo courtesy Rita Beaumont Guirard Pharis.

(left) The Beaumonts—Arthur J., Mary Ann (1857–1914), and son, Arthur W.—in front of one of the family's two plantation homes outside St. Joseph, Louisiana, ca. 1889. Photo courtesy Rita Beaumont Guirard Pharis.

subject but his heart and soul a Southerner, carried on for four years, until the surrender of General Robt E. Lee, at Appomattox Md., in 1865.

In rags and tatters and wearing what was once the uniform of a Captain in the U. S. Navy (This uniform had been taken by my father from the cabin of the Commander of the U. S. S. Indianola) that had been captured by my father's command.

Arthur John Beaumont (my father) surrendered to the U.S. forces at Minden La., in 1865.

A few days later, he rode into the small village of St Joseph,

Tensas Parish, Louisiana, astride a white horse (one of the few possessions allowed in the terms of surrender)

Penniless and forlorn, he applied for work to Eli Tullis, a young planter, who had just returned from the War and was trying to bring back something from a our glorious and prosperous South This same Eli Tullis, later became the father of Mrs Joseph Curry Sr., of St Joseph, Tensas Parish, Louisiana.

Dean Lee Tullis of the Law School of L. S. U.

Hugh Tullis, a prominent lawyer and Judge of the 10th Judicial

Two pages (30–31) from Arthur W. Beaumont's handwritten family history, penned in 1941 for his daughters, in which he recounts his father's service for the Confederacy and extols the Old South and its lost ideals. Courtesy Rita Beaumont Guirard Pharis.

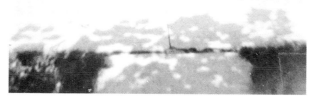

Pearl Brumley Hall, the author's great-grandmother, in front of her house at 6422 Chatham Street in St. Louis, ca. 1925. The photo was given to the author by Rita Beaumont Pharis when they met. The author later copied and framed it as a gift for his mother. Photo courtesy the author.

The author and his mother, Mary Turner Henry, in Seattle in 1988. Photo courtesy the author.

A lunch during a 1999 gathering of the "Tenth Man Classic." Left to right: E.C. ("Uncle Sonny") Turner, Jr., Bobby Henry (brother), the author, and Dr. John R. Henry (father). Photo courtesy the author.

little volume may suit their problems and afford them a great deal of consolation and happiness," he wrote.

As I read through the memoir and history at Rita's kitchen table, I realized with an eerie start that it had been penned more than fifty years earlier in a spirit not unlike the one I felt as I tried to piece together our black family story for myself and, I hoped, for my daughter one day. I had always wanted to produce a story for Zoë to read when she was older, something to help her understand race and racism in America through the lessons of our family tree. Like me, Arthur W. Beaumont was trying to explain to his daughters where his people came from and the things they believed in. Like me, he was proud of his ancestors and hoped his writing would help steel his children with a strong sense of identity and faith.

Yet the lessons this white man was trying to tell in those eighty-eight pages were almost exactly the opposite of what I wanted to convey to Zoë. Beaumont's family story boasted of the glories of white supremacy, of the greatness of enjoying regal bloodlines, and of the enduring values of the Old South that his family's immigrant history illustrated. By contrast, mine was a story of black faith, of the struggle for equal rights, and of progress in the face of bigotry. Their story celebrated traditions that resulted in the oppression of black people. Our story celebrated the overturning of such traditions. We shared the immigrant's blood, but the morals of our two family stories could not have been more diametrically opposed.

As I read the history, I found sorrow and wistfulness at the heart of the white family story. The author, writing in 1941, when he was fifty-six, seemed to be looking backward on things that had been lost instead of looking with hope toward the future. By contrast, Beaumont's half niece and contemporary, Fredda, then forty-five, was simply glowing about her life in St. Louis and her family's future, doing all that she could to prepare her three children to take advantage of it. Already, the next generation was gearing up for the great changes for black people that were on the horizon. In 1941 my father was about to enter Meharry Medical College in Nashville, and my mother was about to become an undergraduate at Harriet Beecher Stowe College in St. Louis. Both were full of youth and, despite the oppression of Jim Crow, brimming with the optimism of their generation. They had everything to look forward to, so many goals to pursue, so many dreams that they would live to see come true. How far removed they were from the small town in Louisiana where Arthur W. Beaumont seemed obsessed with glorifying the past, the splendors of the plantation era, and all that been lost.

I was mesmerized as I slowly flipped through the pages of family history and only slightly surprised by the greatest omission at its heart: that the author had a black half sister—my great-grandmother Pearl—whom he refused to acknowledge, in life or in print.

Beaumont's manuscript traced the family's blood origins to France in the seventeenth century, when a paternal ancestor named Pierre Gustave Beaumont de la Bonnier, who hailed from the province of Beaumont la Chartre, sailed to England as a young *chevalier* along with thousands of other French sympathizers to remove the despot Oliver Cromwell from power and restore Prince Charles to the throne. In thanks, Beaumont the Frenchman was given land in Kent, where he raised his family and became an English citizen.

Thus began, according to Beaumont's family history, a long

association over the next several centuries between the now-Anglicized Beaumont family line and the British military. This alliance saw succeeding generations of Beaumonts fight for Britain in numerous storied battles, from the Napoleonic Wars and the Battle of Waterloo to the Crimean War and the Charge of the Light Brigade. The handwritten family history was full of colorful detail about the suffering, derring-do, and bravery of various Beaumont ancestors on the battlefield.

Arthur J. Beaumont, Arthur W.'s father, was born in Kent in 1839, one of six sons of the Waterloo veteran Peter Alastair Beaumont, who had retired as a "squire and Magistrate and lived the life of a country gentleman." Like his brothers, A.J., as he was commonly known, was educated at Woolwich Military Academy, a privilege given to the sons of Waterloo veterans. But in 1856, when he turned seventeen, he left home and sailed to America in search of his fortune—an act of defiance that caused his father to disinherit him, for his father had planned a British military career for him. Indeed, two of A.J.'s older brothers did serve the crown in the armed forces: Peter Beaumont, whose legs were "shot off during the Kaffir War in Africa," according to the manuscript, and Douglas Beaumont, who earned the Victoria Cross for gallantry in the Crimean War, as a captain of artillery during the Battle of Balaklava in 1854.

A.J. was one of three brothers to emigrate from England to America in the mid-nineteenth century. Clarence Beaumont, a physician, served as a lieutenant in the U.S. Army's Fifth Illinois infantry during the Civil War, then disappeared in the West after the conflict was over. Another brother, Louis Beaumont, also disappeared, somewhere in California during the Gold Rush of 1849.

"My father first settled in Chicago, remaining for about a

year," Arthur W. Beaumont continued. "But hearing so much about the great plantations of the South and the great landholders and slave owners who lived in almost regal splendor, he headed there to seek his destiny." Gradually, before my eyes, the manuscript filled in the details about the white branch of my family tree I had long sought, like dabs of oil paint completing a long unfinished landscape.

"Great opportunities lay in this section [of America]," the younger Beaumont wrote. "He secured a position as one of the assistants to the overseer on the great Frisbee Plantation, of ten thousand acres, in western Tensas Parish, Louisiana. This was in 1858. My father, for whom I am named, remained here until April, 1861, when the thunder roared and the lightning of war struck the entire South."

Then, the arrogant words of the long-dead white man cut through my soul. "Becoming imbued with the spirit of the Southern people," he noted, "my father enlisted his services as well as his spirit in the cause of the Southern people and of course became a soldier of the Confederacy. In April of 1861 he enlisted in Cameron's Battery–4th Louisiana Heavy Field Artillery, Captain [Archibald J.] Cameron commanding, with a roster of 103 men. He was engaged in many battles of major and lesser degree; he was at First Bull Run, also saw the beloved son of Louisiana, General Mouton, killed at Mansfield, La."

As I read these lines, I remembered the years I had spent voraciously reading about the Civil War to understand the broader context of Laura's and Arthur's lives. I was never able to find Beaumont's name in the incomplete rosters of Confederate volunteers from Louisiana in the National Archives, but I did discover in several Louisiana military histories that Archibald

Cameron's artillery battery was well known throughout the state and was one of the first units formed in Tensas Parish after Louisiana seceded from the Union in 1861.

First Bull Run, often called First Manassas, was the first major battle of the war, occurring barely three months after the surrender of Fort Sumter. It was a bloody engagement involving some 28,000 Union troops and 32,000 Confederate soldiers, most of them volunteers under the command of Generals P.G.T. Beauregard and Thomas J. Jackson, who earned his nickname "Stonewall" during this battle. The fighting took place near the banks of a small stream called Bull Run in the Virginia countryside south of Washington on July 21, 1861. To the world's shock, the Union troops were quickly and decisively routed in one of the South's greatest victories, setting the stage for other rebel military triumphs over the next two years.

Arthur J. Beaumont, his son wrote, "suffered the extreme privations and hardships of all soldiers of the Confederacy. Many times having only a small tin cup of meal and small piece of half putrid meat. This was the ration for one day. In the evening, they had to go 'a-foraging.'"

"Barefoot and in rags," the white family history recounted, "this young man, a British subject, but his heart and soul a Southerner, carried on for four years until the surrender of General Robert E. Lee in 1865. In rags and tatters and wearing what was once the uniform of a captain in the U.S. Navy (this uniform had been taken by my father from the cabin of the commander of the U.S.S. Indianola, which had been captured by my father's command) my father surrendered to the U.S. forces at Minden, La. in April, 1865."

A few days later Arthur J. Beaumont "rode into the town of St.

Joseph astride a white horse, one of the few possessions allowed under the terms of surrender. Penniless and forlorn he applied for work to Eli Tullis, a young planter, who had just returned from the war and was trying to bring back something from a once glorious and prosperous South."

I couldn't help smiling as I read those words, my attention grabbed by the name Tullis. The historical portrait filled in as I read on in wonder. *Tullis*—that name was imbedded in the heart of our black family's lore. The Tullis family had owned the cotton plantation where Laura Brumley, my great-great-grand-mother, had been born in slavery in 1850. It was the New England–born mistress of the plantation, Sarah Tullis, who had taught Laura to read and write as a child and saw to it that she ac-quired sewing skills. The same Tullis family had figured promi-nently in Louisiana's political and economic rebirth after the war. It included a state judge and newspaper editor, Hugh Tullis; business and society leaders; and Lee Tullis, a dean of the law school at Louisiana State University. Beaumont's manuscript de-tailed the things that I had already discovered in my research.

As I read about this part of A.J. Beaumont's life, I couldn't help but link it to Laura's. In 1865, the year the Civil War ended, she was fifteen—in the prime of her teenage years—still living and working on the Tullis plantation. Into Laura's life in St. Joseph was destined to come the white man, the English immi-grant and war veteran who would turn out to be the only man she would ever love, the father of her only child, Pearl.

"My father worked for Eli Tullis for several years," Beau-mont's son continued, "he saved his money, and in 1867 with a few dollars and lots of credit he engaged in the cotton planting and general merchandising business. Prospering slowly, owing to

the readjustment of conditions during this period of Reconstruction, by 1870 he had become a man of influence in Tensas
Parish. By 1875 he had prospered still further and become a nat-
uralized American citizen."

And, according to his son, Arthur J. Beaumont worked tire-
lessly, proudly, doggedly against black political rights in Tensas
Parish and his adopted state. What I always had suspected in the
deepest recesses of my mind about his political beliefs suddenly
became clear as I saw it in black and white in the manuscript before me: A.J. Beaumont took "an active part in the banishment of
Carpet Bag rule and the elimination of Negro influence in the
state, by the election of Francis T. Nicholls as the first Democratic governor since the war."

What his son did not point out in the manuscript was that A.J.
Beaumont enjoyed a long relationship with Laura Brumley during that very period, which resulted in the birth of Pearl, my
great-grandmother, in 1877. A year later, in 1878 in St. Joseph,
Beaumont married Mary Ann Sims, a white woman who hailed
from Arkansas. While it was always part of our black family story
that the relationship between Laura and Arthur was very affectionate and conducted with mutual consent over a long period in
the 1870s, it was not clear whether the relationship continued
after Beaumont's marriage. Laura and Pearl continued to live in
the South until the early 1890s, when they moved to St. Louis.

Arthur the younger wrote that he was the only child of the
marriage between A.J. and Mary Ann Beaumont to survive childhood. Two other children, including Florence, whose name I
had found in the 1880 census records in Washington, died at an
early age.

"My mother and father lived for many years in St. Joseph

where they enjoyed the respect, esteem, and confidence of all who knew them," the son continued, echoing all that I had discovered in the microfilms of old Louisiana newspapers. And it was during the last two decades of the century that the family became quite prosperous, turning the immigrant's dream of prosperity in America into reality. In the son's words: "During this maelstrom of events and kaleidoscopic changes in the affairs of the nation, my father acquired two great cotton plantations—Lakewood and Gladstone—which he operated successfully for many years. . . . [In 1901] my father died as he had lived—a man true to the ideals of the land of his adoption."

True to the ideals of the land of his adoption.

How true that was, I thought, as I read the white man's words. For Beaumont believed in slavery so deeply that he staked his life on it in wartime. He believed that black people did not deserve rights equal to those of white people, and like millions of other white men of his age in the South, he worked to erect a system of separatism and inequality that oppressed blacks by law through numerous generations. The evil system lasted all the way into the era in which I, his great-great-grandson, was born. And like many white men of such "ideals," A. J. Beaumont was a hypocrite, siring a mixed-race child in loving union with a black woman in private while maintaining in public his belief in our racial inferiority and enforcing our lower-class citizenship.

Arthur Wilford Beaumont wrote that he was destined to inherit his father's estate, along with the trappings, and traditions of the prosperous plantation life his family had grown to enjoy. But several short years after his father's death, disaster struck. In 1908, he revealed, the boll weevil scourge wiped out not only the family's extensive planting interests in rural Tensas Parish but also the plantation supply business on Plank Road in St. Joseph that his father had worked so hard to build after the Civil War. Arthur W. and his mother, Mary Ann, were ruined.

"Daddy wasn't trained to do anything with his life except to inherit what his father had built," Rita explained as we sat at her kitchen table, drinking soft drinks and awaiting the arrival of the other dinner guests. "He considered himself an aristocrat, a real dandy. I can remember from my childhood that he even used to carry around a pair of dancing shoes. Can you believe it?"

Bobette laughed as she heard this. "You're kidding, Mama. Dancing shoes?"

"He didn't have a penny to his name," Rita said, dragging on her cigarette softly and chuckling huskily as she shook her head slowly from side to side. "But he had dancing shoes."

As she showed me pictures of her father as a pale-faced child, Rita began to talk about her difficult relationship with him. "My mother had grown to despise him by the time I came along, and I think I did too, mainly because I loved my mama so much," she said, sipping her soda from a clear drinking glass, glancing at me over her bifocals. "I remember that I used to love to disobey him. I remember when I was going off to high school—my parents had separated years before—he sat me down to warn me about a few things. He said, 'Now, Rita, high school is a major turning point in a girl's life. And no matter what you do, don't you ever read the works of Guy de Maupassant.'"

She smiled, her face looking younger, brighter. "He said it the French way, you see. He was Cajun that way. 'Gie deh moh-peh-SAWN.' He was very proper. I guess he figured Guy de Maupassant was too sexy for my own good. But, of course, you know the first thing I did as soon as I got to high school was look up the books of 'Gie deh moh-peh-sAwN,'" Rita said, slapping her hand on the tabletop, throwing her head back, and laughing as Bobette and I laughed with her.

"It wasn't sexy at all," she sighed. "Maybe in the nineteenth century it was considered sexy, but I found it pretty dull."

Her father considered himself a very refined gentleman and aristocrat, Rita reiterated, and like many aristocrats he was not imbued with a great deal of worldly ambition. She said her father loved nothing better than to fish for trout and bass, raise prize roses, and read great works of literature. He wrote poetry, short stories, and novels in his spare time and frequently contributed short essays and letters about ethical issues of the day to the editor of the Louisiana Knights of Columbus magazine. He was a dreamer and an artist, his daughter explained, a man raised to live no other role but that of a white southern gentleman.

"Kindness is one of the most potent of God's medicines. It makes no distinction in race, creed or color," Arthur W. Beaumont stated in a verse published by the *Jeanerette, La. Enterprise* in October 1944 and pasted into his book of life's memories. "If it were prescribed more for the ills of this tired and weak old world, I am sure it would be just as effective as of yore and would bring about peace and goodwill to all men."

The manuscript was filled with such clippings from his writing, along with a list of more than twelve novels he said he had written, with titles like "The Last of the Fairmonts," "A Tale of Old Russia," and "The Master of Ravenswood," none of which were ever published.

And like his father, who had worked in the Democratic Party in the 1870s and 1880s to fight Reconstruction, black suffrage, "Negro influence," and carpetbag rule in Tensas Parish, Arthur

W. Beaumont believed deeply in the old southern way of life. He valued racial separatism and the cherished ideals of the Confederacy. Until the day he died, he considered his dearest possession a bronze medal, the Southern Cross of Honor, which the state's Daughters of the Confederacy chapter bestowed on him in 1920 at a ceremony in New Orleans, in recognition of his proud standing as a direct living descendant of a valorous veteran of the War Between the States.

When I read that passage in his family history, on page 45, I couldn't help comparing it to my family's story, for the differences between us suddenly became starkly apparent in my mind. Arthur W. Beaumont's most cherished keepsake all those years had been a medal representing the ideals of the Confederacy, white supremacy among them. My family's most cherished keepsakes also included a medal, but one of a far different kind—the lifetime NAACP membership pin that my grandfather Clifford, Fredda's husband, earned through his many decades of work for and paying dues in the civil rights organization in St. Louis. He had been so proud of it that when he died in 1971, Fredda— Arthur W.'s niece—lovingly insisted that the medal be pinned to the lapel of the suit he wore when he was laid to rest in our old family plot in Illinois.

So valued was his Southern Cross of Honor that in his manuscript Arthur W. Beaumont specified a line of succession for its possession after his death, from his oldest daughter to his youngest, Rita Mary, and from her to the oldest child of his oldest daughter. "It is strictly understood," he stipulated, "that the Southern Cross of Honor is never to be worn publicly, loaned, nor sold."

But today, Rita told me, the medal is missing, along with

much of her father's writing—lost or misplaced somewhere in the line of succession. "I wish I knew where it was," she indicated. "He wanted us all to keep it, but I don't know for the life of me where the thing is."

Near the end of the family history Arthur the younger provided an intricate color painting of what he called the Beaumont coat of arms, which showed a British lion rampant on a field of blue studded with the fleur-de-lis of France. Its motto read: "Erectus non elatus"—Lofty not proud.

While Arthur the younger was a dreamer all his life, a white aristocrat without a plantation to call home, his Italian wife, Anna, seemed always to have her feet firmly planted on the ground. It was Anna who got the family through the trials and hardships of the next forty years, Rita told Bobette and me. "My mother meant more to us as a family than Daddy ever did," Rita asserted. "She was the one who kept us all together."

The Beaumont family holdings were gone by 1910, when Anna first met Arthur, who was working then not as a prosperous landed gentleman but as a foreman for the coal company in Vicksburg, Mississippi. One spring night Arthur asked this fiery daughter of an impoverished Italian grocer to marry him, and she instantly said yes. However, Arthur W.'s mother, Mary Ann, didn't like the young woman and vociferously opposed the marriage. It was bad enough that the girl was just fifteen years old, and worse still that she was dirt poor and could offer little to the family. But what was infuriating to Mary Ann was that her only son wanted to marry an Italian, of all races, a people she considered crass and coarse and unworthy of the proud English blood that flowed through the veins of the Beaumonts.

Nevertheless, marry the young couple did, and soon children

were born: Marie Therese in 1912, Anna Elva in 1915, and Virginia Grace in 1918. Marie gained the nickname "Muggins," or simply "Muggie," after her adoring father told her she looked like a poor ragamuffin as she ate breakfast one morning with her face smeared with dirt. Certainly, Arthur W. was proud of his girls, especially because they were healthy and full of life. Born in 1885 in St. Joseph, he was the only surviving child of a couple who lost two other children to disease, and he believed deeply in his destiny to maintain the Beaumont bloodline in America.

Arthur W. knew his father had had another child by a woman his father had known shortly before marrying Mary Ann. And while the child of that relationship, Pearl Brumley, was his half sister, eight years his senior, he did not regard her as such because she was not white, and he refused to have anything to do with her whenever she tried to contact the family in her letters. In Arthur W. Beaumont's mind Pearl was little more than a half-breed. A mongrel. An old "Indian" woman. She was not white, and therefore her link to him was not valid or real. To Arthur W., the inheritor of his father's ideals, the "colored" relative simply did not exist.

"Daddy didn't even want to discuss such things, these relationships that were outside the formal structure of family and society, you know," Rita murmured softly as she flipped through her father's manuscript looking first at me, then at Bobette. "That just wasn't done. It was bad form. Aristocrats," she noted, holding her nose up to imitate an aristocrat's style and bearing, "never talked about such things. It was beneath them."

Anna looked at Pearl quite differently, though, Rita said. And it was Anna who, on her own, welcomed Pearl as a member of the

Beaumont family, as best she could under the circumstances—
almost as an act of rebellion against her husband. No one knew
when or how they met.

"I just wish you could have found us five years earlier, Neil,"
Rita interjected wistfully at this point, placing her hand on my
forearm for emphasis. "My gosh, the stories my sister Muggie
could have told you. She always knew so much more than me.
And she would have loved to talk to you." I, too, felt the loss
powerfully—if only I had been able to find the Beaumonts two
or three years earlier, Rita's older sisters might have told me so
much.

Somehow Anna and Pearl, who was living in St. Louis, did
meet, and they became very friendly and corresponded regularly
in the mail throughout their adult lives, Rita said. Her sisters had
told her Pearl also visited the family on at least two occasions in
the years before Rita was born. Anna was a very welcoming sort
of woman, Rita emphasized. Anyone of common blood to her
and her family was certainly family to her.

Her husband called Pearl an Indian, and maybe she was. Anna
herself was not immune to judging people by their bloodline. She
made sure to point out to anyone who cared to ask that her ancestors came from the *north* of Italy, where people were blessed
with lighter skin and fairer features—unlike the southerners and
the "Sicilianas," whom her family scorned. "No marry Siciliana!
No Siciliana!" her Italian-born mother had often warned her as
a child in New Orleans.

But in the end, when it came to family, those things didn't
seem to matter to Anna. Once someone was a part of your blood,
they were *family*, no matter the shade or color. And that included
Aunt Pearl, Rita said—"always, no matter what Daddy felt."

Anna, the daughter of the poor Italian immigrant, found that she had something else in common with Pearl, Rita added—a sense of feeling like an outcast, like a stranger in a hostile land. So Anna knew the importance of feeling linked to people. To Anna, the beautiful and exotic-looking woman named Pearl, who sent photographs along with her letters from St. Louis, was simply Aunt Pearl, the sister of Anna's husband. And she became known that way to Anna's children, despite Arthur's firm opposition to maintaining any contact with her. Rita admitted it didn't hurt matters that Anna got some joy out of defying her husband that way.

"When my Aunt Muggie was dying almost two years ago, she would talk a lot about our family history," said Carolyn Layne, Rita's sixty-year-old niece, when she arrived later for dinner after making the long drive from New Orleans with her husband, Jack. "And she always remembered Daddy's half sister fondly. That's the way she described her—Daddy's half sister, Aunt Pearl. We always knew her that way."

Arthur W. and Anna Beaumont moved to New Orleans from Vicksburg in 1918, where Arthur got work in a department store called Maison Blanche. He was not a very dedicated worker, though, and labored sporadically, much to his wife's discontent. He began to drink and they began to argue more and more. They separated and reunited, only to separate again. This happened repeatedly. It was during one of those reunifications that Rita, the last child, was conceived in 1929.

Times were already difficult enough. There was no work, and Arthur W. had suffered internal injuries and a broken pelvis in a car accident, leaving him disabled and sickly for the remainder of his life. A devout Roman Catholic whose mother was named

Crucifixia Aragnona Ventura—"That ought to tell you enough about her faith," Rita chuckled—Anna knew she would never be able to divorce Arthur W. That would have been unthinkable. Still, not long after Rita's birth, she separated from her husband for good.

Anna needed to get to work to support her family, so they moved to Jeanerette, in the heart of Cajun country, where she managed to get a loan to open a grocery store a few years later. Times were tough, not only economically, but socially as well, Rita remembered. A single mother in those days, especially a single white mother, was frowned upon and looked at with deep suspicion and revulsion in the conservative southern culture. Rita used to make up stories when she was a child in elementary school to hide the fact that her mother and father were not living together. "I'd say, 'Daddy's away on a big ship. He's a captain,'" she recalled, with a distant and sad look in her eyes. "Or 'Daddy's traveling and won't come back for a long time.' Anything to avoid the stigma, you know? It just wasn't right in those days that we didn't have a daddy in the house."

They were poor, so poor they sometimes had to rely on handouts from charity. Unlike her husband, who was disabled and never worked after the early 1930s, Anna, as a small shop owner and faithful Democrat, promptly registered with the Social Security Administration after Franklin Delano Roosevelt signed the act into law in 1935.

As Rita remembered her childhood during the Depression, I realized that it was only because of Anna, the mother she loved so deeply, and a quirk of historical fate that I had been able to find the white family at all after so many years of searching. Had it not been for Social Security records, for the "mistake" that brought

Rita into the world as the "cow's tail" in the family line in 1930, and for Anna Beaumont's acceptance and love of my great-grandmother Pearl, I likely never would have heard this story of the white family I was distantly related to—an intricately woven story of human experience and tragedy that stood as a complement, in many ways, to the saga of my family. I was awed by the contrasts between Rita and me but also strangely moved by the human connection we were making.

Still, despite the common ground we were finding, the two of us were products of our separate racial pasts—a reality that struck me again in a flash when Rita confided that one of her sisters had married into a family that was active in the Ku Klux Klan in central Louisiana in the 1950s. She mentioned it almost offhandedly while we were looking at family photos. But from that point on in our gathering, I felt myself withdrawing slightly, becoming wary, more ill at ease than when I had arrived.

When the rest of her family gathered at Rita's house for dinner later, I was welcomed warmly by all and asked to join their circle around the kitchen table as they bowed their heads and held hands to hear Newton Himel, a gray-haired widower in his eighties who was suffering from cancer and heart trouble, lead us in a Catholic prayer. "Bless us, O Lord, for all of our gifts and for these we are about to receive," the elderly man recited in a deep southern drawl, and we joined in to close the traditional prayer with soft "Amens."

Then, clustering around the dining room table, we filled our white Styrofoam plates with Rita's seafood gumbo, crawfish salad, and Boston cream pie and traded stories about our lives.

Jack Layne, Carolyn's husband, a retired records analyst, was especially fascinated to hear about my years working in daily journalism in Washington, D.C., and overseas. "Did you know Bob Woodward when you were in Washington, Neil? Ben Bradlee?" asked Layne, a soft-spoken man with gray hair and a very pleasant demeanor, as he looked up from his bowl of gumbo with eager and expectant eyes.

My years writing for the *Post*, the years in which I finally came into my own as a reporter and as a man more comfortable in my own skin after the lonely years at Princeton, flashed through my mind. I especially remembered a windy autumn night in 1983 when I first spoke to Woodward, my editor in those days, about my idea to try to find my white cousins somewhere in America. He had been intrigued that I had historical documents to begin my hunt, but he cautioned that the sheer effort I would have to put into the search for the mythical Beaumonts might not translate into a good story in the end. And what was journalism if you didn't have a good story to tell? "What if the people you find after years of searching aren't particularly interesting?" he had asked me, leaning back in his chair with his hands folded behind his head. "What if the white guy you find is Joe Six-Pack working on an assembly line or something somewhere? What have you got then?"

I smiled to myself hearing his words in my mind again as I sat at Rita's dining table in Pineville. The irony was that Woodward had turned out to be right, at least in one way. The Beaumonts seemed to be the ordinary white Americans he had warned me I might find after years of searching. But God, how infinitely fascinating these people were to me.

"Yes, I knew both Woodward and Bradlee fairly well," I answered Layne as his eyes grew wide with surprise. "They were my bosses for a few years at the *Post*."

I also was fascinated by Carolyn, a striking woman with reddish hair and piercing, luminous brown eyes. Not long ago, after decades spent as a housewife and a mother raising her two children in New Orleans, Carolyn had started a career as an emergency room nurse at an inner-city hospital. She told me she had always been something of a rebel among the Beaumont clan, very independent by nature, and had married her husband, Jack, partly because his attitude about life was so laid back and tolerant and similar to hers. Despite their conservative southern white backgrounds, each had had black friends for as long as they could remember, she informed me, relationships that consternated their families to no end. "I can't tell you why I was different," she reflected, sitting back in her soft white sweater and smiling over her plate of green salad. "It's just the way I turned out."

She said she and Jack had raised two sons, one of whom was working as a Pep Boys auto mechanic in Baton Rouge, the other as a sales manager in New Orleans for Nextell, a communications company. The two sons had given them four grandchildren so far, distant cousins of my daughter's generation.

An avid skier, Carolyn had traveled around the globe in pursuit of her sport. But at the center of her life now, she told me— her true passion—was her new career in nursing at Charity Hospital in New Orleans. There every weeknight until long after midnight she helped save the lives of shooting victims and the sick in the hospital's trauma ward, where 90 percent of the patients and most of her fellow workers were black. "It's a different sort of life I have now than I ever knew," Carolyn said slowly in her elegant southern accent. "And I wouldn't trade it for a minute."

At the head of the table, observing all this chatter with a studied reserve, the old man, Himel, sat eating his dinner slowly, struggling noticeably and evidently in some pain from his illnesses, including the cancer that would spread to his liver in coming weeks. He sat at the table's edge with his back rigidly against the back of the chair, his pained breathing audible. After a few minutes the old man turned his head toward me. Peering at me through his eyeglasses, he began to speak about his political beliefs. The rest of the gathering listened as Himel talked about Ronald Reagan, the glories of the Reagan presidency, and the age-old conservative politics that he and his people in central Louisiana still believed in strongly, his viewpoint providing a sharp contrast to the moderate, progressive attitudes espoused by Carolyn.

"I probably don't need to tell you this," added the old white man in a thick drawl, coughing twice, his cane resting on the arm of his chair, "because I suspect you already know. But up here we got a lotta rednecks, Neil. Highway 190 is what we call our Mason-Dixon line in Loos-iana. North is redneck, and south is considered Cajun. Oakdale, just south of here, is considered the redneck capital of the state, so that ought to give you an idea of where you are."

Himel (pronounced "ee-mell") sipped some lemonade from his drinking glass, wiped his lips with a napkin, and stared at me through his eyeglasses. "I'm a staunch American," he continued, "and I believe in the rights of man. Huey Long was raised just thirty miles from here, don'cha know. He had his faults, but I always considered him a very good man. We also have a lot of Baptists in these parts—or at least they call themselves Baptists."

The rest of the table giggled.

"Yes, they call themselves Baptists, but I call them hypocrites.

You see, Pineville is supposed to be a dry city—you can't buy alcohol here—but you see more bottles lyin' around here on Sunday mornin's than anywhere else in the state, I reckon."

The gathering laughed again.

"I guess the point I'm trying to make is we believe in things here. We always have. We think people's rights are important and worth protecting."

I knew he was talking about race. I was certain that he was saying to me in a roundabout way that conservatism—conserving the old ways and traditions in the South—was something he and his people continued to believe in deeply, just as they had since the days of A.J. Beaumont in the 1850s. I assumed that when he said his "people" he meant either his family or white people or both. It didn't matter.

I felt a sudden tension in the air and a knot form in my stomach. I gently put my fork down and folded my hands in my lap. I felt my back stiffen, not knowing whether I should challenge the old man at the dinner table—to talk about the rights of *black* people since the days of A.J. Beaumont—or let him continue with his soliloquy.

The elderly white man paused, still eyeing me through his horn-rimmed spectacles, and sipped again from his glass. "But times change," he went on. "Lord knows times change. Circumstances change. And I suppose people do too. So I just want you to know I'm glad you found us. I'm very glad you spent the time and effort to find us. I'm especially glad because you've made Rita so happy."

I felt the tension ease. I didn't press the political point, though it remained awkwardly in the air. I didn't challenge the old man, didn't feel up to a fight, didn't think it was worth it. Inside I knew that fighting and arguing weren't really what I had come all this way to do. I was working, after all. And my work was succeeding in ways I never could have imagined. For one by one the old questions I had long wanted to ask the white family about their lives and feelings about America—the questions that had fueled my search for so long—were being answered in ways both cryptic and clear, and extraordinarily compelling.

It was a short, cordial dinner, after which Himel, feeling ill, expressed his regret at having to leave early. I and several others walked him to the door. Then, as I said good-bye to him there, the old white man suddenly did something unexpected. He placed his dark wooden cane on the crook of his arm, looked at me for a moment, then folded his arms awkwardly around me. He said, "Welcome to the family," in his gruff drawl before slowly heading out into the night.

The words echoed in my mind as the door was closed: "Welcome to the family."

I pondered how unreal and otherworldly the words had sounded coming from him and how uneasy they made me feel. Indeed, for the rest of the night the words reverberated in my mind.

"Welcome to the family"—that wasn't what I had come to Louisiana to hear. It was certainly not what I had expected, and I hoped the Beaumonts weren't mistaking my intentions. I wasn't an orphan or an illegitimate distant heir, and I felt a strange revulsion, at first, over Himel's use of the expression. I couldn't explain exactly why. But, as I mulled all this over nearly six hours later, I wasn't sure what I was feeling anymore in my heart. The intense feelings that had filled me throughout the afternoon and evening were turning into a state of self-protective numbness.

My senses were being pulled in so many directions at once that I felt myself closing off inside in an almost instinctive reaction of self-protection.

Carolyn came up to me a moment after Himel departed and said, "I thought you should know that Newton's the one who insisted that Jack and I come from New Orleans to meet you tonight. He was really insistent about it."

We were standing in Rita's living room then, watching as Rita and Bobette set up a projector to show old slides of family gatherings dating back to the 1950s. "You know, he called us in New Orleans," she continued, "and he said to me, 'Carolyn, if you love me, you'll be there. If you love me, you'll come.' He never said anything like that to me before. He felt really deep emotions about your coming."

"What makes it more surprising," Rita interjected then, almost offhandedly, her southern drawl tinged with remorse, "is that Newton and his family were KKK in the old days." Rita looked at me over her bifocals. "He is the one I was telling you about before, Neil. He is the man whose family was active in the Klan."

The room instantly fell into silence again.

"Oh, come on," Carolyn exclaimed softly after a moment, the shocked disbelief slowly spreading on her face, her bright eyes widening as she stared at her aunt behind the projector. "Come on, Rita."

Rita looked up again. "True," she said softly.

"Oh, you don't *mean* it!" Carolyn insisted, her face reddening with surprise and embarrassment over the knowledge about her uncle.

"It's true. You ask him, Carolyn. He was in the KKK."

"In those days," Bobette interrupted apologetically, "it was more a social thing than anything else, wasn't it? I mean, it wasn't always evil. . . ."

Carolyn glanced first at Bobette, then back in disbelief at her Aunt Rita, as the latter sorted through the pile of family slides.

"What's KKK?" asked Patrick, the nine-year-old, sensing the fierce emotions behind his mother's, aunt's, and grandmother's words. He tapped his mother's arm.

"What's KKK?" he repeated.

I felt myself backing up against a wall near the old photo of Rita's sisters, unable to speak as I witnessed the tense scene unfold.

"Oh, please, Bobette," Carolyn lashed back. "That's just shameful. I can't *believe* we had family in the Klan. It *was* evil. A terrible evil. I get so mad just thinking about it. It's outrageous."

"What's KKK?" the little white boy continued to ask each of the women over and over, finally pulling gently on his mother's sleeve. "What's KKK?"

Bobette placed her hand on her son's head to gently smooth his brown hair. She looked down at him with a sad smile. "Shhhh," she hushed him softly, telling him to never mind.

Rita continued to put her slides together in the eerie silence that filled the living room for several moments. I put my notebook and pen aside, then sat back on a couch, feeling a mixture of surprise, fatigue, and disgust.

"Welcome to the family."

I couldn't get over the feeling of Himel's arms around my shoulders, the awkward welcome the elderly man had issued to me, the emotional reconciliation he had wordlessly sought. It was as if I were reliving something our family had already gone through many years before, something atavistic. I recalled that nearly one hundred years earlier, shortly before his death, A.J. Beaumont had penned a letter of regret and apology to his mixed-race daughter, Pearl, and sought her forgiveness for not acknowledging her as his own for so many years. Now Newton Himel, a white man of similar background, had made an eerily similar gesture to me—and under eerily similar circumstances. (Indeed, he would die barely a year later.)

I felt torn in two different directions as I contemplated all this, desiring renewed connection, yet unable to get over the revulsion I felt. Why were we the ones who always had to understand and struggle to forgive, generation after generation? Most of all, though, I felt an almost overwhelming sense of sorrow.

For the first time in a long time, my parents' words of advice about white racism from my childhood in Seattle returned to my mind with a clarity I hadn't known before: *"It's their problem. It's the white people's problem. Not yours."* It was true, I began to understand just then. For the first time I saw that at least a small part of it was true. White racism was their problem, their legacy in this case, and they were the ones who would have to grapple with it somehow in a way that ultimately had to count. They would have to explain to nine-year-old Patrick what KKK meant. They would have to confess their connection to such evil to a child who didn't understand. Either that, or bury the shame in a tortured, cancerous silence.

I felt deep sorrow. And some sympathy for Bobette, as a parent. But these feelings were also mixed with relief that I would not have to explain such a dark thing from my people's past to my daughter. For the first time I realized, in that sad moment in Rita's living room, that at least one aspect of white racism wasn't my problem at all.

Rita broke the silence a moment later. "I won't lie and tell you we don't have these old feelings in our family," she said, looking up at me from the projector, her voice steady but subdued. "I remember the first time I saw an interracial couple, sometime back in the 1940s. I couldn't believe it. I was a teenager and I was absolutely speechless. I was at a restaurant. I was flabbergasted. I told my companion, 'Gosh, would you look at that!' And my friend said, 'They must not be from around here, because that's illegal.' It was just so unbelievable. I wasn't brought up to accept things like that."

Carolyn nodded, adding, "It's so true. It doesn't make it right, but it's true. When I was child we had a black maid named Rose. Remember Rose, Rita? We loved her like family. When she got sick we took her in and took care of her." Here Carolyn paused slightly, looking at me through her beautiful and intensely deep brown eyes.

"But," Carolyn went on, "my parents made it very clear to us that we could not call her *Miss* Rose, or call her by her last name. Ever. Because there were certain things, certain social rules, that you always had to obey about black people. You couldn't show them the same respect you showed white people. That was clear. That was the order of things."

Whoopi, Kobe, Denzel, Spike . . .

Rita nodded. "To this day I still have some of that feeling inside," she admitted, looking up at me from her slides. "I won't lie. It's a part of me. Like, I'll come up behind someone black in a car, and I'll hear myself saying, 'Come on and move, you black so-and-so. . . .' It's in me. You can't divorce yourself from your past."

"But it's also true," Rita reflected, "that things have changed—

for the better, I think. It's not like it used to be. I've had a couple of black friends in my life. And I promise you, in my little circle we don't have what we used to have—that old animosity toward black people. When I told my white friends about your coming to meet us, they were pretty thrilled. They said, 'I just can't believe you've got a black cousin.' Times change, you know? We probably never could have done this twenty-five years ago."

Rita was right, I knew. There was very little chance that our meeting and attempt at understanding could have happened in an earlier era, before the gains of black civil rights and all the other social changes in America over the last half century, especially the advances that allowed for closer personal relationships between the races. While the very word "miscegenation" remained as emotionally charged as any in our cultural lexicon, and while antebellum laws against interracial marriage had remained on the books in several southern states until 1967, interracial relationships in America—as just one small measure of change—were more common, tolerated, and accepted than they ever had been when Laura and A.J. first loved in the 1870s, even in tiny Pineville in Louisiana, the heartland of Huey Long and Newton Himel.

The fact was our society had changed drastically from the plantation era of A.J.'s and Laura's time. Certainly attitudes and perceptions had changed. A few of the most popular figures in our culture, from sports heroes like Tiger Woods and Derek Jeter to pop singing idol Mariah Carey, were products of loving interracial homes in an America far different from the country A.J. Beaumont arrived in in 1856. Who could have imagined back then or even as recently as twenty-five years ago that Americans would see a black man take the oath of office for the U.S.

Supreme Court with his white wife holding their family Bible at his side?

So Rita was certainly right, in a way. It was true that we had progressed as a society to a point where she and I could meet as social equals, white and black, as we certainly did on that long and emotional March day in the house on Tudor Street in Pineville. It was true that the tentative bonds we forged there, especially those between Rita and Carolyn and me, simply could not have been attempted had it not been for our respective experiences and learning during the era of integration and through other great changes in American society since the 1950s.

But it was also true that a gulf still existed between us as people, as it did between most blacks and whites across our country. We were once joined by blood from a taboo relationship in America's distant past, and some 120 years later we remained two families and two peoples with particular histories and backgrounds, representing two very different branches of a shared tree. Between us there was still a wary divide that awkward hugs could not disguise.

Bobette dimmed the lights in the living room, and soon more than forty years of the white family's memories began to illuminate a wall near the front door. There were slides of Rita laughing joyfully as a young bride in the 1950s, an era coinciding with my birth in the black hospital in Nashville. Rita was truly beautiful when she was young, raven haired, with pretty eyes as dark as coal. Next came pictures of Bobette as a gurgling baby happily eating prunes in a high chair in the late 1950s—about the time my family was settling into Seattle after making the long move from the South. Then the wall was splashed with pictures of Bobette's father and Rita's first husband, Alfred Guirard, a dark-haired fellow wearing a zoot suit at a Damon Runyon costume party from the same period. He was working at the time for United Gas and Electric, like many white blue-collar men in the region.

Photos from countless happy Christmases, Easters, Thanksgivings, Halloweens, Mardis Gras, and Sugar Cane Festivals and from summer vacations at sunny segregated beaches on the Gulf of Mexico flashed on the wall, along with portraits of Rita's cherubic mother, Anna, and her three sisters. Bobette, Carolyn, and Rita laughed hysterically at times, remembering the scenes as if they were yesterday. As I watched, I couldn't help reflecting on where I was and what my family was doing during the same period that our white cousins were leading their lives on the other side of the color barrier.

"These were the happiest days of your life, I guess," I remarked offhandedly to Rita as another photo of her laughing and hugging Alfred and baby Bobette filled the wall. "You all look so happy."

"Yep," she replied softly over the low hum of the projector. "They sure were."

On into the 1960s the photos and family memories hurtled. That was the era of racial integration I grew up in, in the white neighborhood in Seattle. Then Rita came to the year 1968. It was the family's last Christmas before Alfred, the husband she loved so deeply, was incapacitated by the brain disease that killed him seven years later. The room grew quiet, save for the sound of Rita clicking her projector from one slide to the next, as the late sixties dawned on the wall.

Then Rita apologized to me. She said she was too tired to go on.

"That's okay," I told her. It had been a long night. "I'm beat too."

We snapped a few rounds of new pictures then, some for me to take home to Letitia and Zoë and some for them to keep of me. Then, just as we all gathered our things to file out into the night, Rita remembered she had a surprise for me. She beckoned with her finger for me to return to the kitchen. I followed her and watched as she reached into her folder of keepsakes lying on the kitchen tabletop. She pulled out seven small black-and-white photos, each about three by five inches in size. Several displayed old yellow strips of Scotch tape on their borders, as if the pictures had been plucked from an album. The edges of a few others were dog-eared. The pictures were slightly blurred with age.

Rita gently placed the photographs on the table before me. They showed a light-skinned black woman with lustrous straight hair in various poses and scenes. They seemed to have been taken in the 1920s and 1930s, judging by the woman's haircut and style of dress.

"We've had these for such a long time," Rita said, gazing at the photographs through her bifocals, the brown and gray strands of wavy hair atop her head shining in the light over the table. "My mother saved them all those years. We kept them too after Mama passed. It's Aunt Pearl."

I looked closer at the photographs, my eyes disbelieving. I felt the blood of excitement racing to my face once more. There in the pictures before me was my mother's beloved grandmother. They were photos my family never knew existed.

Pearl evidently had sent the pictures to the Beaumonts to share her life in St. Louis with her white kin in Louisiana. One photo showed her smiling in the backyard of her house among shoots of blooming hollyhocks. Another showed her smiling and waving her hand from a bridge in Forest Park. Several others showed her posing on her front porch and in her front yard behind a pretty white picket fence. The backs of two of the photos bore Pearl's cursive handwriting in blue ink faded by time. The jottings read, "In the back yard with the hollyhocks" and "Duck pond, Forest Park."

I couldn't take my eyes off the pictures. Each one offered such a poignant glimpse from the life of a mixed-race woman who seemed to be trying, perhaps vainly, to keep a bridge to her white relatives.

"They're yours, Neil," Rita told me as I peered intently at the photos. "If you could make copies, I'd appreciate it. But they're yours."

I looked up at Rita to thank her, but all I could do was exhale. I couldn't summon a word, not even the simplest expression of gratitude. Rita seemed to understand. All she could do was smile back.

It was then that I began to understand that Rita and I were perhaps more alike than we knew. The revelation hit me with sudden and powerful force, for I began to see clearly that, in a way, Rita had been paying tribute to her mother, Anna, by welcoming me so warmly and by bestowing me with her gifts—just as I had perhaps been trying to pay tribute to my mother all these years, without even realizing it consciously, by searching for answers to the old questions in our family history. We were such different people, Rita and I, from such completely different backgrounds and histories. Yet in the end, despite our differences, we were oddly alike in the heart.

I stared closely at the photos. Then I asked Rita if she had a magnifying glass. I wanted to see something in one of them. The picture showed Pearl standing on her front porch in a pretty sundress. She seemed to be in her middle age. Rita directed me to a reading glass near the living room. I turned a light on and held the picture under the glass to make out the street numbers hung in the porch above her head.

What I saw banished any lingering doubt about our connection. The numbers on the porch of the trim, white wood-frame house with the picket fence read "6422" under the magnifying glass. This was the address on Chatham Street in St. Louis where Laura and Pearl lived in the 1920s and 1930s—and where my mother spent some of the happiest years of her childhood.

I gingerly placed the photos in an envelope, then slipped the envelope into my black canvas shoulder bag along with the Beaumont family history manuscript and the nineteenth-century photos from A.J. Beaumont's family life in St. Joseph that Rita had already given me. Rita walked me to the door. I was still virtually speechless by the time I got there, stunned by her act of kindness, numbed by the experiences of the night.

"You don't know how much this means to me, Rita," I told her as I stood in the entryway under the shining porch light, placing my arms around her to return her hug. "All of it."

"I'm so glad you came," she said.

A moment later we all said good-bye.

CHAPTER SEVEN

Tenth Man Classic

A few weeks after I returned to California from my trip to Pineville, I took Rita's old photographs of Pearl to a professional copier in downtown Davis, who enlarged the pictures for me on a color printer. Next I found a pretty cut-glass picture frame sitting on a silver stand at an art store, which I purchased for thirty-two dollars. When I got home, I slipped the finest photo—the one from the mid-1930s of my mother's grandmother standing proudly in her front yard behind the picket fence—inside the shimmering frame. As I gazed at it, the old black-and-white picture appeared so beautiful and so luminous, despite the blurriness of age, that it almost took my breath away.

"Who's that, Daddy?" my daughter asked me when I brought the framed photo into the living room and placed it on our coffee table to show her and Letitia.

It took me a moment to try to figure the relationships out. "Let me see. It's your great-great-grandmother, Zoë. Yeah, that's right. Two greats," I said. "Her name was Pearl. It's a very old picture. She isn't living anymore. But she was very special."

My daughter gazed at the photo, running her finger over the edge of the frame's silver border. For a moment, with her brown eyes, light brown skin, and curly brown hair, she reminded me almost exactly of pictures I had seen of my mother as a child and of my mother's mother, Fredda, a generation earlier in St. Louis.

"I didn't know her either," I added. "But some people still remember her really well."

It had been some time since I returned from Louisiana, and I had spent a great deal of it in deep reflection about my emotionally complicated odyssey, the story I had heard in Pineville, and what my search meant in the end. I found myself thinking more and more about how it had started in the first place years earlier with the oddly simple intellectual challenge I had posed for myself: try to find out what happened to the white family on the other side of my ancestral tree.

All along in that quest, a part of me had hoped and perhaps expected that I might uncover some earthshaking revelations about race relations and American history—lessons that might help me see my own experiences in this country, and those of my family and other black Americans, in a clearer light. I wanted to discover something so extraordinary and hitherto unknown about ourselves as Americans that it would be worth shouting about to the heavens. It was what kept me going in the search really, the sense that there just had to be some great intellectual treasure at the end of the trail.

There was a part of me too that had secretly hoped that my white kin had faired more poorly than my black kin over the past century. It was the same part of me that had secretly and perhaps vengefully wanted to rub the evil of white supremacy and bigotry in its face. I guess I wanted to show white people—especially the white family I was related to by blood—that blacks were just as smart, courageous, and strong, if not more so, than any people in America, and that all of us could prove it—as my family had through the generations—if given a fair chance.

In the end, as I contemplated my journey's lessons and ultimate meaning for me, none of those things really seemed to matter much at all. I didn't think I had uncovered any clear and definitive truth of universal significance—nothing as profound, sparklingly pure, and important to American race relations as $E = mc^2$ was to the world of physics, say, or the quadratic formula or the law of gravity. No flash of light or searing revelation suddenly exploded in my head, transforming my life forever. In some ways, race and racism in America remained as profoundly complex to me months after my visit to Pineville as they had when I began my search for the white family years earlier. I wasn't sure I understood the roots and anatomy of racial bigotry and ignorance any better, though I did continue to be sensitive to their effects on me, my students, and my family. To be certain, the topic still vexed me deeply, as much as it ever had, and as much as it likely always would.

Nor was I sure I had learned significantly more about the context of my family's struggles and successes in the face of racism—though I did appreciate my family even more in light of the Beaumonts' lives. I had been proud of all my people before the search and was just as proud afterward. And while I did at first feel elated to discover that my family's progress in the twentieth century contrasted with the Beaumonts' downfall after the boll weevil plague, that feeling was momentary, vain, and shallow. The term "poor white trash" in the context of the Beaumonts seemed, in the end, as hollow, useless, and malicious as any black slur or stereotype. For the truth was that Rita had generously opened the door to her house and to her family's remarkable life story to me, and I was grateful, having found parts of that story as moving and admirable as any I had run across in my life and career. Rita's struggles, inner strength, love for her family, and life experiences were no less profound, no less resonant, no less meaningful than those of anyone in my own close family—and don't such things constitute the true measure of a life and human existence?

In the Beaumonts I found a white family that certainly was every bit as human as we were, people who had struggled with their own brand of demons. Both of our families had been crippled to some degree by prejudice, personal trauma, and tragedy, but in the most important ways both branches had endured. So it wasn't what we did for a living that counted, nor what kind of china we dined on, nor what our houses and neighborhoods looked like. Nor, in this one sense, did our skin color even matter very much. What counted most through the generations, far more than any other factor, regardless of our race, was how we treated those we loved and how well we loved. That seemed the transcendent lesson or moral that my search had revealed. And it held true whether the figure was my mother or Fredda on one side of our family tree, or Rita or Anna Beaumont on the other. Simple as it was, it was my $E = mc^2$.

I emerged from my search with a complex web of emotions:

pride, a deeper understanding of human complexity, a sense of professional accomplishment. But I also felt a lingering sadness, sharper than any I had felt previously, over the cancerousness, the sheer wastefulness, of racial prejudice and bigotry, and the sinister way they can replicate themselves from one willing generation to the next.

Yet even in this stark sadness there was an overarching complexity. For I also began to recognize, grudgingly, that racism itself, while oppressing us and limiting our potential for generations, had also deeply challenged us as individuals, pushed us to strive harder, to compete better, to believe in ourselves more fully. That had certainly been true for my father, and it was true for me. Racism was a hurdle, but the pathology also stoked our inner fires to attempt to rise above it. To the extent that challenge and personal struggle are ingredients for a fulfilling, productive, and complete life, it was strangely true that racial prejudice, in a singularly American fashion, had pushed my family to be far better than society expected or even desired us to be. It had presented us with a unique form of challenge that the Beaumonts had never had to face really. And generation after generation, many of us proved ourselves in facing up to it. Indeed, this ceaseless contention with prejudice had concentrated our minds through the generations, helped forge our family bonds and identity as black Americans, and forced us to exceed ourselves at times in ways we perhaps wouldn't have otherwise. It was a thorny truth I was beginning to see, one I had a hard time reconciling with the pathology's pain and crippling evil.

It was also true that my family's advances in the twentieth century, while mirroring the rise of the black middle class across

America in the wake of the civil rights struggle, could not be separated from the chilling reality of abject poverty, failing schools,
poor housing, meager opportunity, and hopelessness in which
most other blacks in this country remained. Such suffering, inequality, and injustice constituted the most salient and overriding
social context of our lives. Within this context my family story
was something of an anomaly, I knew, one whose lessons were
difficult to reconcile with the greater African American experience. What good was such progress, such success for our country as a whole, I often thought, if, with each succeeding generation, so many more of our kind were left in the mire with little or
no way out?

During the years I pursued my project in the mid-1990s, a
new generation of white conservative analysts authored widely
publicized books asserting the racial inferiority of blacks. Richard
J. Herrnstein and Charles Murray's *The Bell Curve* in particular
was the focus of discussion for weeks in the national press and
broadcast media, the stepchild in many ways of the work of the
1970s race theorist William Shockley, the Nobel Prize–winning
physicist whose views on black genetic inferiority and steriliza-
tion had so disturbed me during my college years at Princeton.
Often as I stood at my lectern as a professor at Berkeley, scanning
the crowd of undergraduate faces before me, I made special note
of the brown and black ones sprinkled among the white. At such
moments I couldn't help envisioning my own face as a much
younger man among them and feeling, as I did so many years
earlier, the dull ache of unease and aloneness, the extra psychological burden I remembered having to bear. I began to see a
clearer and deeper sense of meaning in my work—not just in

teaching but also in trying whenever I could to shore up the souls on the edges, to help them believe in themselves and their promise. In this regard, my research helped to crystallize my thinking about the enduring evil and burden of prejudice and the fragile nature of human potential, especially among the young.

It also refueled my dedication and belief in our continuing struggle as a people, I realized. For it was during my research trip to the South in 1997 that I recruited a promising young woman from all-black Clark-Atlanta University to my journalism program at Berkeley. Sherri Day had had little journalism experience in her undergraduate training, but she showed a deep passion for questioning, learning, and writing. I was excited by her potential, and she did not disappoint. During her two years at Berkeley the bright young woman from rural Georgia succeeded beyond all measure, finishing at the top of her class and delivering the valedictory address at her May 2000 graduation before going on to work as a reporter for the *New York Times*. Such were the hidden, almost inexpressible joys of teaching in the difficult post–affirmative action age in California, feelings that carried even greater psychic meaning for me in the wake of my project.

The end of my search did not produce any major changes in the rhythms of my daily life, however, nor did it greatly adjust the mental prism through which I viewed life and American society. When I got back from Louisiana, I picked up my life right where I had left it. I taught my classes, delivered my lectures, researched and wrote, coached Zoë's softball team in Davis, refereed her soccer games, read her stories at bedtime, and went to sleep each night with Letitia, all of us enduring life's small challenges and taking pleasure in life's little joys from one day to the next, like most American families. Still, there were a few small changes as bits of information accrued in the wake of my discoveries, each lending new wrinkles to my life and to the story I had discovered on the other side of the tree. The truest value of my search lay not so much in how it transformed my life but in how it deeply informed it in so many ways.

When I called Carolyn in New Orleans a few months later to get information to fill out a fuller family tree, encompassing the complete span of the white and black sides, she sounded delighted to hear from me. "You'll never guess what happened," she said, struggling to contain her laughter. "The word got around about you among our cousins all throughout the state, but you know how word of mouth can get distorted—it turns out some of them completely misunderstood. They said, 'Did you hear the news? We're *black!*'" Carolyn chuckled. "I had to straighten it all out, to clarify the story for them. But it sure was funny."

I learned from Carolyn then that at least one member of the white Beaumont family, a young man, had recently left Louisiana to settle elsewhere, in San Francisco. He was a rarity, as hardly any of the white Beaumonts had strayed far from Louisiana since A.J. first settled there in 1856. Much as my black ancestors long ago, the young white man had felt somewhat stifled and oppressed by Louisiana's conservative culture and had yearned to branch out on his own to realize his dreams. He was an architect, Carolyn told me, and gay.

Our families stayed in touch occasionally, sending e-mail messages and greeting cards to each other on holidays and at other special times. Rita promised at one point to make a dress for my daughter, remembering the time when she herself was a little girl in the 1930s and her mixed-race Aunt Pearl in St. Louis designed and sewed her a dress that she had adored. But it would be a stretch to say we considered both sides of our tree one "family." Our lives continued much as before, separately, quietly, distinctly white and black.

Still, I think the small victories in life are important—just finding and meeting the Beaumonts was, I realized, significantly fulfilling. When I thought about it months later, it was almost as if all the old keepsakes—A.J. Beaumont's photo, his obituary, his 1901 letter to Pearl—had been handed down for one hundred years in my family not just for sentimental reasons but to bedevil, perplex, and provoke some descendant down the line. I had turned out to be that someone. In the end, if part of God's life plan for me was to unearth and tie together the forgotten and long-concealed threads in my family's racial past, I had at least gained the simple gratification of knowing that I had done so, that I had solved the old puzzle and solved it well.

Researching family history is, for most Americans, an effort to restore links to an old country and culture of origin. We are a restless, transient people by definition, hailing from many places around the planet, and in our sometimes disquieting alienation from our own country and modern society, we seek identity and perhaps solace in the old places we came from and the ways our people once knew. In my case, however, researching my family history was inspired by a deep desire to document, understand, and strengthen ties to my native land, a land that has done much through the centuries to deny black people a basic sense of birthright and belonging. I investigated the past in order to make a more meaningful connection to America, one that many of my fellow citizens perhaps take for granted, yet one that racial division through the generations has made murky, nebulous, ambiguous, fractured. I was interested not in my genetic ties to Africa, the old and disconnected place, but in my hard-earned and far more meaningful roots here, in this dirt, in the country I call home. Indeed, the black and white roots I unearthed proved to be as strong, compelling, and deeply affirming in a human and archtypically American fashion as I knew they must be when I started on my quest.

It was funny, but as the months went by after my visit to Pineville, I began to realize that perhaps my most precious discovery wasn't an intellectual revelation about the anatomy of race and racism in America, or even about white people. It was a slightly surer, purer, and better sense of myself and my own identity—as an American and, far more important, as an African American. That was the treasure I had unearthed. It was as if after all that searching, I had found a kind of mirror on the far side of the family tree. I had set out to explore the white side of my ancestry, but I came back with a stronger sense of my black roots and a deeper awareness and appreciation for those who had made my family history so meaningful and rich.

When I was a kid growing up in Seattle, I didn't know many black people. So the ones I did know I held closely in my heart, as if they somehow carried important keys to life's meaning and my own identity. I didn't realize, though, how tightly and dearly I held them inside until after completing my search for the Beaumonts, when I began to reflect on the deep influence these black people had had on me from the very start. My brothers, Bobby and Wayne, my sister, Sharon, and of course my parents

were central figures in this regard. But so were my parents' closest friends, a group of black professionals who, like them, had migrated from the South to Seattle in the 1950s and 1960s and
begun to form the backbone of an emerging black professional
class in the city. Some were physicians, most of whom had graduated from Meharry in the same seminal era as my father.

I remember cocktail parties and Saturday night card games at
our house, where young black families would gather amid loud
laughter and a haze of cigarette smoke to unwind, trade stories,
and party together while Nat King Cole, Nancy Wilson, Sarah
Vaughan, and Billy Eckstine crooned from my father's record
player. Often I would stand at the living room table next to my
mother, my chin resting on the edge, soaking it all in as my parents played Tonk and bridge with their friends. I remember gales
of laughter, ice cubes clinking in drinking glasses, cold cans of
Rainier and Olympia and Heidelberg beer sweating in the heat,
and moths circling the ceiling light fixture on warm summer
nights. I would listen, smiling happily to myself, as they sprinkled
their conversations with soulful southern expressions that seemed
to melt like chocolate in the air. But most of all, I became mesmerized by everyone's faces and especially their hands—by my
father's, by Drs. Earl and Rosalie Miller's, by Drs. Blanche and
Phil Lavizzo's—smooth, strong, beautiful brown hands with
slender fingers and immaculate nails, hands that worked in
human blood and guts every day healing sick people, hands that
were skilled, noble, and unafraid. These same hands were there
before me, dancing in the lamplight, doing ordinary things—flip-
ping cards, lighting cigarettes, grabbing drinks, covering yawns—
and looking for all the world just like mine, except bigger.

Of all of those black figures in my youth, few were more special than Uncle Sonny, my mother's younger brother, who still lived in our ancestral house in the Ville in St. Louis. Throughout my childhood Sonny represented one of the last living links to our history there, to the city where Laura had moved in the 1890s.

Sonny was born in 1929, three years before the death of Laura, who had held her infant grandson in her arms the week of his birth and exulted that her small family finally had a "man baby" to celebrate. Years later this "man baby" became something akin to the Hope diamond among the jewels in my childhood world—although God knows few other people would have seen him that way. Uncle Sonny visited us often in Seattle, bringing with him all the beautiful jargon, mannerisms, and street culture of the old colored world in St. Louis, which seemed so far away growing up in the Pacific Northwest.

A confirmed and committed bachelor, he was named Edward Clifford Turner, Jr., after my grandfather. But everybody in our family had called him "Sonny" or "Stink" from the time he was a toddler. He had plump lips, skinny legs, a balding pate, and a round pot belly from years of good beer and soul food. Sonny both smoked hard, enjoying his Salems, and drank hard, becoming a connoisseur of Scotch and water on the rocks. He talked loud and didn't care a bit about his appearance when he was on vacation from his work as an architectural engineer in St. Louis, often going for days without a bath or a shave if he felt like it. God, how I loved him and wished I could be as free and seemingly easygoing as he was.

Sonny also was blessed with a rough and ragged vocabulary

that simply thrilled me as a child. He said stuff with his untamed mouth that neither I nor my brothers could even *think* about saying out loud. Despite my mother's protests at his language, the word "motherfucker" would regularly roll off his lips in a smooth Missouri drawl in a way in which every consonant was rounded to perfection—*"muh' fugga."* And he would use it as a verb, noun, adverb, or adjective, and sometimes all four in the same sentence.

To my impressionable ears Sonny was a true virtuoso when it came to the spoken word. He used language the way Willie Mays clubbed a homer, sped around the bases, and caught a fly. He used words the way Jim Brown barreled over tacklers and stormed to paydirt. He played with speech in his deep and resonant baritone the way B.B. King strummed his guitar. He brought such color, life, *blackness* to my world on Lake Shore Drive.

It wasn't ever just "cold" outside to Sonny. It was always "cold as a witch's tit" or "frigid as a whore's heart." When it rained hard it wasn't just *rain*—it was "frog strangler weather," the kind of downpour that sounded like "a cow pissin' on a flat rock." When it was hot, it was as hot "as little sister's wee-wee."

But he saved his best lines for women and sex. A woman wasn't just ugly to my uncle. She was as ugly as "a frog peepin' through buttermilk" or "as homely as ten yards of uncooked chitlins." If a woman was really attractive, she wasn't just sexy—she was "built like a ceramic defecatorium" and might "kill somebody if she got all that shit in mo'shun." If she looked sexually inclined, she was described by my uncle as able to "suck the chrome off a trailer hitch." And if he wasn't getting enough intercourse, Sonny would gruffly complain to no one in particular, "My dick's so clean you could cook greens with it."

I didn't understand half of what Uncle Sonny was talking about when I was a kid, but the *way* he said it—with such flair and animation and gruff theatricality—utterly galvanized me. His words were magic.

"The whole country went to hell when they integrated the armed forces, you know that?" Sonny mused one night as he dragged on a Salem cigarette, me and my brothers at his knee watching television. "Before that, we had a way'a doin' things and white boys had a way'a doin' things, you understand?"

We nodded.

"Back in the old days, if you wanted sex, you'd say, 'I gotta get me some cock.' That's the way we said it. 'I need me some cock.' Cock meant sex back then. Wantin' a little sex meant wantin' a little cock. You understand?"

We nodded again.

"Then they integrated the armed forces after the war, and everything's been fugged up ever since. Black men *never* ate pussy before integration, you know that? Only white boys did that. Then niggas started doin' it, and our whole goddam vernacular changed. Hell, you say, 'I want me some cock' now and people look at you like you're *queer*."

Bobby, Wayne, and I would nod our heads in almost perfect unison again, as if in complete understanding and agreement, although we did not comprehend half the exotic words our uncle was using.

"Don't you ever eat pussy, you hear?" Sonny would sagely go on, his booming voice lowering an octave. "Black men should *never* eat pussy. It's bad for your teeth."

Uncle Sonny might be loud, obnoxious, and crude, but I

loved him dearly for his stories, his independence, and the stark and beautiful contrast his very being presented to the white world I was coming to know. Indeed, it was Sonny whose passionate storytelling first opened my mind as a boy to the proud heroism of the Tuskegee airmen, the courage of Jackie Robinson and Marion Motley, the legends of Josh Gibson and Dr. Charles Drew, the incomparable beauty of Dorothy Dandridge and Lena Horne, and the creative genius of scores of black artists, from Duke Ellington and Louis Armstrong to Miles Davis and Thelonious Monk. My uncle was a veritable window to an enchanting world of blackness my white world in Seattle could not offer.

White people were many things to Sonny—"ofays," "honkies," "peckerwoods," "paddies," "Mr. Charley," even "Mr. and Mrs. Lynch," depending on his mood and circumstance. But "crackas" and "cracka muh-fuggas" were his pejoratives of choice. Black people enjoyed a similar variety of appellations in his Old World lexicon—"ziggaboos," "splibs," "cheegroes," "spooks," and his personal favorite, "club members," which he uttered with a loving drawl. That's what all of us were, even me. Club members!

I coveted the soul of the language my uncle brought from St. Louis on his visits to us nearly every summer. But no matter how hard I tried to mimic him, in private to myself, under my breath, I could never make "muh-fugga" or "nigga" or any of those other words trip off my tongue quite the way he could, my boyhood diction having been shaped forever by the clear, precise, upstanding English of the hopelessly white Pacific Northwest.

My uncle considered himself an expert on fishing, cooking,

hunting, fighting, engineering, politics, and practically every-thing in between. He was a blowhard. A blowhard's blowhard. But he was a true troubadour of opinion when it came to the op-posite sex. My uncle was married once. To an abrasive woman named Ethel, who I guess yelled at him a lot and made his life miserable. It was a mistake he rued for years. The marriage didn't actually last very long. Sonny remembered the duration exactly: "Ten months, ten days, thirteen hours, and twenty-five minutes," he would soberly intone every time the subject of marriage, in any context, came up. He recited those numbers so often that we, his nephews and niece, knew the marriage's duration by heart, as if it were a sacred psalm from the Old Testament.

His experience of marriage had left Uncle Sonny feeling much wiser about male-female relationships, especially black male–black female relationships. He rarely used the expression "black women" in ordinary conversation with us, preferring instead to use the word "Sapphire" to sum up that half of our race. "Sapphire" was akin to another all-encompassing term he used for black people— "The Ten Percent," as in ten percent of the American population. "Sapphire" and "The Ten Percent" con-stituted a special kind of shorthand for him.

After his fateful but blessedly brief marriage to Ethel in the 1970s, Uncle Sonny said he had a good working title for the book he intended to write someday about his life and times as a black man in America: *The Sapphirization of the Tenth Man*. He claimed it was sure to be a national bestseller.

Our family was blessed in having a colorful figure like Sonny in every generation, around whom so much of our story could be told. But there was one person in particular, Pearl, whose story seemed the most colorful of all, the one that joined together the black and white branches of our extended family tree.

I never knew Pearl. She died ten years before I was born. But Pearl's story loomed large in our family, a true morality tale about black and white in America. I knew that she was born in 1877 in St. Joseph, Louisiana, and died in 1944 in St. Louis, and that she was the daughter of a black woman born in slavery and an Englishman who had come to America to seek his fortune before the Civil War.

Pearl was married once, in the 1890s, to a black man, Frank Hall, who fathered her child Fredda in 1896. But she enjoyed numerous relationships with men of both races after the marriage ended in divorce, for she did love men very much. At one point, in the 1910s, she ran away with a jazz singer, but that affair eventually fell apart.

Pearl spent many happy years in the 1920s with a Jewish man named Jacob Bronstein, her second husband, an immigrant from Russia, who worked as a carpenter in a St. Louis clothing factory. In his jovial Russian accent, Bronstein used to tell Pearl exciting stories about his unusual arrival in America through a cold and distant place called Sitka, Alaska. Like Pearl, Bronstein was a figure not fully accepted in the mainstream of American society, an ethnic Jew relegated to the fringes. But the Russian immigrant and his mixed-race American wife, both orphans from their past, loved each other well and found great comfort in their strange alikeness.

After "Mr. Jake" died, Pearl became involved in the 1930s and 1940s with a white handyman named Charley James, who lived with her in her white frame house on Chatham Street. Charley used to call her "Poyle" in a heavy Brooklyn accent and loved her dearly until the day she died.

A gorgeous, vivacious quadroon, Pearl lived her life in the lonely twilight between the white and black worlds, never feeling fully accepted in either. At that time there was little or no room in American society for very light brown when it came to race. Pearl never felt fully comfortable in her own skin, and because of this, people who loved her remembered a kind of sadness always hovering over her. "She just never fit in," my mother recalled about the grandmother she loved so deeply. "She just never felt at ease with herself."

Pearl was even estranged at times from her daughter, Fredda, who viewed her mother's inexplicable fondness for the South and her secretive attempts to maintain contact with her white relatives there, the Beaumonts, as beneath her. "Those white people never did anything for us," Fredda used to chide her. "Those people don't want anything to do with you. Stop living in the past."

"I'm just an orphan girl. A poor little orphan girl," Pearl once moaned in Fredda's living room when she was feeling especially sorry for herself in the early 1940s, not long before she died.

Fredda exploded: "You ought to be ashamed, Mama! Here you have a daughter, grandchildren, great-grandchildren for goodness' sake, a family that loves you, and you sit here in my living room talking like an old fool. You ought to be ashamed!"

But despite her sense of isolation, one thing remained constant in Pearl's life: her undying love for and devotion to her grandchildren, Fredda's kids—Vivian, Sonny, and Mary—who adored her just as much. They knew her by her beloved nickname, "Mam-ee," a derivation of the French *ma mère* ("my mother"). And Mam-ee, to the children, was the cat's meow. They idolized this woman who dressed and walked like a Paris model and loved to tool around St. Louis in her Model T Ford. It didn't bother them that she could curse a blue streak—so much so that Fredda's husband, Clifford, used to call her the "old battle-ax."

Pearl doted on the kids, especially on holidays. Whenever she visited, Pearl promised a nickel to little Mary, my mother, if the little girl could put just one curl in her grandmother's straight and silken hair, anything to make Mam-ee look a bit more "colored." It was ironic. While many black people at the time were processing their coarse hair in a struggle to make it look "white," Pearl insistently headed in the opposite direction, trying her damnedest to make her hair look "black."

As a little girl, my mother would go at this unusual task with all her energy and creativity, filling Mam-ee's hair with curlers and pins. But no matter how long the curlers and pins were kept on Mam-ee's head, her hair would return to its natural straightness once they were taken out. Mam-ee just had too much white blood in her.

During the Depression my mother and her family moved in with Mam-ee and Charley in the tidy little house at 6422 Chatham Street. It was there, in her adolescent years, that my mother discovered the joy of books, of the public library, of reading and writing—a joy she passed on to me many years later in Seattle. The house on Chatham Street also figured in my mother's earliest memories when, as a toddler in the mid-1920s, she and her mother would visit Pearl and her mother, Laura, then in her twilight years. My mother remembered sitting on Laura's lap and watching the old woman sip coffee from a saucer, then retiring with her later to a second-floor bedroom, where they would fall asleep together watching the white lace curtains ruffle in the afternoon breeze.

Some of my mother's most cherished memories, long before her years in Atlanta, Nashville, and Seattle, came from those years on Chatham Street in the 1920s and 1930s. And no person figured more prominently or lovingly in those memories than Pearl, my mother's beloved Mam-ee. It was Pearl who showed her how to use elbow grease to clean the grime from the bathtub, Pearl who taught her what class and style meant in fashion and music, Pearl whose language was so salty that my mother and Uncle Sonny used to practice saying "shit" in just the right soulful, southern way she did—"sheeee-it."

And it was Pearl who showed my mother and her brother how to stand up to white people when they messed with them, how to put them in their place—like the time a white boy repeatedly took Sonny's tricycle from him, reducing him to tears. "You go out there and beat that little cracka's ass," Pearl told her five-year-old grandson, "or I'm gonna beat yours." And Sonny did just that, because he feared Mam-ee's wrath more than any white boy.

Pearl, the daughter of an Englishman and a woman born into slavery, may have looked white, but she taught all of her family a great deal about what it meant to be black.

Memories of Chatham Street and Pearl, I knew, occupied some of the dearest places in my mother's heart. Once on a visit to St. Louis she, Bobby, and I tried to find the graves of Laura and Pearl at an old black cemetery near Lambert Airport. The cemetery had been neglected for many years, though, making the task impossible. At the end of our long, unsuccessful search that chilly February day, my mother concluded, "It just goes to show—all this doesn't mean anything." She waved her arms toward the expanse of lonely headstones, many of them chipped or broken or fallen over in the mud and overgrown with weeds and wildflowers. "Folks don't live on in graveyards. It's what you remember in your heart that counts."

On Thursday, May 14, 1998, after my classes at Berkeley were finally finished for the term, I flew from Sacramento to Seattle for a small family reunion. Every six months or so, my brother Bobby, Bobby's grown son, David, Uncle Sonny, and I would get together to play golf on various courses in California and Washington. We called this regular gathering of black males in our clan "The Tenth Man Classic" in honor of Uncle Sonny's favorite expression for black folks, "The Ten Percent." We usually played miserably. And Uncle Sonny often won these informal tourneys, despite his advancing years. But winning or losing was never the point, despite the intensity of our competition. Drinking lots of beer, smoking good cigars, eating soul food, celebrating the latest accomplishments of Tiger Woods, and joking around with each other were.

This time our weekend gathering was set for the golf courses of Seattle, and I was looking forward to seeing everyone even more than usual, especially my mother and Sonny. The plane flew northward high over California in the bright blue afternoon sky, which turned gray and cloudy by the time we entered

Oregon over the Cascade Mountains. All the while, brimming with excitement and eagerness, I thought about how much time had passed and how much our family and American society had changed since 1956, when my parents migrated from segregated Nashville to make a new start for themselves in the Pacific Northwest.

My father, so stern, unyielding, and hard-working throughout my childhood, had changed, becoming far more reflective in the years since his retirement in 1988. "If I had to do it all over again," he had told me during one of my more recent visits, "I probably never would have even gone into medicine. I probably would have enjoyed forestry or oceanography a lot more. But in my day and age there was never even an option like that for black men, as there is now." That, he said, was the reason the larger struggle by his generation and the push for racial integration had been worth it. The mere fact that talented black men and women could aspire to success and greatness in so many different fields these days, not just a few, was to him the greatest and most worthwhile change he had seen in society in his lifetime.

My father had also become a surprisingly emotional man in more recent years. During my visits, whenever he and I hugged to say good-bye, he would begin to cry. I could feel his frail body tremble almost uncontrollably in my arms. It was amazing. This old black man, who had rarely betrayed any real emotion or pain for so many years, for fear of betraying any weakness to his children, suddenly began to display a great deal of emotion in his old age. During those partings in Seattle, I could literally feel my father releasing the great sadness inside himself. Finally, in a life spent with such tight emotional restraint and guardedness, he seemed to be allowing himself to let loose all kinds of hurts and sorrows he had kept pent up inside for so long. In those moments I felt closer to him than I ever had as a child.

After my plane landed in Seattle, as I slowly walked into the terminal with the legions of other travelers, my satchel on my shoulder, I heard a familiar voice. It was unmistakable over the din of greetings, as gruff, loud, and obnoxious as it ever was in my childhood.

"Hey dummy, you ready to get your ass kicked?"

I smiled as soon as I heard it.

"Sonny, I brought my driver this time," I informed my sixty-eight-year-old uncle, punching him gently on his soft, round shoulder. "And I'm not takin' any prisoners. So be prepared for your whuppin'."

"All right, that's enough of that," my mother said smiling, joining us amid our laughter and placing her arms around my neck. "You're looking good."

"So are you, Mom."

She was looking fabulous, in fact. But of course, she always looked that way to me. Her dark hair was short, curly, sprinkled with silver and gray, her twinkling eyes a deep brown, her face tanned and elegantly lined with age. She was wearing a blue sweatshirt, sweatpants, and running shoes—her usual outfit for her morning exercise, a four-mile walk along the shore of Lake Washington—but she managed to carry even the most ordinary clothing with singular personality and style.

"Flight okay?"

"Yeah, sure was," I said, kissing her on the cheek. "Zoë and Tish say hi."

"Let's go get something to eat, okay? Wanna?" she asked, slipping her arm inside mine.

"Yeah, I'm starved."

"Good," Sonny growled as we went to retrieve my golf bag and then headed for my mother's car. "You can pay for it too. We're senior citizens."

In the years since our move to Seattle, perhaps the one thing that had stayed mostly the same was Sonny, I realized. Retired from his engineering career, my uncle now loved to monitor the world's happenings through the satellite dish he had installed on the roof of the old house where he and my mother had grown up in the Ville. But he remained a frequent visitor to Seattle, still carrying a potbelly on his stovepipe legs, still loving his Scotch and water, still cursing about the "Sapphires" and "crackas" who made his life hell. He had stopped smoking, though. And while the top of his tan-colored noggin was still as shiny and bare as a cue ball, he had decided several years back to grow the remaining hair on the sides of his head as long as he could and then pull the strands back into a hip little ponytail that he bound with a tie. With his ever-present Greek sailor's cap on his head and the ponytail down his neck, Sonny looked like he had a full head of hair underneath, which I suppose was the effect he desired.

We piled into my mother's green Honda Civic, and she drove us through the rain-soaked streets of Seattle to a favorite restaurant, a seafood grill about a half hour away from the airport on Lake Washington, in the city's Leschi Park section. As we caught up with each other's lives, I felt like a nervous kid again, harboring an amazing secret and badly wanting to share it but not knowing how or when.

Years earlier I had confided my idea of searching for the Beaumonts to my mother, but the quest had been so fruitless for so long that I had long ago stopped discussing it with her. I was almost certain I would fail, and I figured she felt the same way after a while. And I had certainly never discussed my search with Sonny, not since the first time back in the 1980s when my uncle had growled his disdain and disapproval of any attempt to find the white family. "Forget them goddamn people," he had muttered to me over the phone when I told him I was going to search for his white cousins. "If you wanna write about something, write about the black folks in your family. What the hell's wrong with you?"

Now, years later, I finally had the full story to tell and the priceless photos of Pearl in my satchel. But for the life of me I didn't know where to begin or how. I realized I was feeling almost as hesitant and apprehensive about the prospect of telling my mother and uncle about their white cousins as I had been in making my first telephone contact with Rita.

The Seattle I saw passing outside my mother's car window that night certainly was remarkably different from the city I had known as a boy in the 1950s and 1960s. Back then Seattle called itself the "Queen City of the Pacific Northwest," but in reality it was little more than a sleepy backwater in a far corner of the continent, an afterthought in our national consciousness. For decades Seattle was known for Boeing aircraft and Weyerhaeuser lumber and little else, except its climate, in which rain fell seemingly year-round. It was a happily unsophisticated place that reveled in its provinciality, a town where folks liked to wear lumberjack outfits and hats with floppy ears in the winter, à la Elmer

Fudd, and where there was no such thing as a traffic jam or a car horn honked in anger. I still saw Seattle as it used to be. I remembered the summer fishing trips my father and I took to catch salmon off the Pacific coast. And I recalled the minor league baseball games my brothers and I enjoyed as we sat high in the wooden bleachers at Sick's Stadium in Rainier Valley, where, by night, we could watch the stars and moon peek between the clouds, and where, on clear sunny afternoons, Mount Rainier loomed majestically beyond the right field wall like a giant snow-capped sentinel.

Now, however, the city I grew up in called itself the "Emerald City," a place where Oz-like fortunes were indeed being made. Gone were the days of 1969, when Boeing ordered massive layoffs at its manufacturing plants and plunged the city into a terrible recession, prompting the cynical refrain, "Will the last person leaving Seattle please turn out the lights?" Now Seattle had much bigger shoulders of economic might and a population that had more than quadrupled since the days of my boyhood. Distant hillsides once green with virgin firs and pines were gradually being replaced by growing satellite towns like Bellevue with skyscrapers of their own. Multimillion-dollar homes, golf courses, and developments had been carved into these hillsides. The once sleepy backwater I had known as a child was now a city of international renown, one that had seen the birth of new technologies that were fueling the longest sustained period of economic growth America had ever known. Traffic clogged Seattle's streets and freeways now, smog poisoned its air, and sport fishing for coho, king, and silver salmon off the coast was now much more tightly restricted because so many species of the fish were endangered.

One thing hadn't changed. The rain that seemed to fall relentlessly on the pretty city when I was a boy was falling now, and my mother's windshield wipers flipped back and forth in a steady lament as she turned her car onto a quiet street called Lake Washington Boulevard. We arrived at the Leschi Grill after a few minutes, and as we waited in the entryway for the waitress to show us to a table, I put my arm around my mother's shoulder and gave her a quick, warm hug.

"You don't get older. You just get better, right? Isn't that what they say?" I said smiling.

"Maybe," she chuckled, her hands shoved into her windbreaker. "But old age isn't for sissies, just the same. You remember that."

In recent years my mother had thrown herself into an array of travel and writing projects that had made her retirement one of the busiest and most creative periods of her life. She had journeyed to Africa, Europe, and around the country over the past decade and found herself growing in ways that went far beyond the social. In 1985 she was awarded a highly competitive humanities fellowship for educators to spend a month studying the works of Alice Walker, Flannery O'Connor, Eudora Welty, and other southern writers at the University of Mississippi at Oxford. It was a privilege that would have been unthinkable for a black woman in the era of racial segregation, some forty years earlier, when she had attended college.

For much of her life, my mother had been fascinated by minority history in Seattle, and in 1983 she joined the Black Heritage Society of Washington State, a group of black educators dedicated to preserving artifacts and commemorating the achievements of the state's black population. In 1997, at the age

of seventy-four, she authored a book that told the personal sto-
ries behind the parks, swimming pools, and other landmarks in
Seattle named after twenty-three distinguished black Americans,
Medgar Evers, Martin Luther King, Jr., and Thurgood Marshall
among them. Published under a grant by King County, *Tribute:
Seattle Places Named for Black People* was lauded by reviewers in
Seattle and appeared on shelves in libraries and bookstores
throughout Washington. One reviewer, a columnist for the
Seattle Times named Jerry Large, wrote this about my mother on
December 7, 1997, in a long column devoted to her book:

> Henry was the librarian at South Shore Middle School in the
> midst of a 27-year career when she noticed how much children
> struggled with a black history quiz. Many of the children were
> cared for at the Odessa Brown Clinic and swam at Medgar Evers
> Pool, but had no idea who the people were who lent their names
> to those landmarks.
>
> Henry is of that generation of black people for whom dignity
> was paramount. Her home is immaculate and tastefully deco-
> rated. Her bearing and her language are gracious and graceful.
> She is the product of segregated schools whose teachers saw
> each child as a great hope not just for herself but for a whole
> race of people.
>
> This country's movement forw ard and the people who kept
> it moving mean something to her.

After we took our seats in the restaurant, my mother, Sonny,
and I toasted each other with martinis—still their drink of
choice, dating from the 1950s—and we laughed long into the
night as we recalled events from my childhood in Seattle and
from theirs in St. Louis. It wasn't until the next morning that I

was able to begin to tell them about the story on the other side of the tree.

I showered and dressed for our "Tenth Man Classic" golf game while Sonny prepared breakfast. The day was cloudy and overcast, but the sun was beginning to peek through the mist in the east. It promised to be a clear and sunshiny day for our outing.

As I entered the kitchen, where my uncle was cooking scrambled eggs, I noticed my mother seated nearby in the dining room. Dressed in her walking clothes, she was eating a bowl of cereal in skim milk and reading the morning paper. I took a seat across the table from her and watched for a moment as she chewed her raisin bran. She continued peering at her newspaper through her tortoiseshell eyeglasses.

"Whatcha doin' today, Mom?" I asked.

"Oh, nothin' much. I've got a doctor's appointment at noon," she replied idly, her eyes still skimming the front page. She took another bite of her cereal. "Annual checkup. Then, well, I guess I'll cook a salmon for you all and Bobby. I think Sharon and her kids will be by too."

"But you're more or less free for the day? You have some time maybe to read some things?"

She nodded. "Yep. Reckon I'll just relax."

"Good. I've got somethin' to show you. You too, Sonny."

I felt my heart beating in my throat as I went to the bedroom, quickly returning to the dining table with my satchel. I sat down with the bag in my lap and looked up at my mother, who had finished one newspaper article and started to turn the page.

"You know I've been researching all this time for my book," I began, reminding her about the research I had been doing about

Meharry, the family's move to Seattle, and the white neighbor-hood I grew up in—research in libraries, courthouses, and archives.

"Yeah, I know," my mother answered softly, looking at me for a moment, then returning her gaze to the newspaper's world news page.

"And you remember a long time ago I also had an idea to try to find the Beaumonts, to compare their story to ours."

She nodded again. But then, as she began to turn the newspaper page once more, she looked up and cast a brief glance at my face.

"I found them, Mom. In Louisiana."

She fixed her eyes on mine, holding the newspaper page suspended with her left hand. Her expression was quizzical.

"They never left, after all these years. I found them and I got in touch with them."

"Say, what?" I heard Sonny mutter in disbelief in his gruff baritone as he stood behind her now.

"And they invited me down there to have dinner with them."

"Oh shit," Sonny grumbled.

"What?" my mother exclaimed, echoing his disbelief as she dropped the newspaper and softly tapped her left hand on the table.

"And I did. I went there," I told them, feeling my words catching in my throat and hearing my voice quaver with emotion. "In March. I flew to Louisiana. I met them and I heard their story."

"*What?*" she exclaimed again, leaning forward now, her face electric with surprise. "You've gotta be joking, Neil."

I pulled out my copy of the fifty-six-year-old handwritten history of the Beaumonts and placed it on the table before her, along with the photos from the white family's life in St. Joseph before the turn of the century. Sonny looked on with her, standing over the table with a cup of steaming coffee in his hand, his brow furrowed as his eyes scanned the material.

"Why, you little shit . . . ," he said, starting to laugh in spite of himself.

"Here are the Beaumonts in front of their house in the country, at about the same time Laura moved to St. Louis," I indicated, my finger pointing at the old photo before them. "The little boy with the bike is Beaumont's son. That's the half brother Pearl never knew."

My mother pushed her empty cereal bowl aside. She touched the photo with her finger and placed her other hand on her heart as she leaned forward to look closer.

"And this one," I went on, pointing to another picture that Rita had given me, "this is A.J. Beaumont's store in St. Joseph. But they had a hard time after that. After Beaumont died. A really hard time."

I told Sonny and my mother about the fall of the white family's fortune, about their suffering after the boll weevil plague and on into the Depression, about the tragedy and heroism of both Anna's and Rita's lives. I told her about Newton Himel and about Carolyn too, and Carolyn's work at the black hospital in New Orleans.

"This is their story. This is what happened to the Beaumonts after Laura and Pearl moved to St. Louis," I said then, pointing to the manuscript before her. "It's a family history that was written by Beaumont's son in 1941."

My mother opened the small bound book, just as I had weeks earlier at Rita's kitchen table in Pineville. She couldn't take her eyes off the family history as she slowly turned from page to page, with Sonny leaning closely to peer over her shoulder.

"They had some very hard times after 1900—broken marriages, alcohol abuse, personal tragedies," I continued. "But the book isn't about that really. A lot of it is about how wonderful slavery and the plantation era was for them."

"And I bet there's nothin' in there about Mam-ee, right?" Sonny interjected, still leaning over but raising his eyes to mine. "Nothin' about the child that was born on the wrong side o' the blanket."

"Right. Not a word," I replied. "But they do remember her down there, Sonny. That's what's most amazing."

I looked at Mom again as she leafed through the book. Her eyes seemed riveted on each page she turned. I reached across the table to place my right hand on my mother's left.

"All those years, Mam-ee stayed in touch with them. Throughout her life in St. Louis. She tried her damnedest to stay in touch. She wanted them to know her."

I looked back at Sonny.

"And all this time they thought she was an Indian," I added. "They called her Aunt Pearl and thought she was Indian . . ."

"Typical whities!" Sonny exploded, his laugh booming now.

". . . because Beaumont figured 'better Indian than black.'"

"Typical!"

My mother still seemed too surprised to speak. All she could do was shake her head from side to side, an uncomprehending look frozen on her face. She alternately moved her gaze from the old photos to the manuscript and back. Her reaction seemed to suggest that something in her universe had suddenly, weirdly, shifted, but she wasn't sure exactly what had happened.

"But . . . how? *What?*" she stammered, focusing her deep brown eyes intensely on mine. "What was it like, Neil? What happened? What was it like to be with them?"

I answered as best I could, but no matter how hard I tried, I couldn't find the words that would do justice to what I had experienced in Pineville, or to what I was feeling then.

"They were an ordinary southern white family," I said slowly, finally, emphasizing each word distinctly. "And here I had come from out of nowhere, a black cousin suddenly flying across the country to meet them, representing a family of doctors and teachers and engineers."

Sonny began to chuckle again. "You sneaky little shit."

"And we sat together and ate gumbo at their dinner table. I learned some things I really despised. I found out one of those people was in the Klan. . . ."

They continued to study me with their eyes.

"So it was emotional. That's what it was, most of all. It was just like you always used to say, remember? Race in America is never a simple thing to understand or to explain to anyone. But one thing is always true: being black in America can be a powerfully rewarding experience. Remember how you used to say you wouldn't want to go through life any other way? Because being black in this country is such a meaningful and *interesting* life? That's exactly what it was like. That's what I felt."

I looked up at Sonny again, then back at my mother. They waited for me to go on.

"I found out so much that was different about us. We're so incredibly different. But I also found some things that were the same."

And then I looked down at the satchel in my lap again and remembered the gift I wanted to give her. I reached into the bag and pulled out the framed photo of Pearl.

"They had pictures, Mom. They had pictures of Mam-ee," I exclaimed, spreading all of the old photos of their grandmother on the table before them, placing the prettiest one in its frame near a vase of tulips at the table's edge.

My mother stared at the images for a moment. Then, as it dawned on her what exactly was before her, she gasped with delight. The enchantment began to spread on her face.

"Sonny, look!" she cried.

And it was in that instant, seeing the happiness in her eyes, hearing the laughter in her voice, that I knew my long search was finally reaching its true end and that it had been worth all the effort in ways far dearer to me than I could ever have expected. She and my uncle remembered every detail of every old blurred picture I showed them, just as I knew they would. And for a moment I felt myself once again joining them in their childhood some sixty years earlier in the house behind the white picket fence in St. Louis.

My mother would spend much of the rest of that sunny spring day lost in reading the book and looking at the old black-and-white photos Rita had given me, marveling, she would tell me later, in the memories they evoked, the questions they inspired, and the new knowledge about the past they offered. But for now, as we hovered together over her dining room table in Seattle, her gleeful words and memories tumbling out, there was simply the wonder of discovery.

"I love you, Mom," I heard myself saying as she and my uncle took turns cradling in their light brown hands the old photograph of their grandmother glimmering in its cut-glass frame.

"I love you guys. . . . ."

I'm not sure they heard me above the laughter.

COMPLETE FAMILY TREE

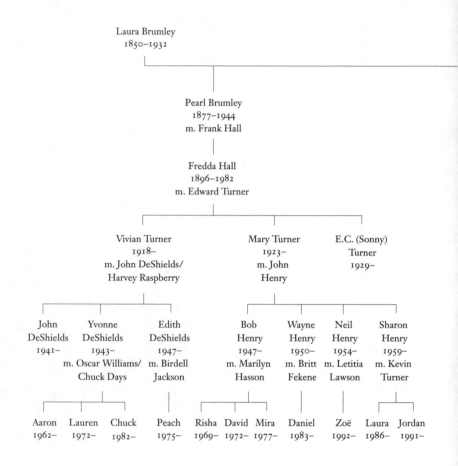

Laura Brumley
1850–1932

Pearl Brumley
1877–1944
m. Frank Hall

Fredda Hall
1896–1982
m. Edward Turner

Vivian Turner
1918–
m. John DeShields/
Harvey Raspberry

Mary Turner
1923–
m. John
Henry

E.C. (Sonny)
Turner
1929–

John
DeShields
1941–

Yvonne
DeShields
1943–
m. Oscar Williams/
Chuck Days

Edith
DeShields
1947–
m. Birdell
Jackson

Bob
Henry
1947–
m. Marilyn
Hasson

Wayne
Henry
1950–
m. Britt
Fekene

Neil
Henry
1954–
m. Letitia
Lawson

Sharon
Henry
1959–
m. Kevin
Turner

Aaron
1962–

Lauren
1972–

Chuck
1982–

Peach
1975–

Risha
1969–

David
1972–

Mira
1977–

Daniel
1983–

Zoë
1992–

Laura
1986–

Jordan
1991–

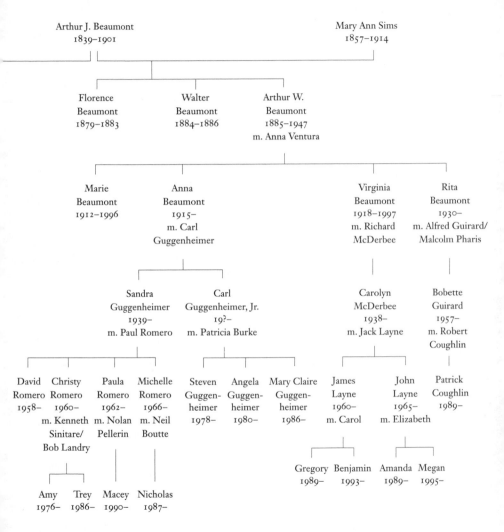

Acknowledgments

I thank my mother, Mary Turner Henry, and my father, Dr. John Robert Henry, Jr., of Seattle, for their love, support, and assistance with the research that led to this book. With patience, wit, and infinite understanding my mother in particular endured many hours of questioning in which I tried to piece together the narrative of my parents' lives in St. Louis, Winston-Salem, Heidelberg, Nashville, and Seattle. Without her consent, criticism, and generous help this book would not have been possible.

I also thank my brothers, John Robert Henry III of Seattle and Wayne Turner Henry of Boston, and my sister, Sharon Theresa Henry of Mercer Island, Washington, for their friendship and constant good humor. My siblings remember as well as I the unusual racial journey we experienced during childhood, an adventure that continues to the present day, and their keen insights along the way have proved extraordinarily helpful and reassuring at many turns, not least during the period of my research and writing.

I extend special thanks to Rita Beaumont Guirard Pharis and her family in Louisiana, who opened the door to their lives and shared their remarkable family history with me that eventful March evening in

Pineville. By doing so they allowed me a chance to reap the full rewards of my project. For that, I will always be grateful. I also express special thanks to Carolyn M. Layne of New Orleans for her help in constructing the Beaumont genealogy.

I'm very grateful to my aunt, Vivian DeShields Raspberry, and my cousins, John DeShields III and Yvonne DeShields Days, all of St. Louis, for their generous support of my work and the use of photographs and other historical documents in their possession. I also thank my uncles, Dr. Frank Demby of San Rafael, California, for sharing his wisdom, especially his recollections of his teaching and training at Meharry Medical College, and Edward Clifford Turner, Jr., of St. Louis, for his storytelling skills and exquisite taste in single-malt Scotch, soul food, and Cuban cigars.

As a kid growing up in Seattle, I was fortunate to count as family friends a number of black professionals, many of whom pioneered like my parents from the Deep South to the Pacific Northwest in the 1950s. I thank them for their family friendship, love, and example. They include the late Philip and Toby Burton, Frank and Janice Fair, Hon. Judge Charles and Lazelle Johnson, Dr. Bill and Helen Lacy, the late Drs. Philip and Blanche Lavizzo, Drs. Earl V. and Rosalie Miller, and the late June Smith.

I'm also grateful to three brilliant teachers who inspired me in my school years: the late Lee O. Schmalbeck at Sharples Junior High School in Seattle, the late Professor H. H. Wilson at Princeton University, and Professor Penn Kimball at Columbia University.

Numerous libraries and historical societies were very helpful at many turns in my research, including the University of Washington, Louisiana State University, the University of California at Berkeley, the University of California at Davis, the Yolo County Public Library in Davis, the British Imperial War Museum and British National Army Museum in London, the Church of Jesus Christ of Latter-Day Saints Family History Center in Woodland, California, the Tensas Parish Public Library in St. Joseph, Louisiana, the National Archives and Library of Congress of the United States in Washington, D.C., and the historical societies of St. Louis, Missouri, and Tensas Parish, Louisiana. I especially thank Gordon A. Cotton, curator of the Warren County Court House Museum and Library in Vicksburg, Mississippi, for the public records expertise and assistance he offered during my visit, and Quinton L. Jones, curator of the Archives of Meharry Medical College in Nashville, Tennessee.

Many friends, professional colleagues, and students played an invaluable role in supporting and encouraging me to complete this book. I am very grateful to them and will attempt here to name all of them, apologizing in advance for what may be an incomplete job. I thank my colleagues, first, on the faculty at Berkeley's Graduate School of Journalism, including Joan Bieder, Lydia Chavez, Mark Danner, William J. Drummond, Clay Felker, Cynthia Gorney, Paul Grabowicz, Ken Light, Paul Mason, Marcia Parker, Susan Rasky, William B. Turner, and Carolyn Wakeman, for their unfailing good cheer and camaraderie. I'm especially grateful for the expert editorial eyes of Jon Else, Tom Goldstein, Thomas C. Leonard, and Orville H. Schell, all of whom offered valuable comments and criticism on early drafts of the manuscript. I also thank the administrative staff at the journalism school, including Roy Baril, Mimi Chakarova, Andre Des Boine, Johnny Dong, Ida Fowler, David Martinez, Paulette Powell, Michele Price Rabin, and Kean Sakata. I especially am grateful to former staff members Mitsuru "Mitch" Ikuta and Natalie Smolensky, who never tired in their assistance to me in my transition from newspapering to academia.

Leon F. Litwack, the Alexander F. and May T. Morrison Professor of American History at Berkeley, offered a keen eye and terrific suggestions for improving the book at a critical time in its creation, and for that I will always be thankful. I'm grateful, too, to Naomi Schneider, James Clark, and Ellie Hickerson at the University of California Press for believing in this book, to copy editor Virginia Croft and designer Nicole Hayward, and especially to project editor Sue Heinemann, who made timely suggestions and wielded a terrific pencil during the editing process. I also thank my agent, Jill Kneerim, for her literary expertise and counsel.

Among the hundreds of undergraduate and graduate students who have passed through my "Mass Media and Society" lectures and my news reporting and writing seminars in the seven years I have taught at Berkeley, a number have supported me in my work as well as assisted me in my teaching. They include Lauren Barrack, Gregg Bell, Anita Chabria, Sherri Day, Karen D'Souza, Charlotte Fadipe, Eric Gran, Emelie Gunnison, Damon Hack, Tyche Hendricks, Matthai Kuruvila, Andrea Lampros, Harry Mok, Suzanne Pardington, David Pescovitz, Rob Selna, Jackie Spinner, Jessica Thaler, and Elliot Zaret. I also thank the many students in my Journalism 200 classes through the years, who provided the grist for informing and improving my work as an educator. My respect and affection to all you guys.

I also express appreciation to the following San Francisco Bay Area journalists, whose work I have come to admire and who have generously assisted me on occasion in my Berkeley classroom and lecture hall: John Diaz, Richard Gonzalez, Adam Hochschild, Tim Keown, Ann Killion, Gwen Knapp, Teresa Moore, Carl Nolte, Lori Olszewski, Bob Porter-field, Manuel Ramos, Dennis Richmond, Gary Rivlin, Joan Ryan, Barbara Shulgasser, and Ruthe Stein.

Professional colleagues and dear pals from my days in Washington, D.C., and Africa when I wrote for the *Washington Post* supported me consistently, through the bad times as well as the good. I thank, above all, David Maraniss, Bill Hamilton, and Janet Philips. I also treasure the support and friendship of these kindred spirits: Paul Addison, Jeffrey Bartholet, Jerri Eddings, Johanna Janssens, Jennifer Parmelee, and Rehana Rossouw. In addition I'm grateful to Leonard Downie, James V. Risser, Roger Wilkins, Juan Williams, and Bob Woodward for considering and commenting on early drafts of the manuscript. Thanks, too, to editor Donna Frazier, my old friend from our days in graduate study at Columbia's Journalism School; Dr. William E. Matori; and Tansey Thomas.

During my formative years as a reporter and writer in New York City and Washington, D.C., I was very lucky to be surrounded by colleagues and counterparts whose camaraderie I treasured, whose excellence I admired, and whose zest for the craft inspired me. I thank them for demonstrating from the very start how rewarding journalism could be. They include my splendid brethren from the *Washington Post* summer intern class of 1977: Sandra G. Boodman, John Feinstein, Ted Gup, Carla Hall, Vanessa Barnes Hillian, and Lexie Verdon. I also thank Charles R. Babcock, Gene Bachinski, Karlyn Barker, Jamie Baylis, Dudley Brooks, Warren Brown, Milton Coleman, Denis Collins, Leon Dash, the late Herbert Denton, Jackson Diehl, Lewis Diuguid, Maureen Dowd, Bill Elsen, Patrice Gaines, Joyce Gemperlein, Michael Getler, Dorothy Gilliam, Donald Graham, Nell Henderson, Craig Herndon, Michael E. Hill, Alison Howard, Gwen Ifill, Michael Isikoff, the late John Jacobs, Janis Johnson, Robert G. Kaiser, Laura Kiernan, Athelia Knight, Charles Krause, Steve Luxenberg, Jim Malone, Dennis McAuliffe, Michelle McQueen, Eugene L. Meyer, Reid Miller, Courtland Milloy, Morton Mintz, Thomas Morgan, Beth Nissen, Angus Phillips, William Raspberry, David Remnick, Eugene Robinson, Wendy Ross, Ann Rutherford, Mike Sager, Deborah Schwartz, Jane Seaberry, the late Howard Simons, Molly Sinclair, Dita Smith, Christine Spolar, Valerie Strauss, Fred Sweets, Karyn Taylor, Pat Thompson, Vernon Thompson, James M. Thresher, Loretta Tofani, Judith Valente, Paul Valentine, Elsa Walsh, Martin Weil, Benjamin Weiser, Michael Weisskopf, Larry Whiteside, Tom Wilkinson, and Brad Wye.

I am grateful, too, to the following wonderful souls whose companionship and confidence in me I found deeply rewarding and nurturing at different times, and in many different ways, since I moved west and made Davis, California, my home: John and Melissa Gates, Robert B. Gunnison, John Samples, the late Richard C. Sinopoli, Andrew and Melissa Skalaban, and Dave and Cindi Unmack.

Finally, I thank my wife, Letitia Lawson, whose editorial assistance, endless patience, sympathy, common sense, laughter, and loving support saw me through this odyssey in one piece, sane and whole. To her I owe everything.

Text:	10/15 Janson
Display:	Rotis Serif
Design:	Nicole Hayward
Composition:	BookMatters
Printing and binding:	Haddon Craftsmen